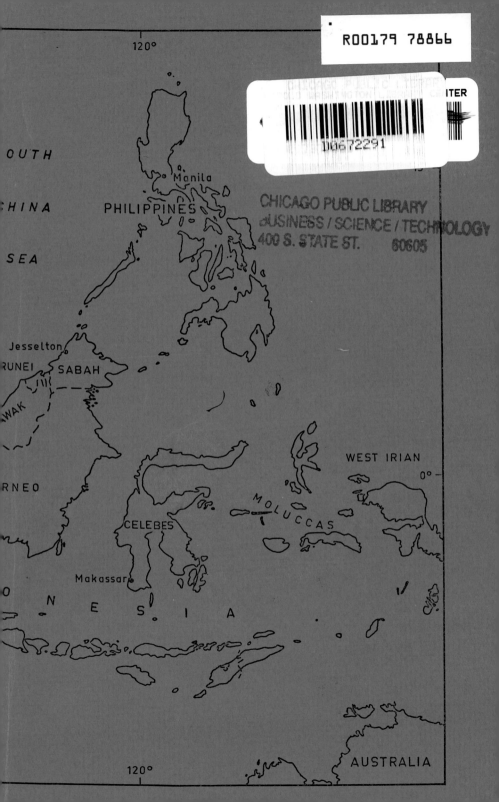

120°

OUTH

CHINA   PHILIPPINES

SEA

Manila

Jesselton

RUNEI   SABAH

WAK

RNEO

WEST IRIAN

0°

M O L U C C A S

CELEBES

Makassar

O   N   E   S   I   A

AUSTRALIA

120°

The Economic Development of Thai Agriculture

The Economic Development of Thai Agriculture

T. H. Silcock

Cornell University Press

ITHACA, NEW YORK

© T. H. Silcock 1970

First published 1970

Standard Book Number 8014-0545-9
Library of Congress Catalog Card Number 77-87010
Printed in Australia

To
MARGARET

Acknowledgments

This book was written during the tenure of a Senior Research Fellowship at the Australian National University, and the field work during the early part of 1967 was also financed by that University. Assistance and office accommodation were provided by the Applied Science Research Corporation of Thailand, which also negotiated on my behalf with the National Research Council, and gave most valuable help in arranging the field work.

The background work on Thailand on which the book is based was mostly financed by a grant from the Ford Foundation through the Australian National University. In particular my field work in the south was undertaken under this grant. During that period of field work I was attached as a special lecturer to the Graduate School of Chulalongkorn University and derived much help from this position and from my colleagues. To all these organisations which made the work possible I wish to express my thanks.

Some six pages of the text of the book are appearing more or less simultaneously, in my chapter on Thai Agriculture in R. T. Shand's book on *The Development of Asian Agriculture*; tables 2.1 and 9.1 and parts of some other tables are also used in that chapter.

Tables 2.3 and 4.3 and 4 are in large part taken from tables previously published in the author's *Thailand: Social and Economic Studies in Development*, A.N.U. Press, 1967. Permission from Dr R. T. Shand and from the A.N.U. Press to reproduce the material is hereby acknowledged. Permission from the Editor of

Australian Outlook and from Dr D. H. Penny to reproduce the Appendixes is also gratefully acknowledged here.

It is next a duty, which I can discharge with real pleasure, to acknowledge personal help received in the collection of material and the writing of this book.

First to many Thai farmers, village headmen, agricultural officers, district officers and various specialists and administrators in provincial headquarters, my thanks for time generously and patiently given, for friendly attention and consideration which largely overcame my ignorance of dialect and my errors in their language, and also for much generous hospitality. Professor M. Wagner of Kasetsart University gave me valuable help in the early stages of the work and showed me some of his own material in draft form. Mr Chumnian Boonma, who had also been working on regional specialisation in Thai agriculture, translated my questionnaires into Thai.

Next a word of special thanks to my two research assistants, Nancy Viviani and John Merritt. Both performed many tedious calculations and much laborious checking for me, and both, by their thoroughness and scholarship, saved me from errors—John Merritt from one serious one. They are not, however, responsible for any errors that remain.

To Dr R. T. Shand and Dr D. H. Penny my thanks for criticisms of earlier drafts. These have been most helpful.

My friends Dr Chote Khumbhandhu and his wife Lamyong have given me hospitality and help far beyond any reasonable claims of friendship, and a great deal of sound and useful advice, for which I shall always be grateful.

I wish to thank also the cartographers of the Geography Department in the Research School of Pacific Studies who drew the two maps.

Mrs E. R. Wilkie typed the whole manuscript, with much ingenuity in tabulation and with infectious cheerfulness. Both were often badly needed and are acknowledged with gratitude.

Finally to my wife, to whom this book is dedicated, my loving thanks for bearing so generously the many trials which its preparation involved.

T.H.S.

Canberra
16 April 1968

Contents

Tables

Abbreviations

F.A.O.   Food and Agriculture Organization
I.B.R.D. International Bank for Reconstruction and Development
I.L.O.   International Labour Organization
N.E.D.B. National Economic Development Board
N.S.O.   National Statistical Office
U.S.O.M. United States Operations Mission

Thai Weights, Measures, Spelling, etc.

Weights and distances in Thailand are often reckoned in the metric system, though a standardised Thai system is also used. In this book the metric system is followed.

The only traditional Thai measurements used in this book are two which are still almost invariably used in both daily business and official publications. These are

1 *kwien* = 2000 litres   = 440 gallons capacity
1 *rai*   = 1600 sq metres = 1914 sq yards area

The Thai unit of currency, the *baht*, has the following parities in terms of International Monetary Fund values

1 *baht* = 0·0427245 grammes of fine gold   US\$1 = 20·80 *baht*

Thai words have no suffix for the plural, and the plural of *baht* is usually written *baht*. This practice is followed here. Other Thai words, when occurring in transliterated forms in English sentences are here given a final s, e.g. 'the six *changwats* of the West Sub-region'. Some scholars, while following this practice in general, make an exception of the word 'Thai', when used to mean inhabitants of the country. This exception can, however, lead to misunderstandings and in this book inhabitants of Thailand are called 'Thais'.

Thai words have, in general, been avoided in the text except for the administrative terms *changwat* (province), *amphur* (district) and *tambon* (roughly, parish). For place names the spelling of the U.S.O.M./N.S.O. *Statistical Year Book* is followed, or failing this, the U.S.O.M. *Changwat-Amphur Statistical Directory*. Where the titles of Thai books are transliterated (as well as translated) in notes, the spelling used is the same as that in the author's *Thailand: Social and Economic Studies in Development*, A.N.U. Press, 1967.

1

Introduction

One respect in which Thailand is often praised for its policy towards economic development is its emphasis on the importance of agriculture. Unlike many of the less developed countries it has put a good deal of money and effort into developing agricultural infrastructure—the irrigation, the roads and railways, even the research and extension activities, which raise productivity (N.E.D.B., 1964: ch. 6; 1967: ch. 9). Moreover there is a good deal of evidence that this policy is succeeding. Thai agriculture is, in fact, becoming more diversified, and at the same time productivity in the traditional main crop, rice, is improving, so reversing a trend towards falling yields which had been in existence for many decades (Ingram, 1955: 48-9; Trescott, 1968).

This lends special interest to the agricultural sector of the Thai economy, though we must be careful to avoid accepting the obvious implications too readily. If we infer that the Thai government gives special attention to agriculture out of concern for the welfare of the farmers who constitute some three-quarters of the population, our inference will probably be wrong. The large expenditures on roads, irrigation, etc., did not even result from a rational analysis of the best methods of promoting overall economic growth. Nor can we be sure that the improvement in productivity—still less the diversification—is a simple consequence of the expenditure of government funds on agricultural infrastructure. A closer look at Thai agriculture reveals other explanations and implications. Yet the interest of the subject is such that a closer look is justified.

1

In Silcock (1967) some attention was given to agriculture; three chapters were almost wholly concerned with the agricultural sector, and it was given some attention elsewhere also. Yet, because of the previous interests of the participants, agriculture was not given as much attention as it deserves. This book attempts to make good this deficiency by concentrating almost exclusively on the development of Thai agriculture. However, within agriculture it aims at reasonable comprehensiveness, so that some aspects of the rural economy covered particularly in chapters 9 and 10 of the former studies have also been included in this work, though with a different approach.

It is not sufficient to look at Thai export agriculture alone. This is obvious when we consider rice, of which over half is grown as a subsistence crop, although it is also Thailand's leading export. Thailand has, indeed, been successful in expanding its export crops, but it has at the same time apparently greatly expanded its output of crops and other products for consumption within Thailand. It is an 'outward-looking' economy (Myint, 1967), devoting much of its attention to export promotion rather than to import-substitution; yet it has succeeded in doing this without subjecting its own agriculture to any serious outside competition.

There are, however, special obstacles in the way of any detailed study of the structure and the changes of an agriculture producing for the Thai market. The published figures are neither very extensive nor very reliable. The process of change is also extremely complex: transport is simultaneously widening the area of exchange and increasing local real incomes, in some areas very rapidly; but the process is certainly not one of a straightforward increase in regional specialisation. Moreover the period of time for which figures are available for most of the questions one wishes to ask is still very short; although it is long enough for perceptible change to have taken place, it is certainly not yet long enough for elimination by reliable statistical methods of all random influences due to weather or flooding.

Some of the development problems raised in this book might well repay study in Thailand by a considerable team of investigators working together; but that is not the basis of the present book. It is based on the work of a single individual, using the statistical sources and existing secondary material supplemented by a very limited amount of field work. Nevertheless it has been thought worth while to publish it because of the interest and importance of the subject.

Not only did I work alone; I can claim no competence in the techniques of Thai (or any other) agriculture. There is always rather a tendency for a rural Thai to expect any European—except perhaps a soldier—to be an expert on any scientific matter. Particularly when I came to interview farmers, they could be forgiven for feeling some disappointment when I could give them no indication of the fertiliser or weed-killer best suited to their needs. Their questions were often informative to me, helping me to understand attitudes, and the nature of the service they received. I often wished that the exchange of information could have been less unequal.

Theoretical Considerations

The analysis of the agriculture of a country such as Thailand may be assisted by taking up first some theoretical questions. Perhaps one of the most interesting theoretical aspects of Thailand's development is the very considerable and rapid growth of a road transport network, reducing the costs of specialisation and increasing the integration of the economy. It is surprising that, in the general expansion of economic development theory in recent years, so little attention has been paid to general problems of 'opening up', or the impact of communications on the internal structure and characteristics of an economy. We shall attempt to set out briefly here the micro-economic and macro-economic characteristics of a contact economy, where new transport is opening up an area which previously produced mainly on a subsistence basis.[1]

At the beginning of contact with an external market economy,

[1] Economists appear to have followed very inadequately the lead given by Sir Keith Hancock in interpreting economic development in colonial areas in terms of frontier concepts. His breadth of vision made it possible to give unity to the 'opening up' process into regions both lightly and densely populated where the original economies were very different. See Hancock, 1942: vol. ii, pts 1 and 2. There are, however, advantages in looking specifically at the opening up process in a previously populated and culturally unified area. Since the use of the term 'frontier' has been largely pre-empted by American writers to describe advance into formerly 'empty' territory, I here use the term 'contact economy' to describe the characteristics of an economy on the frontier, in Hancock's sense, when studied from its own point of view and not from that of the specialised system in which it is being absorbed.

one of the chief characteristics of a contact economy is that the price of any given product in different places within the area will be subject to very wide, but also rapidly diminishing, differences. All goods from the outside world will be much cheaper at the ports of entry, much dearer at points far from these ports; farm prices of export crops will be much lower in remote areas, much higher near the ports; where there is rudimentary specialisation in tools or handicrafts, these will be much cheaper where they are produced, much dearer elsewhere.

New entrepreneurs, in these conditions, earn high profits from investment in transport equipment, premises, credit, and stock-in-trade. These, however, are not usually their only investments. They normally encounter an unspecialised, customary society in which the new trade tends to upset social customs and the basis of authority. They have to invest a good deal of effort in persuasion, education, and conciliation. When they have initiated new lines of trade they may easily be in the position of an inventor unprotected by patents, or an author unprotected by copyright. Imitation is much easier after the initial step has been taken.

The first in the field may enjoy some advantage in initiating further changes; but we need, in each situation, to look into the character of the enterprise generated by the circumstances, and at the factors that would make either continued innovation on the one hand or effort to prevent further competition on the other more likely to be profitable. In an initially unspecialised society the first entrepreneurs may well become closely involved in the social structure and the framework of authority. There will be at least some factors which will incline them to protect their investment by using social and political power, based on wealth, to check the growth of competition.

In so far as competition is allowed to develop, the advantages of improved transport accrue to the primary producers, in ways which will be discussed later. Yet analysis of a contact economy is seriously incomplete if it does not discuss the social and political conditions which prevent or favour competition. For it is competition which diffuses traders' profits by raising costs or lowering prices. The entrepreneur in a contact society is not normally made in the pattern described by Schumpeter (1949: 74-94). He is normally involved in efforts to stabilise the initial abnormal profits or political struggles to capture them from rivals. The Thai rice premium, for example, can be partly interpreted as a successful capture, for the public purse, of most of the profit resulting from improved transport of Thai rice during the twentieth century. The later stages of this political struggle are discussed in detail in Appendix I.

If the transport and trading interests are unable—either alone or in combination with the politicians—to stabilise the profits resulting from lower transport costs, the farm price of the goods exported will rise. This will be simply a redistribution, which does not directly affect the size of the gross domestic product; but if, as commonly happens, some of the export goods are also consumed within the country, the value of these also rises, and the gross domestic product, measured in terms of internationally traded goods, is raised by the amount of this rise in price (Usher, 1963: 140-58; 1965).

When, as in Thailand, one of the main exports is also the country's staple food, an improvement in the transport system which raised the farm price of that food would lead to a very great rise in the gross domestic product. It can be argued that much of this is illusory—a mere statistical accident—so long as the amount of rice consumed on farms is unchanged (Usher, 1965); yet in fact the change in the relative value of this rice and of other consumption goods is the source of possible specialisation which may come later, while the change in relative value of rice and fertilisers may stimulate new and more productive methods. The higher income is certainly there, even before the option to use it is exercised.

Low transport costs do not, of course, only raise the farm value of the original subsistence crop. They also increase the range of crops that it is now possible to produce, as well as increasing the range of consumption goods available. In some measure also, falling transport costs themselves add to the difficulty of establishing permanent and effective monopolies, so that the process of diffusion, once begun, is cumulative.

In Thailand the rice premium has prevented most of the advantages of falling transport costs from diffusing to rice farmers, but they can secure these advantages by switching to other crops. There is thus a much greater inducement to switch to other crops than would arise from lower transport costs alone. This is partly a distortion of the Thai economy; but in part it is an acceleration of the process of transition from a subsistence economy to one based on specialisation and exchange. The effect of this pressure needs to be examined in more detail. Some of the implications are discussed in chapters 2 and 3.

Turning to the macro-economic characteristics of a contact economy, we must recognise that the high cost of transport produces discontinuities which often make it more useful to apply Keynesian analysis to particular districts than to apply it to the country as a whole. Aggregate demand in Thailand as a whole may be a less useful concept than aggregate demand in Chon Buri Province or Takhli District. We can probably sensibly speak of a multiplier effect resulting from any autonomous increase in exports from Chon Buri, or any investment in Takhli, because of the proportion of the additional income that will be spent on products of that area. The analysis differs in some respects from that of an entire national economy, but it has more in common with it than would any regional study within a more developed economy with smaller price differentials.

One of the important differences relates to mobility of factors. Regional analysis is profitable because the mobility of factors is restricted by certain institutional barriers. Yet changing transport costs and manageable institutional changes can modify these restrictions. We can look at regions as economic entities with fixed factor supplies and later consider changes which may permit more growth by an influx of scarce factors from elsewhere.

Much of the recent growth in Thailand has been concentrated in quite limited regions. Some of the macro-economic implications are discussed in chapters 6 and 7.

Sources and Field Work

Most of the published material on Thai agriculture is available in English. Of the statistical sources virtually the only ones for which a knowledge of Thai is necessary are the annual crop reports and the annual reports of the provincial governments. Even the interpretations of the statistics of agriculture and the special research projects on particular problems of agricultural economics have, for the most part, either been written in English or translated into it. Among these, however, there are a few significant exceptions. Perhaps the most important is the series of annual reports on the production of rice. These have been delayed so much—the latest available in 1967 was that for 1962—that they tend to be little used. There is, however, some excellent analysis, very inadequately summarised in English; most of the statistical tables in these reports are given in English. Some of the special agricultural economics surveys by Kasetsart University are available only in Thai and a very full study of market structure—particularly in the livestock trade—in the Northeast is also in Thai only.

Since the present study has been mainly concerned with rice and the movement out of rice, and has sometimes needed to survey the structure of agriculture by provinces, it has been necessary to cover this Thai material as far as possible. In particular extensive use has been made of the two series of crop reports—by crops and by provinces—which the Department of Agriculture has published, extending from 1961 to 1965. Some provincial reports have also been used.

In addition I made two visits to rural areas, to verify and supplement statistical data. The first, a relatively informal visit, was made to the southern provinces in 1964, with a view to achieving three aims. First I wished to compare the rubber industry in south Thailand with that which I already knew in Malaysia. Next I wanted to inquire in the field, from officials whose confidence I could gain and from other responsible people, about the methods of collecting regular agricultural data and about local experiences in the 1963 Agricultural Census. Finally I wanted to form a general impression of the economy of the South Region, which has been much less discussed in the literature than the Central, North, and Northeast Regions.

Being at this time a special lecturer at Chulalongkorn University I had the great advantage that I could approach both government officials and private individuals and be accepted as a research worker, without affiliation to a government scheme. The corresponding disadvantage was that I had to rely on contacts arranged through my university colleagues, through the Bangkok Bank network, through Chinese merchants with whom I had contacts from Malaya, and other contacts arranged on a more casual basis. It was not possible to arrange any systematic plan of interviews in each province. I was able to visit Trang and Phuket on the west coast, Nakhon Si Thammaret, Songkhla, Yala, Pattani and Narathiwat on the east coast.

I had hoped to be able to interview both Thai-speaking and

Malay-speaking farmers, but in fact was unable to interview Malay-speaking ones except on the island of Phuket. The Malay spoken in the South Region proved to differ far more from standard Malay than the southern dialect of Thai from standard Thai. Moreover my movements were restricted by the government because of communist terrorism in the country areas. Thus my main sources of information on this occasion were bank officials, rubber dealers, government officials both administrative and technical, and school-teachers. The comparatively few farmers I interviewed were all Thai-speaking.

The second visit in 1967 was a more formal piece of field work, with interviews with approximately a hundred farmers, and the application of formal questionnaires to some seventy of them; though on this occasion too I also interviewed almost an equal number of officials, merchants, and teachers informally in addition to the formal interviews. My method on this occasion was to select eight provinces which—on the basis of a previous scrutiny of the provincial crop reports—appeared to have interesting character-istics, and to be well scattered over all regions except the South, and then to choose, by a more or less random method, one village in each province in which I could stay in the temple or in a villager's house for a few days, try to win the villagers' confidence, and interview villagers with a range of different incomes, and growing different crops.

I had not the resources, the previous knowledge, or the time, to attempt a sampling technique which would make it possible to specify with any precision the representativeness of the sample. The method of making the selection and the villages selected will be described here, since I have used the information derived as one type of evidence, and there may be unknown sources of bias which another worker may detect.

The provinces selected were two in the north (Chiang Mai and Nakhon Sawan) and two in the northeast (Roi Et and Nakhon Ratchasima), one (Chon Buri) in the southeastern and one (Ratcha-buri) in the southwestern extension of the Central Plain, and two (Sing Buri and Ang Thong) in the Central Plain proper. The reasons for selecting these provinces were that Chiang Mai and Nakhon Sawan were the leading provinces, respectively, of the small-scale irrigated farming area in the far north, and of the new maize and mung-bean (*Phaseolus aureus*) export area just north of the Central Plain. Roi Et was central in the northeast, part of the kenaf area but not confined to kenaf, while Nakhon Ratchasima was the nearest northeastern province to Bangkok and an area of many new developments. Chon Buri was the leading producer of cassava and sugar-cane for export, while Ratchaburi had developed highly capital intensive methods of vegetable growing that were influencing the farming of the rest of the southwest. Sing Buri and Ang Thong were rice-growing provinces of the Central Plain, the former with rather better irrigation and transport, the latter nearer to Bangkok.

Within the provinces there were no published data to use as a basis for selecting districts.[2] I eliminated the district in which the provincial capital was situated and chose one other at random for each province. Within the districts there were no adequate lists or maps from which to choose; to avoid having a specially convenient or successful village selected for me, I specified a distance in kilometers from the district office, asking the district officer, if this left him a choice, to choose not on the basis of convenience but to give preference to villages with a range of different crops. The greatest distance from a district office that I nominated was ten kilometers. Three of the eight villages selected had no road; one had neither a road nor a navigable waterway and mechanical transport could reach it only over the fields—by boat in the middle of of the wet season, by truck in the middle of the dry season.

In each village the headman was asked to select at least two poor farmers, two of medium income, and two of the wealthier ones, and I also selected as many as I could on the basis of casual contact. These last were intended to enable me to notice any obvious bias in the headman's selection.

It will be clear from this account that the farmers interviewed were not intended to be typical of all Thai farmers. I was studying changes, and the farmers were chosen from areas where change was actually taking place. In every province I visited the provincial government office, and discussed policy and development with such relevant officers as were there. I also usually visited the market and talked with merchants in the provincial capital. My deliberate exclusion of the district in which the capital was situated thus gave additional information, but introduced an element of bias by under-

---

[2] In some instances I found that the provincial *Annual Report* gave this information, but most of these were not available in Bangkok.

estimating the impact of official action; for this impact is naturally strongest near the provincial office.

An unintended bias was introduced by my giving the district officers the criterion—when selecting between equidistant villages —that they should choose villages with more than one crop. I believe that the district officers appreciated that I did not want them to choose either a good village or a convenient one, and acted accordingly. They did not, however, take the distance I had given as more than a rough guide, and consequently the need for choice among a number of alternatives was commoner than I intended. In all the eight provinces I encountered only one village which grew virtually only one crop. The others all had quite a range of alternative crops. I suspect that the proportion of villages growing virtually only rice for subsistence and export would, in Thailand as a whole, be much higher than one in eight. It would, in particular, have been helpful to see one such village in the Northeast Region, where they are probably still common in the relatively crowded land near the Mekong Tributaries but away from the main roads (Platenius, 1963). I was certainly influenced by the differences between the village in Ang Thong, which depended almost wholly on rice, and the other villages which I saw, though I have tried to express the resulting conjectures tentatively.

The questionnaires which I used are given in Appendix II. It must be emphasised that these were, in the main, simply the basis for extended interviews. Some results can be expressed statistically and a few of these are used in chapter 7; but the main reasons for using formal quantifiable methods were to enable me first to focus the discussion without discourtesy, when I wished to do so, next to hold extensive interviews with farmers, by-passing the village headman, without appearing to criticise his information, and finally to conform to the stereotype of a research worker which the current American fashion appears to have imposed on the Thai National Research Council, through which I had to work.

I normally sought replies to questionnaires 1 and 6 from the headman, 2 from the schoolmaster, and 3 from two or more traders. Questionnaires 4 and 5 were put to all farmers, while a few farmers were given questionnaire 7 and others questionnaire 6. One questionnaire had to be rejected because translation difficulties produced misleading replies.

To avoid misunderstanding it must be emphasised that the purpose of describing the method of work is not to enable another worker to repeat it, but to give some indication of possible distortions in my information. I was attempting to collect and pass on information, as reliably as I could, about a little-known economy. I was not propounding a hypothesis for verification nor do I see any advantage (in the present state of our knowledge) in presenting the information in this form.

Information based on these two visits to farmers, traders, schoolteachers and merchants in Thai rural areas is used in the various chapters which follow. The actual villages I visited are briefly described and set in their regional settings in chapters 6 and 7.

Historical Background

Some of the special features of Thai society that have a bearing on its present economic development are discussed in chapter 3. It is not necessary, in the introduction to a book on agricultural development, to say much about Thai history; but there has been a continuity in Thai development which makes it necessary to go back into Thai history to explain some of these important features, for example the flexible attitude to land, the late development of road transport, the comparative absence of large plantations, the role of the Chinese, the position of the Irrigation Department, and the extension of rice-growing into the dry Northeast Region. These can all be explained in terms of the characteristics and policy of the absolute monarchy which ruled Thailand until 1932.

During the Ayuthaya monarchy, from the fourteenth to the eighteenth centuries, the Thai state developed a system of absolute rule partly derived from the god-kings of the Cambodian Empire (Wales, 1965). Cambodian officials helped the Ayuthaya kings to develop a functionally specialised bureaucracy in place of the more common system in Asia of rule through territorial chiefs. The specialised officials lived on the rents of a measured quantity of land which they held from the king, but were not assigned a definite region. Peasants too were attached to a particular patron, but could change to another by mutual consent. Movement from place to place was thus fairly common, and no strong political attitudes to land or enduring village loyalties developed within the considerable area under direct royal control (Wijeyewardene, 1967).

In the nineteenth century the monarchy's successful leadership in modernisation—training of students abroad, liberalisation of

trade, promotion of public health, abolition of slavery, introduction
of a cabinet system—explains the people's respect and readiness
to accept official suggestions for social and economic change. The
preoccupation of King Chulalongkorn (Rama V, 1868-1910) with
keeping Thailand solvent, when strategic railways had to be built,
explains much of the country's economic framework up to World
War II (Ingram, 1955): the extraordinary centralisation on Bangkok, the key role of the railway in development, the need to maintain its revenues, and the consequent refusal to build trunk roads.
Roads could play a leading role in post-war Thai rural development largely because several other features of a modern economy
existed without a road system, and the need for roads was clearly
felt.

The monarchy's relations with the colonial powers also affected
the structure of the rice trade. European (mainly British) firms
dominated the Bangkok rice export business. This was because
most rice importing territories were either under British control or
supplied from Singapore or London, and after the Bowring Treaty
of 1855 the British had greatly expanded this trade (Ingram, 1955:
ch. 3; Skinner, 1957: 1-2).

Chinese were, however, the main intermediaries in this and
several other trades. Their strength originally arose from the
Bangkok dynasty's family connections with leading Chinese (Skinner, 1957: ch. 1).

The cultivation of rice as the chief occupation of the great
majority of Thais can be attributed mainly to geography. The
great plain around Ayuthaya and Bangkok, with its flat surface,
annual flooding, and limited rainfall, is extremely suitable for a
single crop of rice, though in large areas other crops can be grown
only with difficulty. Outside the Central Plain, however, rice as a
principal crop is less a result of geography itself than of history:
Thais grow rice for their own consumption because they were
already rice-eaters before they occupied their present territory. In
the Northeast Region Thailand, in the nineteenth century, established its authority in an area previously administered as many
small states between the Thai and Cambodian kingdoms, and this
ensured the persistence of a mainly subsistence agriculture. There
was little active interest by Bangkok in the economy of the area
until World War II, and trade was mainly the exchange of the rice
surplus for a few imported products.

Outline

This is a relatively short book, attempting to set out the limitations of our present knowledge of the facts of the Thai rural economy, to summarise some of the more important facts, as derived from such evidence as we have, and to apply to them some of the basic concepts of a contact economy.

At the very beginning, in the next chapter, we discuss the principal problems of measurement involved in any discussion of the facts of the Thai economy. This suggests that we should be somewhat wary of aggregates; yet a preliminary outline is necessary. This is presented in chapter 3, in the form of a relatively brief description of the development of the principal rural products of Thailand up to 1950, with a largely descriptive overall account of recent developments. It is explained that analysis in terms of particular products and particular regions is necessary, to obtain a clear picture of recent events.

Chapters 4 and 5 approach the development of the rural economy in terms of particular crops, the growth in the area applied to the cultivation of each, important changes in conditions, changes in yield and major problems. Three of the principal crops, rice, rubber, and kenaf, are treated in chapter 4 and the others in chapter 5.

In the course of this analysis it becomes clear that the growth of output for some of these crops is extremely localised, and that in others also the distribution of output over the map of Thailand is a most important factor. The next two chapters therefore consider regional questions including the economy of particular villages visited within the different regions. Chapter 6 considers the Central Region, including the Central Plain proper and extensions of it to the southeast and the southwest. Chapter 7 considers the North, the Northeast, and the South.

These chapters prepare the way for Chapter 8 which attempts to draw together material from the previous four chapters and to suggest some interpretations. It includes some quantitative analysis of the rural sector as a whole. Chapters 9 and 10 then attempt some criticisms of current policy and suggestions for the promotion of development in the light of the analysis undertaken.

2

Problems of Measurement

Relative Size of the Rural Sector

In any discussion of Thai agriculture it is desirable to compare the size of the rural sector as a whole with the rest of the economy, to gain some idea of the relative magnitudes of the different parts of the rural sector and to show how they are changing relative to one another. Unfortunately it is impossible to do these things in an unequivocal and reliable way. An attempt is made in chapter 8 to discuss growth rates for the rural sector and relative changes in the importance of different crops, but before this can be done it is necessary to discuss a number of problems of measurement.

Some of the difficulties can be indicated by attempting to present a picture of the relative importance of the rural sector in the whole economy. For this we define the rural sector as including the whole of agriculture—all crops and livestock—and also forestry and fisheries. Table 2.1 uses official figures to show the relative share of the rural sector in the Thai gross domestic product, the exports of Thailand, and the Thai labour force.

This picture needs qualification in a number of important respects. It is not a matter of simply correcting the official figures. We need to raise certain conceptual problems, particularly in relation to the gross domestic product, and also to decide which of alternative statistical sources we are to use for different purposes, and what are the limits of our knowledge as derived from these sources. It is by no means impossible to derive information from the available statistics but the inconsistencies must be recognised.

In discussing the contribution of the rural sector to gross domes-

14

Table 2.1 Division of gross domestic product (1961-5), domestic exports (1961-5) and economically active population (1960 Census) between parts of the rural sector and the rest of the economy

	Gross domestic product 1961-5 average		Domestic exports 1961-5 average		Economically active population 11 years and over (1960)	
	m *baht*	% of total	m *baht*	% of total	000	% of total
Rice	7,924[a]	11·3	3,830·5	36·1	11,187	81·2
Other crops and livestock	13,236[a]	18·9	5,103·1	48·1	36	0·3
Forestry	2,014	2·9	340·4	3·2	111	0·8
Hunting and fishing	1,675	2·4	84·9	0·8		
Total rural sector	24,849	35·6	9,358·9	88·3	11,334	82·3
Rest of economy	44,999	64·4	1,245·9	11·7	2,438	17·7
Total	69,848	100·0	10,604·8	100·0	13,772	100·0

[a] The division between rice and other crops is not reliable, for the 1964-5 detailed figures for GDP were not available at the time of writing. Figures for agricultural crops were calculated for 1961-5 and divided between rice and other crops according to percentages calculated for 1961-3. Probably relatively higher prices for rice approximately offset relatively lower increases in output. For detailed comparison the new national income figures to 1966 should be used.

Sources: N.S.O., *Statistical Year Book, 1965*; N.E.D.B., *National Income Statistics of Thailand*, 1964; Ministry of Agriculture, *Agricultural Statistics of Thailand, 1965*.

tic product we can clearly distinguish conceptual problems from statistical ones; moreover the conceptual problems require separate consideration because they relate to the rice taxes and are clearly relevant to the consideration both of the causes of change and of appropriate economic policy.

It will be apparent that the contribution of the rural sector to the gross domestic product contains both a value component and a quantity component. Our main conceptual problem relates to the value attributed to agricultural products and particularly to rice. The main statistical problems relate to outputs—usually estimated from acreage and yield—and they concern most agricultural products other than rice and rubber.

Conceptual Problems

There is a systematic distortion of values in the Thai rural economy through heavy taxation of rice affecting the economy's relations with the outside world (Usher, 1966: 430-41). This distortion is, however, complicated by the fact that the rice taxes merely prolong an undervaluation of Thai domestic income which was formerly a natural consequence of high transport costs.

Following a lead given by Usher we can classify contact economies as mining camp types and surplus-export types (Usher, 1963: 140-58). In the former, contact with the outside world takes the form of an outside demand for a product not previously significant in local production or consumption. It is necessary to attract labour into the new production and bring in subsistence goods from outside. If transport costs and entrepreneurial profits are high the local money incomes will be high, costs of living will be high, and even real incomes will be high enough to attract some immigration to the area. This may or may not be international migration. Competition, and the cheapening of transport, will introduce forces tending to raise local money incomes but also forces tending to lower them —fares will be lower, so that a smaller real wage will be enough to attract labour to move in; and the cost of living will be lower, so that a smaller money wage will mean the same real wage as before. Because the most likely justification for building new transport is the availability in a region of some scarce mineral, or the possibility of producing a scarce plantation product, mining-camp types are common in contact economies.

In Thailand only the northern teak forests and the southern

tin-mines approximately conform to this type. One of the characteristic results of this type of economy is the effort to import labour under supervision by employers; but in Thailand this was never carried very far. For an agricultural analysis the surplus-export type of economy is more relevant to Thailand.

In surplus-export economies the good first exported is one previously produced for local consumption. Here, the higher are transport costs and entrepreneurs' profits, the lower will be local real and money incomes. Competition, and the cheapening of transport, will raise local money incomes, and raise real incomes more.

The way in which this occurs can be understood if we can assume that transport costs between the ports of different countries are zero. Farmers' incomes will be valued mainly in terms of the goods exported overseas; but farm prices of these will at first be low because of the high internal transport costs. They will rise as these transport costs fall, unless merchants are able to maintain a monopsony.

Thailand has always been a surplus-export economy. The higher the cost of transport, and the greater the element of monopsony in marketing, the lower will be both Thai prices and Thai incomes, expressed in terms of Thai currency converted at free exchange rates. In fact, the margin between the farm price of a ton of paddy and the corresponding world price of rice has remained not far short of 100 per cent of the farm price, in spite of greatly improved transport and increasing competition in the rice trade, because of the heavy taxation of rice exports. Vegetables, eggs, and other products which are both produced and consumed by the farmers will have low prices in sympathy with rice. For on the one hand farmers will be driven by low returns from rice to producing more of them, while low rice prices will also reduce farmers' demand for them. This applies of course only to crops which enter negligibly into international trade. The resulting low cost of living keeps wages relatively low in comparison to both import and export prices, so giving some support to Thai industry and also encouraging a switch to export crops other than rice.

In assessing the importance of the agricultural sector in Thailand, how should we deal with the distortions in the price structure introduced by the rice premium? The Thai government's attitude is quite straightforward. The rice premium is an indirect tax. Its proceeds must be deducted from gross national product in order to

C

derive net national product. At first this seems odd, when it is a tax which keeps incomes down, until we recall that the object in national income calculations is to assess income in terms of goods and services at their local factor cost (Sherwood, 1956: 73-83). The Thai system of reckoning has two merits: first it draws our attention to the absurdity, in international comparisons, of taking the exchange rate, uncritically, as the conversion factor; and second, it shows that if we can think in terms of Thai factor costs the exchange premium is like a general tariff on imported foreign goods.

The convention by which the actual proceeds of indirect taxes are deducted, without any allowance for elasticities of demand and supply, is at best approximate. In the Thai case we are left wondering uneasily just what is the appropriate Thai price level when these deductions are made. There appears to be no wholly satisfactory solution.

The impact of the rice taxes on the economy can be clearly understood only if we see them in their historical context. The conditions from which these taxes emerged are discussed in Appendix I. Here it must be pointed out that these taxes merely represented an alternative form of interception of the gains which falling transport costs might have distributed to rice farmers, had there been no monopsony in the rice trade during the period between World War I and World War II.

To what extent had the farmers benefited from improved transport in the pre-war period? Certainly in areas near Bangkok the margin in the early 1930s was little more than might be accounted for by transport costs. In remoter areas, however, the proportional difference between the farm price and the export price was as high as it is now. Since there were already barges with motor traction on the main rivers this difference probably represents margins kept up by monopsony of transport or tying of suppliers by indebtedness.[1]

Table 2.2 shows the average difference between the Bangkok wholesale price of rice and the farm price of the equivalent quantity

[1] See Zimmerman, 1931, ch. IX. Zimmerman records the monopsonistic conditions binding farmers to particular dealers, but appears to think that large numbers of dealers would help to ensure low margins. This study was prepared in Harvard just before the publication of Chamberlin's *Theory of Monopolistic Competition.*

Table 2.2 Farm price for rice expressed as a percentage of Bangkok prices, 1929 and 1930

| Provinces | 1929 | | 1930 | |
	White rice (Khao Na Suan)	Glutinous rice	White rice (Khao Na Suan)	Glutinous rice
Northeastern	51·24	35·51	60·88	34·86
Northern	54·63	50·80	64·20	49·53
Central	81·75		83·17	
Southern	80·22		84·46	

Source: C. C. Zimmerman, *Siam Rural Economic Survey, 1930-31*, Bangkok Times Press Ltd, 1931, Tables IX B to F, pp. 186-93.

of paddy, expressed as a percentage of the Bangkok price for various provinces in the years 1929-30.

It is impossible to get much accurate information about marketing conditions in the inter-war period; but it is certainly widely believed by the Thais that there was a great deal of monopsony by the Chinese at this time, and it is unlikely that this is a baseless belief.

This belief sometimes leads Thai officials today to argue that the rice taxes cannot be a significant source of change in the economy, since they merely replaced a system of formal rice monopsony and exchange control after World War II and a system with a good deal of informal monopsony before that.[2] This is a misunderstanding of the position. The significance of the rice premium is that—in a period in which pre-war education, wartime industrialisation and post-war development efforts were modernising the economy—the old process of extracting most of the subsistence farmers' surplus did not cease, but turned into a formal tax. Hence the pressure to move into untaxed alternatives became more obvious, whether these were other lines of agriculture or non-agricultural production.

If we are to measure the relative importance of agriculture or any branch of it, at a point in time or over a period, we cannot simply neglect the fact that the farm price of rice is approximately half the international price, because the government taxes away about 45 per cent of rice export proceeds.[3] For rice is not only

[2] This is a reference to conversations with Thai officials and their advisers, rather than to literature.

[3] Based on Table 2.3. There are various ways of assessing the average size of the rice premium. This is one of the highest.

much the largest user of rural land and rural labour; it also has close economic relations of transformation, substitution, or both with almost all important products in the Thai economy. Most rice farmers produce some subsidiary crop, wages and rents are often paid in rice, and rice, as the most important constituent in the cost of living, dominates the level of unskilled wages.

The simplest way to allow for the rice premium is just to raise the value of all rice produced by the average amount of the rice premiums. Table 2.3 shows the proportion which the rice premium bore to the total export price of rice for the mixture of grades found in Usher's 'typical' ton of paddy. This typical ton, however, was merely a specimen designed by him on the basis of his studies. It has no statistical significance in relation to the country as a whole. It includes, for example, no parboiled rice or cargo rice. The proportions in which rice is exported do not correspond to the proportions in which it is grown; and some of the export gradings on which the premium is based do not apply to rice milled for home consumption. Usher's typical figure is appreciably larger than the average obtained by dividing the rice tax proceeds by the total rice exported; moreover this applies only to white rice; glutinous rice is about a third of the crop but only a tenth of the exports, and is taxed at a lower rate. Strictly we should raise the value of the glutinous rice crop by this lower figure.

Moreover it would be misleading merely to raise the value of rice only; as indicated above, the lowering of the rice price lowers many other internal prices, and an accurate estimate of the relative importance of the rural sector has to allow for all of these. The income from rice as a proportion of total agricultural income has first fallen and then risen in recent years (N.S.O., 1964: t.7); in 1963 it was 38·5 per cent. About a quarter of non-rice agriculture consists of crops such as rubber and maize the value of which is quite unaffected by rice taxes, because they are sold in a competitive world market. All other agricultural products—crops mainly or wholly home consumed, fishing, livestock, and forest products— are in some measure reduced in price by the rice taxes;[4] other products outside agriculture are also affected in some degree.

To indicate the orders of magnitude involved, we estimate in

---

[4] Partly through effects on demand, because rural incomes are lower and people also substitute rice for other consumption; partly through effects on supply because people are driven to produce other crops.

Table 2.3 The chain of rice prices in Thailand, showing incidence of costs, profit margins, and taxes[a]

(all values in *baht*)

			Costs	Taxes	Price of rice (cumulative)	% of total selling price
Paddy price at the farm					770	46
Transport to the mill			30			2
Miller's account (rice sold at Bangkok)						
		Costs				
Paddy price at the mill					800	48
Unloading		5				
Labour		35				
Tax		36		36		
Transport to Bangkok		18				
Commission		5				
Other selling expenses		10				
Profit		12				
Total milling cost			121			8

Milling out-turn		Proceeds at Bangkok				
Grade of rice	kg	Price per kg	Value			
100%	420	1·62	680			
A Special	42	0·97	41			
A	170	0·87	148			
C	40	0·62	25		894	54
Bran	90	0·30[b]	27[b]		27[b]	2[b]

			Costs	Taxes	Price of rice (cumulative)	% of total selling price
Export tax (4·2%)				69		4
Rice premium						
950 *bt* per ton on 100%						
A Special and A		599				
800 *bt* per ton on C		32				
Total rice premium				631		38
Exporter's gross margin 60 *bt* per ton			40			2
Selling price of rice f.o.b. (excluding bran)					1,634	98
Export price including bran sold at mill					1,661	100
Total taxes				736		

[a] One ton of paddy yielding mainly 100% rice, milled 30 km from Bangkok, 1965.

[b] Bran is normally sold at the mill but its price is a component of the total price of the initial paddy and it must therefore be included.

Source: D. Usher, 'The Thai Rice Trade' in T. H. Silcock (ed.), *Thailand: Social and Economic Studies in Development*, Canberra, 1967.

Table 2.4 Estimate of upper limit of agricultural income revalued to allow for effects of the rice premium, 1961-5

	1961	1962	1963	1964	1965
1 Rice output converted at 66% to rice grain = 000 tons	5,978	6,330	6,505	7,127	7,306
2 Premium per ton of rice: bt	563·6	550·2	632·2	649·6	618·1
3 Increase of GDP from rice through adjustment for rice premium (1 × 2) m bt	3,369·2	3,482·8	4,112·4	4,629·7	4,519·5
4 Increase in GDP from home consumed agriculture through adjustment for rice premium m bt[a] [c]	1,648	1,445	2,002	2,224	2,629[a]
5 Increase in GDP from partly exported agriculture through adjustment for rice premium m bt[b] [c]	183	155	212	294	317[b]·
6 Increase in total GDP from agriculture through adjustment for rice premium (3 + 4 + 5) m bt	5,200	5,083	6,326	7,148	7,466
7 Official GNP from agriculture m bt	23,166	24,307	25,110	25,368	26,294
8 Adjusted GDP from agriculture m bt	28,366	29,390	31,436	32,506	33,760
9 Adjusted total GDP m bt	65,169	70,390	75,287	81,964	87,652
10 Adjusted ratio of GDP from agriculture to total GDP %	43·5	41·8	41·8	39·7	38·5
11 Official ratio of GDP from agriculture to total GDP %	38·6	37·2	36·4	33·9	32·8

[a] It is assumed that the value of output of the following might be adjusted upward by a proportion not great than $\frac{2}{3}$ of the proportional adjustment of rice: forest products, less teak; livestock, less buffaloes; sugar-cane, all vegetables, all fruit. (For notes b and c and sources see p. 23.)

Table 2.4 a rough upper limit to the relative importance of agriculture from 1961 to 1965. The figure for the average rice premium per ton is one supplied in 1965 by the Export Division of the Department of External Trade. It leaves out taxes other than the premium, is lower than Usher's figures (given above in Table 2.3), and differs slightly from the figure given in the budget documents, no doubt as a result of differences in timing; the approximation here is so crude that there is little point in attempting detailed reconciliations. If other rice taxes were included the figures could be about 15 per cent higher, but it would be unreasonable to set the maximum as high as this without allowing an offset for the lower premium on glutinous rice which would work in the opposite direction, and be of the same order of magnitude.

We allow for the effect of the rice premium on other agricultural prices in lines 4 and 5: crops and other rural products produced for local consumption are allowed to increase by not more than two-thirds of the percentage by which rice increases;[5] products which are exported in relatively small amounts and for which the local price cannot be assumed to be export-determined, for various reasons are allowed to increase by not more than one-third of the rice percentage. This is not, of course, a figure that should be treated as more than a very approximate guess.

For what it is worth, this table indicates that the 1961-5 decline in the relative importance of agriculture could have been from

---

b It is assumed that the value of output of the following might be adjusted upward by a proportion not greater than ⅓ of the proportional adjustment of rice: coconuts, groundnuts, sesame, tobacco, buffaloes.

c The proportional adjustment of the rice price is calculated by expressing the premium per ton of rice given in line 2 as a percentage of the Bangkok wholesale price of rice given in Table 184 (p. 376) of the *Statistical Year Book, 1965*. For 1965 the wholesale price of 1406 has been taken from Usher's Tables. See Table 2.3.

Sources: N.E.D.B., *Performance Evaluation of Development in Thailand, 1965*; N.S.O., *Statistical Year Book, 1965*; Ministry of Agriculture, *Agricultural Statistics of Thailand, 1964*; Export Division, Department of Foreign Trade, 'Rice Premiums' (mimeo.), 1965.

5 There is no theoretical or statistical basis for choosing the fractions ⅔ and ⅓. It is not even possible to prove rigorously that the first ratio is greater than the second and both lie between one and zero, though this seems likely.

about 44 per cent to 38 per cent instead of from just under 40 per cent to just under 33 per cent if different conventions had been adopted about the true value of rice and other crops. For purposes of policy and analysis we should realise that Thailand's agricultural sector is probably undervalued; though, as already indicated, theory does not give us very clear guidance as to what the correct valuation should be.

Statistical Problems: Production

Probably the most reliable source on Thai agriculture is the trade figures. Net exports, however, are useful only for crops where local consumption is known to be negligible; and this applies to few crops. Up to World War II, for example, exports gave a fairly good indication of the output of rubber. Since the war rubber export figures have been much less significant, first because of smuggling in the immediate post-war years (Silcock, 1967: 10n.), and later because an unknown amount is manufactured locally; the latter discrepancy is, however, unlikely to exceed 10 per cent. Maize and castor beans are the only other crops for which exports approximate reasonably closely to output.

Table 2.5 Exports and production of maize and castor beans and exports of castor oil, 1950-65

| | Maize 000 metric tons | | Castor beans 000 metric tons | | Castor oil metric tons |
	Exports	Production	Exports	Production	Exports
1950	11·8	27	7·2	3·2	226
1951	22·6	42	12·7	12·5	282
1952	25·2	45	18·7	10·0	11
1953	34·7	51	20·9	9·2	—
1954	37·0	62	14·4	16·2	87
1955	68·2	68	13·6	15·5	20
1956	81·5	115	22·2	23·9	—
1957	64·3	137	26·0	32·5	—
1958	162·9	186	15·7	28·6	—
1959	236·8	317	31·4	34·0	—
1960	514·7	544	24·0	43·0	—
1961	567·2	598	32·6	32·8	—
1962	472·4	665	54·0	43·6	26
1963	744·0	858	40·1	52·9	50
1964	1,115·0	935	36·2	39·0	41
1965	804·4	1,021	28·2	31·6	47

Source: Ministry of Agriculture, Agricultural Statistics of Thailand, 1958, 1965.

Table 2.5 compares the official output and export figures for maize and castor beans since 1950. These figures can be used as evidence concerning the reliability of the output figures. There is very little local use of castor beans, though a small amount of castor oil is manufactured and in 1950-1 some 200 tons a year were exported. A little of the maize produced is used for human consumption and in the last few years a beginning has been made with using it for animal feed in Thailand.

The table shows, however, that castor bean production figures were probably too low in the immediate post-war period, and that the recent growth in the production of maize has probably been slightly overestimated.

Turning to the figures for production we find that there are two independent statistical sources. The different departments of the Ministry of Agriculture publish annual figures of area harvested and yield for rice, and also for upland crops and vegetables.[6] Regular livestock figures are also published. Independent of these figures are those given in the Agricultural Census for 1963 (N.S.O., 1963).

There are great discrepancies, for most crops other than rice, between the Ministry of Agriculture figures and the census figures. These discrepancies are much larger for individual crops by provinces than for the same crops considered over the country as a whole. Table 2.6 shows, in the form of a frequency table, the extent to which census data and ministry data for the same crop and province differ for 1962, for several important crops. Table 2.7 gives a comparison of the whole kingdom figures for the same crops and some others for which comparable figures exist. If we could rely on the census, the size of the discrepancies shown in these two tables would indeed virtually compel us to discard the evidence of the crop reports altogether. However, the export figures for three important crops, maize, kenaf, and cassava, make it difficult either to ignore the ministry's figures or to take the census as wholly reliable.

A comparative study was made by Gajewski (1965), of the

---

[6] These figures are taken from the Ministry of Agriculture, *Agricultural Statistics of Thailand, Sa-thi-ti-kan-pluk phüt-rai lae phüt-phak* (*Statistics of the Planting of Upland Crops and Vegetables*) hereafter referred to as *Crop Reports*, Changwat Series and Crop Series (in Thai). Annual since 1961.

Table 2.6 Frequency table showing comparison between Ministry of Agriculture figures and Census of Agriculture figures for each province, for area harvested, output, and yield per *rai* for selected crops in 1962

Crops and particulars	Total no. of provinces in both ministry and census figures	No. of regions in which remainders included[a]	Number of provinces in which $\frac{\text{Ministry of Agriculture figure}}{\text{Census of Agriculture figure}}$ gave the quotients as stated below							
			less than $\frac{1}{2}$	$\frac{1}{2} - \frac{9}{10}$	$\frac{9}{10} - \frac{11}{10}$	$\frac{11}{10} - 1\frac{1}{2}$	$1\frac{1}{2} - 3$	3-6	6-9	9 and over
Maize										
Area harvested	41	3 (30)	7	8	4	6	3	2	2	12
Output	41	3 (30)	7	6	3	4	6	5	0	13
Yield per *rai*	41	3 (30)	1	1	13	18	10	0	0	1
Groundnuts										
Area harvested	52	3 (15)	5	6	4	5	18	13	3	1
Output	52	3 (15)	3	6	4	7	17	10	4	4
Yield per *rai*	52	3 (15)	1	16	11	19	8	0	0	0
Mung-beans										
Area harvested	26	4 (32)	10	5	2	4	4	2	2	1
Output	26	4 (32)	4	3	1	4	4	5	5	4
Yield per *rai*	26	4 (32)	0	0	0	2	19	9	0	0
Soya beans										
Area harvested	13	3 (29)	4	4	2	2	2	2	0	0
Output	13	3 (29)	2	4	0	3	4	3	0	0
Yield per *rai*	13	3 (29)	0	0	2	5	9	0	0	0

Castor beans[b]

Area harvested	28	2 (13)	5	8	2	0	9	5	0	1
Output	28	2 (13)	1	4	1	4	4	10	4	2
Yield per *rai*	28	2 (13)	0	1	1	3	20	5	0	0

Cassava

Area harvested	22	4 (46)	1	7	2	5	6	5	0	0
Output	22	4 (46)	0	7	4	5	4	5	1	0
Yield per *rai*	22	4 (46)	2	10	3	8	2	1	0	0

Sesame[b]

Area harvested	26	3 (20)	11	4	3	2	4	4	1	0
Output	26	3 (20)	7	4	1	0	6	6	2	3
Yield per *rai*	26	3 (20)	0	0	0	3	18	7	1	0

[a] Ministry of Agriculture *Crop Reports* give an entry for every province for which they have an observation for a particular crop; the Census of Agriculture gives no figure for certain provinces but includes their area harvested, output, etc. in a total for the region. For provinces covered in this way in the census no detailed comparison can be given, but the remainder for the region was treated as one entry and used as a divisor for the sum of the provinces in the region which were listed in the crop reports but not in the census. The number of such remainders is shown for each row, and the number of provinces aggregated in this way is shown in parentheses.

[b] In two cases, provinces Buri Ram (N.E.), and Prachuap Khiri Khan (S.) the Census of Agriculture gave an observation for castor beans and sesame respectively, but no entry was recorded by the ministry.

Sources: Ministry of Agriculture, *Statistics of the Planting of Field Crops and Vegetables* (Crop Series), 1963; N.S.O., *Census of Agriculture, 1963, changwat* volumes, regional volumes and *Whole Kingdom* volume.

Table 2.7 Comparison between Ministry of Agriculture figures and Census of Agriculture figures for area harvested, output, and yield per *rai* for the whole kingdom for selected crops in 1962

Crop	Area harvested 000 *rai*		Output metric tons		Yield kg per *rai*	
	Census	Ministry	Census	Ministry	Census	Ministry
All rice	37,228	38,696	9,252,696	9,279,478	249	240
Maize	1,636	2,009	507,041	665,429	269	345
Chillies	222[a]	173	n.a.	34,265	67[b]	198
Watermelons	121	110	n.a.	118,016	n.a.	1,072
Ramie	2	6	133	823	68	133
Kenaf	518	670	60,002	134,048	116	200
Jute	192	45	20,066	6,690	105	150
Cotton	245	361	16,973	41,308	69	114
Mung-beans	522	307	43,684	53,710	84	175
Soya beans	137	170	14,669	30,023	107	176
Sesame	112	109	5,953	16,008	53	146
Groundnuts	291	533	37,886[c]	112,406[d]	130	211
Tobacco	258	255	99,215[e]	47,944[f]	385	188
Castor beans	229	275	17,131	43,604	75	158
Cassava	504	761	945,363	2,076,928	1,876	2,729
Sugar-cane	433	628	1,689,588	3,154,648	3,902	5,021
Pineapples	171	185	83,217[g]	320,778	487[h]	1,737
Bananas	598	599	313,560[i]	652,490	524[j]	1,087

[a] Fresh and dried.
[b] Dried only.
[c] Shelled.
[d] Unshelled.
[e] Fresh leaf.
[f] Dried leaf.
[g] 000 pineapples.
[h] Fruits per *rai*.
[i] 000 bunches.
[j] Bunches per *rai*.

Source: N.S.O., *Census of Agriculture, 1963, Whole Kingdom* volume.

National Income Office, checking the census figures against those of the ministry by reference to exports and other information. The National Income Office is, of course, reluctant to make major revisions without good cause, and the mere fact that for most crops the ministry figures are to be retained as a basis for the regular national income series should not be given too much weight. We may summarise the study, so far as it bears on the relative reliability of the two series for various crops as follows:

Kenaf and maize: The census figures are so far below the total export figures that they cannot be considered reliable, especially as there is substantial local consumption; the ministry figures are reasonably compatible with exports.

Cassava: The computation of exports involves complex conversion factors, which, however, are believed to be reasonably reliable. Census figures, though slightly greater than exports, would leave insufficient for local consumption. Ministry figures, however, are almost certainly inflated—they imply more local consumption than export, and this is most improbable.

Jute: There is evidence that the census or the ministry—more probably the census, in view of the trade figures—confused jute with kenaf.

Cotton: Independent inquiries have been made into use in manufacture, yield per *rai*, and province by province comparisons. These suggest that the yield figures of the ministry are much too high and those of the census about right; however, a good many provinces have been missed altogether by the census.

Tobacco: Imports and exports are both relatively small. The use of dried tobacco by the Thai Tobacco Monopoly is about 10,000 metric tons a year. The use of local types of tobacco not passing through the monopoly is difficult to gauge. Census figures suggest that it is equal to about half the amount of tobacco used by the monopoly; the ministry figures suggest that it is more than three times as great. Though the Gajewski study gives no decision on which is more likely, the *Household Expenditure Survey, Whole Kingdom* volume, (published since that study appeared) suggests that rather more than three times as much tobacco is consumed in villages as in towns (making allowance for cheaper qualities at lower incomes). Some village tobacco is, of course, bought from the monopoly; but the census figure is likely to be too low. The ministry figure could be right but is more likely to be high.

Sesame, soya beans, and mung-beans: Higher ministry figures here are mainly due to higher yield; exports are inadequate to indicate which figures are better, and local consumption is unknown and difficult to estimate.

Castor beans: These are nearly all exported and export figures tally reasonably with ministry figures (which are more than double the census figures mainly because of higher yields).

Coconuts: Ministry figures for area are 30 per cent higher than those of the census; yield figures are almost double. No adequate check is possible, but the ministry admitted there had been no recent field checks and yields probably did not allow sufficiently for old and exhausted trees. However, ministry officials would not accept the census average yield of only 25 nuts per tree.

Chillies, garlic, and onions: Figures here are not comparable because census figures show the commercial dried chilli, garlic, and shallots (small onions) only, while some cultivation is grouped under truck crops (where yields are not given) and some under kitchen gardens for home use, where neither yields nor areas by crop are given.

Groundnuts: Ministry figures are 80 per cent higher than census ones, this time mainly because of larger area. Ministry figures are for unshelled, census for shelled, nuts; if a ratio of 5 : 3 is taken to allow for the shells, average yield for both is about 130 kg per *rai*. At least two-thirds of production is locally consumed, in a number of different forms which cannot be identified in the Household Expenditure Survey.

Sugar-cane: This can be checked against refining figures which tally with the census. The ministry total, which is nearly double, seems too high.

Rubber: Here ministry data are based on exports. Census figures for smoked sheet tally with them satisfactorily on a national basis, but the census does not cover other grades.

On the whole the study suggests that neither set of figures can be unequivocally preferred to the other, but that on the whole the ministry figures stand up to tests better than the census.

Not all the differences between ministry and census figures are due to errors. The census measured activities within the year from 16 April 1962 to 15 April 1963; the ministry used a different crop year for different crops, but the greater part of the yield for each crop listed for 1962 coincides with the census year. Without detailed farming knowledge it is not possible to estimate the significance of this difference; April is the end of the dry season for most of Thailand, and generally only off-season crops would be affected.

Next, in principle the ministry includes all holdings, the census only holdings of at least two *rai*. This may have some influence on crops normally grown in very small areas, such as some vegetables.[7]

[7] The relevant question is the size of the total holding not the holding of the particular crop. There are many crops which are, on occasion, grown in small areas but probably only vegetables would normally be grown in a holding with a total size of under two *rai*.

Thirdly there appears to be a difference over the location of holdings. The ministry publications do not reveal their practice, but inquiries made locally suggest that village headmen report on all land physically lying within their area. The census, since it is much concerned with the size of holdings, lists all holdings in the area in which the holder—the actual operator—resides. Absentee owners are not holders so this difference affects only border areas.[8]

Fourthly, the ministry states clearly that if a crop is not listed in a particular province, this means that none of the crop is grown there. The census states that a table (or entry) relating to a particular crop, may be omitted if the output is insignificant (N.S.O., 1963);[9] and the census total for a region normally exceeds the total for listed provinces. For kenaf, for example, 78 tons are listed as produced in the Central Plain area though no kenaf is listed in any Central Plain province. This means that the census often appears to miss altogether provinces mentioned by the ministry. Although this probably does indeed happen, it happens less often than a superficial study of particular provinces would suggest.

Finally there is a difference due to the treatment of multiple crops. Wherever one crop is harvested twice, or wherever two crops are harvested from the same area, the census lists the area twice. The yield per *rai* is correspondingly reduced. The ministry does not publish the instructions (if any) which it gives, and local practice is not consistent. However, the ministry aggregates the total area of field crops, and of garden crops, for each province; probably it attempts to count each area once only, but many areas planted to off-season crops in the paddy fields may be listed twice,

---

[8] From Table X of the *Whole Kingdom* volume of the census, we can assess the importance of holdings across provincial borders. Over most of the kingdom between 1 per cent and 1·5 per cent of the holdings overlap boundaries and since the differences would be likely to work both ways, the effect can hardly be statistically significant. In the Central Plain area 8 per cent of the holdings over 60 *rai* have parts held in other provinces. This affects an area of nearly half a million *rai*. Moreover large holdings can include a higher proportion separated from the home plot, and cash crops other than rice are more likely to be involved. If these holdings are concentrated in a few provinces and a few special crops they could significantly affect the distribution of output between provinces; for example the distribution of maize among the provinces of Central Plain.

[9] This statement is not included in the definition or notes, but is a footnote to the table of contents. I am grateful to Mrs N. Viviani for drawing attention to it.

since rice and other crops are separately reported, through different departments. It may well be that low census yields for some crops are explained by multiple cropping.

These are legitimate differences between the two series of figures; but unintended distortions also affect them differently. Both series rely ultimately on a relatively suspicious farmer's statement to a government servant about his operations. There was no physical measurement and no reference to land records for comparison. The channel of transmission is therefore important.

The ministry returns are sent in by village headmen to district agricultural officers. Area figures are usually accepted without query; yield figures, however, are merely used as evidence, and a uniform yield figure is sent on, based on this and other evidence. In most provinces a rounded estimate is given for the whole province; in a few—particularly where a provincial annual report with an agricultural section is published—a separate figure may be estimated for each district, but the headman's estimates are certainly not merely transmitted unchanged.[10]

The headman is usually on the side of villagers and would probably normally co-operate in saving income tax for his wealthier farmers;[11] however, understating yield would be easier than understating area, and this would have relatively little effect on the published figures, since agricultural officers also use market information and personal inquiries to estimate overall yield. We must remember, however, that the agricultural officer is responsible for promoting agriculture as well as reporting on it. This probably would not affect the treatment of areas; but it may well make for optimism in reporting yields.

[10] Agricultural officers are apt to be evasive about the way they arrive at yields. The prevalence of round figures for whole provinces shows that there are very few instances in which any straightforward averaging can be used. Provincial agricultural officers clearly vary greatly both in their knowledge of the facts and in the importance that they attach to reliable figures.

[11] This and other judgments in this chapter are based on two field trips in which I had discussions with twelve agricultural officers, twelve village headmen, eighty farmers, as well as bank officials in country towns, village schoolteachers, traders, and more senior officials, in December 1964 and February-March 1967. Two or three nights were spent in a fairly remote country village in eight separate provinces, in a district other than the headquarters district of the province, in every region except the South (where I stayed in country towns and visited rural areas by day). Seventeen provincial capitals were visited and interviews held with relevant officials there.

The enumerators for the census were usually village school-teachers. Their supervisors were not usually well informed about crops or local conditions, but were experienced in checking that questions had been properly put. There was less point in stating a false figure to the census enumerator; but the enumerator had both less chance and less inducement to correct understatements based on natural caution.

We might therefore draw the following tentative conclusions. There are good reasons for the ministry and census area figures to differ; these reasons suggest that the ministry figures, while open to some question, are likely to be the more accurate. For the yield figures, where the two sources differ appreciably, the choice is more difficult; the census represents detailed and careful questioning, with rather less inducement to distort for reasons of taxation; but the questioners would be more easily deceived by systematic understatement based on habitual caution towards government; moreover census practice on multiple crops and off-season cropping, and possibly also the omission of the smallest holdings, lower the annual yield figures. Ministry yield figures are all informed guesses, perhaps biased upwards by the responsibility of the reporting officers for agricultural promotion, and downwards by the concealment of the highest yields for tax reasons. Here the census figures are likely to be a useful check on the ministry ones, particularly when discrepancies are large; but it would be unwise to prefer the census figure when the ministry one is moderately higher.

Clearly 1962 is the best single year for comparative study of different crops or provinces. Over time, only the ministry figures are available. It seems preferable to use area rather than output figures. Changes in yield per *rai* for a particular province probably correspond to genuine change in the same direction, absence of change is not necessarily significant, and aggregations of yields for different provinces probably conceal differences of attitude and skill between different provincial offices.

The most recent national income figures have taken some account of the different factors mentioned here, though only for the more important crops where national or regional aggregates are likely to be seriously affected. For several of the fruit and vegetable crops the official national income figures still approximate to output by assuming constant consumption per head per day (Prot, 1967: 105-27).

D

Other Statistical Problems

When we consider the share of the rural sector in exports we have
to bear in mind that normal classification of exports includes as
agricultural products rather more than is so included in the national
income figures. Rice is exported in sacks, and has been milled;
most of the sacks have been made in Thailand and the rice-sack
manufacture and the rice-milling are listed as industrial activities
in the national income statistics and the census. Timber is exported
sawn, and much of it roughly shaped; national income and census
figures list sawmills under industry. Probably this inflation of the
rural sector is more important (relatively) in timber than in rice
(Usher, 1967: 206-30).

For some purposes it is quite proper to include rice-sack manufacture, rice-milling, rubber-milling, and sawmilling in the rural
sector. These are indeed industries closely related to primary production. Yet they happen to make up a fairly high proportion of
all Thai industrial employment. In the 1960 population census
approximately one-fifth of the industrial labour force was employed
in these processing industries. Allowance should be made for this
in assessing the importance of the rural sector in Thailand's exports.

In comparing the proportion of the rural sector with other sectors as a provider of employment we must make two adjustments,
both of which tend to make the figure of 82 per cent in Table 2.1
seem too high. One is a simple trend factor. Since 1960 the rate of
urbanisation which prevailed between 1947 and 1960 has probably
continued or perhaps increased (Caldwell, 1967: 27-64). Labour
force surveys, undertaken in 1963 and 1964 (N.S.O., 1963) are
confined to municipal areas and do not enable us to say how much
drift to urban occupations there has been, but this drift would make
it unlikely that in 1965 employment in the rural sector would be
as high as 80 per cent.

A further adjustment is necessary to allow for the fact that the
1960 Census lists as productively employed a higher proportion of
women (mainly unpaid family workers) in rural than in urban
occupations. Usher (1966) refers to this as a statistical accident,
arising from the difficulty in a subsistence economy of distinguish-
ing productive from unproductive work, particularly of women.
The Thai rural economy is one with much less specialisation of
work between the sexes than is usual in traditional societies (Sharp

et al., 1953); both in the home and on the farm the family works as a virtually unspecialised team. Thus even if it is true that most of the women do actually perform 'productive' work, some of the men's work is, by this reckoning, unproductive. There is probably no more justification for reckoning the women as full-time productive workers in rural than in urban occupations, even though rather more sexual specialisation may occur in the towns.

The proportion of the male labour force working in the rural sector in 1960 was 78·5 per cent, and this seems a more accurate measure than the 82 per cent given above. It would probably therefore be more accurate to say that the rural sector employs about three-quarters of the labour force than to say (as is usually done) that it employs over four-fifths.

Conclusions

The analysis given in this chapter does not suggest any clear-cut way of correcting official figures. Probably a good case could be made for the view that, taking all purposes together, the official figure is usually better than any other that could be officially given. The analysis does, however, suggest certain reservations and certain shifts of emphasis.

For many purposes we should give rather more weight to the rice output than the official figures encourage us to give. The pressure of the rice taxes causes rice to be undervalued and some corrections need to be applied to offset this, though we should recognise that some of the dynamic effects of a low price of rice are beneficial in stimulating change and diversification.

As for the rest of the rural sector, some of the official figures tend to overstate, others to understate its importance. Trade figures and employment figures tend to make the rural sector seem more important than it is. National income figures, however, tend to understate its importance; part of the sector is undervalued because its price is kept down indirectly by the rice taxes; part is simply carried at a conventional figure based on population, e.g. firewood, fruit, and vegetables (Prot, 1967), because of the difficulty of calculating any consistent and reliable figures—though at least for fruit and vegetables the ministry's area figures suggest a much greater increase in production (*Crop Reports*, 1961-5).

Another general result of the analysis is that the Ministry of Agriculture's province-by-province figures for each crop—particularly the area figures—seem worthy of rather more attention than they normally receive. Probably no Thai statistics are as reliable as those of some of the more developed countries; but it is paradoxical that the aggregates compiled in the annual Agricultural Statistics of Thailand are widely used, while the published material on which they are based is rarely cited. Independent checks show that the Census of Agriculture relating to the one year 1962 is for most crops no better than the ministry's figures and for some crops appreciably worse.

A final conclusion is that in any construction of aggregates for the whole economy the weighting of the different components is likely to be more arbitrary even than is usual in such cases. Whether we are dealing with rice or with labour widely different conventions are defensible for different purposes. It is unlikely that aggregative models will have much general usefulness in Thailand.

3

Growth of the Rural Sector

Little has been written about the growth of Thai agriculture up to World War II except for three products, rice, rubber, and teak. Because of poor communications and the traditional pattern of Thai life, Thai farmers nearly all tried first to grow enough rice for their own family. Other crops were always regarded as supplements. This does not mean, however, that there was no growing of crops for sale apart from rice and rubber. Some specialisation undoubtedly occurred, and there are records of output of at least some other crops going back before World War II (*Statistical Year Books of the Kingdom of Siam*).

Before World War II

(a) *Rice.* Skinner (1957) has shown that a rice surplus was exported even under the Ayuthaya monarchy (fourteenth to eighteenth centuries). It was a trade carried on by Chinese, as royal agents or as monopoly holders by royal favour.

Regular steamship routes to Bangkok in the late nineteenth century greatly expanded the international demand for Thai rice; they also made possible an inflow of Chinese labour for digging new canals and later building the railway. The population spread out over the Central Plain along new canals opened up both by private initiative and by government. The railway unified the whole country.

Table 3.1 shows both the expansion in the output of rice and the fall in yield per *rai*, continuing until several years after World War II. It is clear that the chief cause of the expansion was the increas-

Table 3.1   Production figures for rice

Year	Area harvested 000 *rai*	Output 000 metric tons	Yield kg per *rai*
1907	8,658	2,582	298
1912	12,324	3,670	298
1917	10,979	2,989	272
1922	15,013	4,340	289
1927	15,960	4,564	286
1932	18,821	5,116	272
1937	18,396	4,556	248
1942	17,973	3,854	214
1947	26,901	5,506	205
1952	32,064	6,602	206
1957	26,794	5,570	208
1958	32,306	7,053	218
1959	32,893	6,770	206
1960	35,270	7,835	222
1961	35,349	8,177	231
1962	38,696	9,279	240
1963	39,715	10,029	253
1964	37,316	9,558	256
1965	37,034	9,218	249

Sources: To 1962, Ministry of Agriculture, *Annual Report on 1962 Rice Production in Thailand*; 1963 to 1965, Ministry of Agriculture, *Agricultural Statistics of Thailand, 1965*.

ing demand for Thai rice, generated partly by the impact on South-east Asia of demand from other parts of the world than the traditional market in China—markets in Europe and Africa, a newly industrialised Japan and new rice-deficit plantation economies in the Netherlands Indies, British Malaya, and Ceylon. The increased demand led to an increasing export, not only absolutely but per head of population. Yet Zimmerman (1931) shows that the typical size of farm was much larger in the more commercialised areas than in the subsistence areas.

The population was clearly spreading out along the canals, and later along the railways, into areas with lower productivity per *rai*, as the demand increased (Ingram, 1955: 43-50). This is a rather puzzling phenomenon. The most natural explanation would be that the increased demand made labour scarcer, so encouraging more extensive farming. Farms would grow larger in the central areas and many small farmers would sell their land and move out, finding they could do better by buying more land more cheaply.

This explanation indeed fits some of the facts. Farm sizes by 1929-30 were perceptibly higher in the Central Region than in the Northeast and other less commercialised areas, as shown in Table 3.2; and average incomes were also considerably higher in the Centre. Yet this does not fit all the facts. It is not as if the areas opened up by the railway were previously uninhabited. Much of Thailand was already producing rice on a subsistence basis, and even in 1930 considerable numbers of subsistence farmers were newly being brought into the commercial economy. The total area of farms where yield per *rai* would increase because of a new market for their surplus would, in these conditions—at least at first—greatly exceed the area of the new farms in which surplus farmers who had sold their land in the commercialised areas would now be farming more extensively. Moreover there is some evidence that the movement into new lands was made reluctantly and under pressure; for example the historical comments on the settling of Bangchan (Sharp *et al.*, 1953), and the earlier efforts of King Mongkut to encourage new settlement in the mid-nineteenth century (Ingram, 1955: 76).

Table 3.2 Land farmed and average cash income and wealth by four regions for 1930

	Area farmed *rai*	Average cash income per family *baht*	Average wealth per family *baht*
Central	24·14	279	2,436
Northern	10·14	176	1,052
Southern	6·20	126	897
Northeastern	6·80	83	460

Source: C. C. Zimmerman, *Siam Rural Economic Survey, 1930-31*, Bangkok Times Press, Bangkok, October 1931, Tables II E-H and p. 129.

A more probable explanation would appear to be that the increased demand for rice was indeed leading to some scarcity of labour, with a tendency for the optimum size of farms to grow, but that this did not in general lead to much higher earnings of labour, but rather to reactions by entrepreneurs and by the government to deal with the situation. The government felt a shortage of population and reacted both by accepting a considerable influx of Chinese as paid labour and by offering special tax inducements, in various pieces of legislation from 1857 onward, for farmers to open up new land (Ingram, 1955: 76-87). The entrepreneurs, chiefly Chinese merchants, reacted at first by introducing methods to increase labour productivity—the steel ploughshare at the beginning of the twentieth century, or even earlier, was one such device, the large steam rice-mill another—but a more important reaction was the attempt by each merchant to secure a tied source of supply. This could partly be done by supplying imported consumption goods on credit or by gaining control of transport equipment (Zimmerman, 1931; Udhis, 1963). Chains of credit stretched out from the large Bangkok merchants and millers to remote parts of the country, and the pressure of competition forced new entrepreneurs to follow immediately any new transport route, and try to gain control of the surplus of the farmers who, up till then, had farmed for subsistence and grown a surplus mainly as an insurance. In the more closely settled areas, with better transport, some of the farmers themselves were able to increase the area of their land, and perhaps become landlords as well as large-scale farmers. In these areas the merchants could often obtain a safe source of supply only by actually securing ownership of the land. Normally this would occur only in the second generation; most of the merchants were Chinese, and only their sons would have Thai nationality and be able to own land.

The stereotype of the Thai farmer is always that he owns his land, and since the Thais came to their present homeland vacant rice land has always been available for new settlers. Nevertheless tenancy has certainly become fairly widespread in the Central Plain since World War II and it had probably been spreading for at least two decades before it (Wijeyewardene, 1967).

On the whole, over the period up to World War II, in spite of favourable conditions of demand for Thai rice, there was insufficient growth in the output of this crop to generate significant overall development of the economy. This was partly because of the fact that so much of the competitive effort of entrepreneurs was devoted to establishing a hold over particular sources of supply. Neither permanent indebtedness of farmers to a particular supplier nor ownership of farming land by merchants to ensure a source of supply is likely to promote effort to improve yields. It is perhaps significant that the period of most rapid growth—in the second decade of the twentieth century—was one in which the main railway network had just been constructed and entrepreneurs could be presumed to have not yet built up much hold over their sources of supply.

At the time of the 1932 coup a good deal of emphasis was laid on the fact that the merchants were foreigners and that their profits were remitted abroad (Chote Khumbhandhu, personal communication). This may well be important; but it assumes that wide margins mean large profits to merchants. If, however, competitive effort is successfully directed to insulating a group of suppliers (or customers) large profits occur only when entry is limited. Otherwise, as Chamberlin showed many years ago, equilibrium is reached with excess capacity (Chamberlin, 1950). The damage, when competition takes an exclusive, insulating form in a contact economy, does not depend on the entrepreneurs enjoying large incomes.

(b) *Rubber*. Rubber was first introduced from Malaya to the Thai southern province of Trang by a Sino-Thai nobleman, Kaw Sim Bee na Ranong, who was governor there, in 1901 (Puey and Suparb, 1955: 39). Probably, therefore, Chinese traders from Malaya were involved in the trade from the very beginning; for Kaw Sim Bee, and two brothers who governed other southern provinces, were sons of Kaw Su Chiang, a Hokkien merchant from Penang ennobled by King Chulalongkorn (Skinner, 1957: 151).

From Trang rubber spread southward. The leading rubber provinces are now the mainly Malay-speaking provinces of the far south, Yala and Narathiwat. Probably Chinese traders, accustomed to Malay conditions, have found the Malay-speaking provinces more congenial than those further north. It is not certain how early Chinese squatters began coming in to plant rubber illegally in south Thailand. Some may have come during the Stevenson restriction scheme in the 1920s when prices were high and rubber was being smuggled into Thailand, or during the period of unemployment in the 1930s when many Chinese began squatting in remote areas in Malaya, and some may have found their way to Thailand. These squatters—many of them already long-established and prosperous—were driven out in the early 1950s, after armed resistance.[1]

Thailand was a member of the second international rubber regulation scheme, but statistics of Thai production have never been as satisfactory as those of the other members. The figures

[1] Information obtained from interviews in the field in and around the Rubber Industry Organisation's estates at Nabon.

given to the committee for the period of the restriction, for example, differ from those published by the Thai Department of Customs (*Statistical Year Book of the Kingdom of Siam*, 1934: 168; Puey and Suparb, 1955). There was much illegal planting at the time, and the Thai government made no serious effort to prevent it but demanded new planting rights as a condition of joining the scheme. Both sets of export figures almost certainly included some rubber smuggled in from Malaya for re-export. The committee plainly winked at a good deal of evasion by Thailand, so long as it was small in relation to the world total. It merely wanted to prevent Thailand wrecking the scheme—as Netherlands Indies peasants had wrecked the previous one—by a vast increase in its output. Thailand was permitted to export 30,000 long tons in 1935, four times as much as it had produced in any year up to 1934 (McFadyean, 1944: 224-5). It was also permitted to increase its exports up to 41,000 tons and to plant 31,000 new acres of rubber at a time when other countries were prohibited from new planting.

The scheme proved a source of corruption in south Thailand, since the issue of export rights rested with the bureaucracy. Coupons were still being issued several years after the international scheme had lapsed.[2]

The main significance of Thailand's membership for our purpose is that it led to the one attempt in pre-war times to analyse the age structure of the Thai rubber holdings; and from this and from the export figures we can reconstruct approximately the pattern of growth of the industry up to World War II. The figures are not, however, sufficiently consistent or reliable to do this with any precision. Smallholding rubber has normally a higher short-run elasticity of supply than estate rubber, but possibilities of increasing output from existing trees are limited (Wharton, 1967: ch. 6). Rubber holdings in Thailand are not, as in parts of Indonesia and Sarawak, remote by-products of shifting cultivation that may not be tapped at all at low prices. Most Thai rubber growers have secondary crops and can switch their effort and overtap some rubber trees to increase their yield. The main elasticity is a long-run one, high prices leading to more planting with increased yields about seven years later.

[2] Royal Thai Government Gazettes of 30.12.49 and 19.5.50 give quotas and regulations under the 1938 scheme.

The main expansions in planting in Thailand appear to have occurred during World War II and the Korean War, each leading to a large expansion of output about seven years later. In the pre-war period the lag at first sight seems to be too long. The high prices of 1909-11 appear to lead to a large increase in exports about twelve years later, and the high prices of 1925-7 to a large increase nine years later. Table 3.3 reproduces McFadyean's series of export figures from 1910 to 1940, together with the average prices of rubber cited by him; these are only one set among several of Thai export figures, but they were the ones accepted by the committee. It will be seen that the main expansions in exports occur in 1922-5 and in 1934-6.

The lag may have been longer when the industry was new. More probably new planting did occur in response to the high prices of 1909-11 and 1925-7 but production did not expand seven years

Table 3.3 Net exports of crude rubber, 1910-40 and average price per pound in London

Year	Exports in long tons	Average price per lb		Year	Exports in long tons	Average price per lb	
		s	d			s	d
1910	13	8	9	1928	4,813		10¾
1911	63	5	5¼	1929	5,052		10¼
1912	102	4	9	1930	4,349		5$\frac{15}{16}$
1913	92	3	0¼	1931	4,514		3⅜
1914	56	2	3½	1932	3,555		2$\frac{5}{16}$
1915	84	2	6	1933	7,373		3¼
1916	42	2	10¼	1934	17,714		5⅛[a]
1917	43	2	9¾				6$\frac{13}{16}$[b]
1918	29	2	2¾				6¼
1919	54	2	0¾	1935	28,327		6
1920	44	1	10½	1936	34,578		7¾
1921	412		9$\frac{9}{16}$	1937	35,551		9½
1922	736		9$\frac{5}{16}$	1938	41,618		7$\frac{7}{32}$
1923	1,718	1	3$\frac{5}{16}$	1939	41,753		8$\frac{5}{32}$[c]
1924	2,962	1	1⅞				10$\frac{23}{32}$[d]
1925	5,377	2	11$\frac{1}{16}$				9
1926	4,028	1	11¾	1940	43,940	1	0$\frac{1}{16}$
1927	5,472	1	6$\frac{7}{16}$				

[a] Pre-regulation.   [c] Pre-war.
[b] Regulation.   [d] War production.

Source: A. McFadyean (ed.), The History of Rubber Regulation 1934-1943.

later because of an acute wartime shortage of shipping in eastern waters in 1916-18 and exceptionally low prices in 1932 and 1933.

Table 3.4 analyses the figures prepared for the International Rubber Regulation Committee concerning the ages of trees still standing at the end of 1940 and the replanting that occurred between 1934 and that date. From this we can see that probably half of all the rubber standing in Thailand at the end of 1940 was first planted during the years 1926-30. Probably there was an equivalent rate of planting in 1925, when prices were very high.

Table 3.4 Analysis of date of first planting of rubber

Since all rubber areas replanted must have been planted twice
total area planted $\geqq$ total stand at end 1940 + total area replanted 1934-40[a]

Total stand at end 1940	= 1,048,135 *rai*
Total area replanted 1934-40	= 188,343 *rai*
Total area planted up to 1940	$\geqq$ 1,236,478 *rai*

Minimum acreage planted

Date of first planting	Cut out and replanted	Still standing, end 1940	Total
1936-40	0	300,743	300,743
1931-35	0	166,822	166,822
1926-30 ⎫ Before 1926 ⎬	188,343[b]	451,542 ⎫ 129,028 ⎬	768,913
Total	188,343	1,048,135	1,236,478

[a] This omits all rubber cut out and not replanted, accidentally destroyed, or replanted before 1934. The sum of all these is probably small.

[b] There is no firm basis for allotting the replanted rubber according to age. There would be a strong preference for replanting rubber at least 15 years old, and we might suppose that at least as high a proportion of the older rubber as of the newer would be replanted. However, the great expansion in output did not begin until 1934.

Source: A. McFadyean (ed.), *The History of Rubber Regulation 1934-43*, pp. 224-5.

It is interesting, however, that the rate of planting was so much lower in Thailand than in Malaya or Indonesia. In both Malaya and Indonesia there was a good deal of European planting by large-scale methods, sometimes importing all the labour (Rowe, 1936). This kind of planting was against Thai policy. However, there was a great deal of planting by peasant cultivators in both Malaya and Indonesia. The main pre-war period for such small-scale planting in Malaya was in the second decade of the century

(Figart, 1925). During this period peasant producers planted over a quarter of a million acres in Malaya while in Thailand, though the crop was introduced to small growers at about the same time as in Malaya, hardly a tenth of this amount was planted. Moreover in Thailand the government was trying to encourage rubber planting by peasant producers, while in Malaya there was a marked preference for estate development at this time.

The explanation here must be mainly the estate rubber boom in Malaya. At first both Malays and Chinese planted rubber with the aim of selling the holding to European companies at a profit.[3] Later a great many potential small planters were available with experience of tapping on estates. The impact of World War I checked the expansion of European estates and gave the small planters their opportunity. In south Thailand, though Chinese merchants were trying to stimulate rubber growing, there was no visible example of large profits, and rubber is a crop requiring a seven-year investment.

In the next decade the export of rubber was restricted in Malaya and comparatively little planting was allowed.[4] Thai small planters planted more during the whole decade than small planters in Malaya; but of course Malaya by this time had a substantial lead. Moreover it is natural in this period to compare Thai performance with that in Indonesia. During this decade, when exports in British territories were restricted and the world price rose, small growers in the outer islands of the Netherlands Indies (as they were then called) planted a vast area of rubber—probably over two million acres (Bauer, 1948; Silcock, 1964: Section III). Of course both the area and the population in these outer islands were vastly greater than those of south and southeast Thailand where the corresponding increase took place; yet there is another factor favouring Indonesian rather than Thai planting. Large parts of Sumatra, Borneo, and the Celebes were still farmed by shifting cultivation. The Indonesian cultivator who had planted his rice in a cleared area for the normal two seasons, would plant rubber

[3] Records to which I was given access by the firm of Guthries in London show early purchases of rubber land planted by Chinese, and there are accounts in the Administration Reports of the Malay States of Malays selling rubber land that they had planted to European companies.

[4] Nominally the restriction scheme covered exports not production, and some new planting took place, but the government was clearly discouraging it and did not normally alienate new land for rubber.

seeds and move elsewhere, allowing the rubber to grow up among the jungle growth. The result was hardly a rubber farm, but when the world price of rubber reached a satisfactory level, the trees could be tapped and produce some income. Shifting cultivation—though it is practised by hill tribes in north Thailand—has disappeared in the south.

The main contributions that these discontinuous expansions of the rubber industry made to the economy of Thailand were—in conjunction with the tin mining—to build up a few relatively prosperous trading centres in south Thailand and to contribute both to official Thai government revenue and to the incomes of Thai government officials. Several of the banks that grew up before and during the war were partly financed by rubber and tin from the south.[5]

(c) *Teak*. Teak was not an article of trade in the Ayuthaya period or for nearly a century after the establishment of the Bangkok dynasty in 1782. Up to the middle of the nineteenth century it was cut by corvée labour for public building, and some for private use (Krit, 1957: 1-2). Chinese merchants first established sawmills and exported teak soon after the middle of the nineteenth century. The trade expanded after about 1880 when Europeans, who had already largely worked out the forests in Burma, began financing Burmese contractors to obtain licences from local chiefs and exploit the northern Thai forests.

Unco-ordinated cutting by rival firms began to deplete all the more accessible areas. In 1895, to ensure some control, the government established the Royal Forest Department, bought out the local chiefs, and renegotiated agreements with lessees. Exports continued to expand, but large firms using more selective methods, and operating inaccessible as well as accessible areas, were now given preference. In 1909, when many of the leases expired, new and more conservative terms were laid down. Exports never regained the level of 122,000 cubic metres attained in 1905-9, though this was partly due to increased local use as well as better control.

Table 3.5 shows the figures for output and export of teak before World War II, given by the Royal Forest Department (Ministry of Agriculture) and the *Statistical Year Book* respectively. Clearly in the inter-war period Thailand was using more of its own teak locally, as well as controlling over-cutting.

[5] Information derived from field investigation in south Thailand.

Table 3.5 Pre-war output and export of teak, and unit value of exports, 1925-6 to 1939

	Output cubic metres	Total all forms of teak exports cubic metres	Unit value of exports *baht*
1925-6		60,672	93
1926-7		84,018	98
1927-8		99,940	100
1928-9		108,837	103
1929-30		105,292	106
1930-1		93,568	104
1931-2		60,805	81
1932-3		53,404	62
1933-4		64,938	66
1934-5	231,813	63,943	72
1935-6	217,215	63,051	80
1936-7	174,219	100,128	86
1937-8	194,500	94,357	97
1938-9	168,657	82,555	81
1939-40	110,811	83,796	89

Source: S. Mahaphol, *Teak in Thailand*, Ministry of Agriculture, Bangkok, 1954, p. 31; *Statistical Year Book*, no. 19, p. 162, no. 21, p. 282.

(d) *Minor crops*. Although much less attention has been given to the pre-war planting of other crops, Thailand was clearly an economy with some agricultural specialisation, mainly for consumption within the country, as well as much subsistence cultivation of rice. Sugar—an important mid-nineteenth-century export—was grown for Thai consumption only, most of it in Chon Buri province.[6] In the southwest, chillies and onions had been grown for the national market for decades before World War II, and the vegetables and fruit grown on a specialised scale in the neighbouring maritime provinces also probably date from this period. Tobacco was grown in several parts of the country for the British American Tobacco Company, which was taken over by a government monopoly in 1941. Pickled tea and opium were special products of northern villages (Van Roy, 1967: 421-32). Buffaloes, reared in the northeast, were sent over long-established routes into the Central Plain (Ministry of Agriculture, 1964: 17).

It is unfortunately not clear whether—and if so how far—

[6] It had originally been grown along the Nakhon Chaisi river, in Samut Prakan and Nakhon Pathom, but this cultivation gave way to rice and later fruit and vegetables; see Ingram, 1955: 123-5.

specialisation of this kind increased as a result of the unification of the country by a railway system. One would expect at least that, with the growth of Bangkok, appreciably more of these specialised products would be sent to the metropolis. There is little evidence that this occurred. Ingram (1955: 133-48) has shown that there was little if any net gain in manufacturing activity. Table 3.6 indicates that for most minor crops there was little if any gain in the area planted. Some of these crops were, of course, grown partly for export.

Table 3.6   Average areas planted in 000 *rai* for various crops, 1915-19 to 1935-9

	1915-19	1920-4	1925-9	1930-4	1935-9
Rice	13,876·9	16,292·0	18,055·5	20,083·3	21,221·0
Tobacco	58·9	60·2	58·7	69·4	62·3
Maize	32·8	39·4	47·9	42·2	48·6
Cotton	29·4	30·6	22·6	20·4	38·6
Sesame	7·1	9·2	10·2	6·8	7·1
Pepper	23·1	15·3	10·2	10·0	5·5

Sources: *Statistical Year Book of the Kingdom of Thailand*, no. 4, pp. 248-51; no. 15, p. 361; no. 19, pp. 162 and 168; no. 20, p. 423; no. 21, pp. 282, 290 and 466.

Yet Thailand, even if it was not developing much, was by no means a pure subsistence economy. Wherever rice could be grown Thai farmers grew enough for their own use. Because of the dangers of flood and drought they normally aimed to grow a surplus, which in good years they could sell. Over the years, an increasing share of this surplus had been secured by the greater commercial skill and economic foresight of Chinese merchant families; the aristocracy had also in some places transformed old political rights into modern landholdings. In some areas where rice would not grow, other crops were grown for a livelihood. There was already some specialisation even in areas where rice would grow, for example there appear to have been specialised farmers, not growing rice, in Ratchaburi (chillies and onions), Chon Buri (sugar-cane and perhaps cassava), Yala (rubber), but in general the fairly considerable trade was a trade in surpluses after the rice base had been provided. Many textiles were home-woven from home-grown cotton and locally reared silk worms, but textiles too were traded within Thailand, not produced only for family use.

After World War II

(a) *The rice situation.* During the post-war period several other crops became important in addition to those already considered. Some of the reasons why different methods of weighting should be used according to the purpose in view, and why these will give sharply differing results, have been given in chapter 2. The performance of the more important crops is discussed in the next two chapters. Here a quantitative outline of some of the main features of the economy is attempted.

Probably the two most important features of the rural economy in the post-war period have been the continuing pressure of taxation on the internal price of rice and the development of greatly improved transport and irrigation services.

After a brief resistance Thailand had become a half-hearted ally of the Japanese in World War II. The rice export trade was disrupted except for shipments in the early war years to Japan and a substantial smuggling trade to Malaya (Silcock, 1949).[7] Considerable stocks of surplus rice accumulated, although the Thai estimate that there were in Thailand, at the end of the war, one and a half to two million tons may well have been an exaggeration.

This rice surplus played an important part in Thailand's post-war development. Most of the actual surplus that was held was smuggled out and sold on the black markets of Southeast Asia, making immense profits for merchants, soldiers, and civil servants of various nationalities. The profits which remained within Thailand played an important role in Thai monetary, industrial, and political history, but need not be considered further here.[8] More important for Thai agriculture were the institutional consequences of the attempt to get the rice surplus for international distribution (Bank of Thailand, 1949-55).

The Prime Minister, Seni Pramoj, had been virtually forced to offer, in the peace negotiations, to supply the surplus rice, up to a total of 1½ million tons, free of charge, as an indication of Thailand's willingness to co-operate with the United Nations. An indem-

[7] I was teaching in Singapore in 1946 and was given information about this trade by a student who had engaged in it during the war.

[8] A fuller account of this is given in Silcock, 1967: 1-26. This was based on interviews and on research in the bulletins issued by the United Kingdom Commissioner-General's Office in Singapore, 1946-9.

E

nity would almost certainly otherwise have been exacted;[9] this method kept some Thai control over the economy.

To collect the surplus an official rice-buying monopoly, the Rice Bureau, was established. This was unsuccessful in getting much of the surplus rice which was to be delivered free. In May 1946 a new agreement granted Thailand payment of £12.10s sterling per ton, a figure still well below the market price (Bank of Thailand, 1947). The combination of some payment with stricter control of internal movement of rice produced improved deliveries. The European exporters' Chinese compradors, who collected the rice, still smuggled their best abroad and delivered broken rice to the United Nations for rations.

The rice trade was still based on private enterprise. The Rice Bureau bought from the Chinese rice merchants and millers, and sold to the Siam Rice Agency, a consortium of the former European exporters acting under the control of the International Emergency Food Control. An attempt to impose a government monopoly of milling and the internal rice trade was at first successfully frustrated by diplomatic pressure organised by the Chinese and European merchants.[10] In 1949 the international allocation system was dismantled, and government-to-government contracts were arranged with most of Thailand's customers. The Rice Bureau made large profits, which were very inadequately controlled. A little private trade was allowed, on payment of a premium to the Rice Bureau. It was this premium which determined the form of the main taxation of rice—the rice premium—from 1955 onwards. For in 1955 private trade was restored (Corden, 1967: 151-69).

In form the rice premium remained an administrative levy; but the amount paid per ton was greater than before 1955, because in 1955 the multiple exchange rate system also came to an end, and under this system rice had been in effect heavily taxed. Moreover the Bank of Thailand, which had hitherto used the exchange control system to capture some of the rice profits and prevent them falling into politicians' hands, after 1955 used its influence to secure better accounting for the whole new rice taxation system. Hence the rice premium is now not merely flexible enough to use in

[9] The negotiations and their effects on the economy are discussed further in Appendix I.

[10] Information supplied by business sources in Bangkok (name not to be revealed).

adjusting the internal cost of living; its proceeds are fully used for public purposes and it has helped to finance development.

It is a matter of some interest and importance that this was not a system that was planned by any group either within Thailand or outside. The British attempt to extract rice from Thailand to relieve distress in British dependencies forced the centralisation of the elements of monopoly in the rice trade in the Rice Bureau. The subsequent victory of the Bank of Thailand in its struggle with the politicians converted these profits into a form of tax.

It is impossible to show quantitatively the changes in the levies on rice before 1955. The charges made by the Rice Bureau, and its accounts, have not been published. It is possible to show from official records that substantial diversion occurred (Corden, 1967; Ingram, 1955: 186; Yang, 1957). It would be naive to suppose that the records have been so drawn up that all such leakages can be detected.

Since 1955 accounts have been kept of the charges made in the private trade, though some of these, and also the premium charged in the government-to-government trade, is kept secret. Table 3.7 shows the various rates of rice premium levied from 1955 to 1965. In addition to the premium there is a milling tax, which in 1965 was 3·85 per cent of sales, and a regular export duty of 4·2 per cent (Usher, 1967; Office of the Prime Minister, 1967).

Since Thailand's rice deficiencies reduced rations in neighbouring countries in the post-war years, international interest was

Table 3.7 Levels of rice premium by grades for the more important grades
(*baht* per metric ton)

Grade	Before Aug. 1959	Aug. 1959	Dec. 1959	Dec. 1960	Apr. 1961	June 1961	Apr. 1962	1965
White rice 100% and 5%	935	935	890	890	890	890	950	950
White rice 10%, 15%, 20%	935	935 840 }	840	840	840	890	950	950
White rice 25%	650	650	650	600	600	650	700	700
White rice more than 25%	650	600	600	550	600	650	700	700
Broken rice A1 super special	730	730	720	720	720	720	780	780
Glutinous rice	600	600	800	600	600	600	800	700

Sources: Ministry of Economic Affairs 'On the Rice Premium', mimeo., 1963 (Thai); Office of the Prime Minister, *Budget Documents Vol. II Receipts*, 1965, p. 348-9, 1967, p. 336.

aroused in Thai transport and irrigation. The Thai government secured loans from the International Bank for repairing railway lines, increasing rolling stock, and improving the port of Bangkok, and also for a greatly expanded irrigation program (I.B.R.D., 1959: 271).

From this there has developed a substantial improvement in the transport network and in the vehicles available. This cannot be adequately gauged from official planning figures, which give little emphasis to feeder roads and none to the improvement of transport vehicles, both by land and by water, in recent years. Casual impressions, the evidence of road maps, bus time-tables, etc. can be supplemented by the evidence of a great expansion in the numbers engaged in transport even in the 1960 Census, and the higher proportion in road transport (Caldwell, 1967: 27-64). In rail transport diesel engines have been substituted for steam, the track has been improved and the number of freight cars increased (N.E.D.B., 1964: 109-10), and this—together with some diversion to road transport—has reduced the difficulty and cost of obtaining freight space. Water transport has become more specialised, with fast outboard motors for passengers and long trains of barges for freight.

This might be expected to extend the cash economy, increase specialisation, and enable more land to be brought under cultivation. Moreover it is bound to affect marketing systems both of agricultural products and of consumer goods.

Irrigation has also been expanded, particularly in the Central Plain; but the effects of this on output need to be interpreted in terms of the standard pattern of agriculture of the Thai Central Plain, as well as of other regions. In many parts of the world irrigation primarily enables wet rice agriculture to take the place of dry rice in the drier areas, and double, or even treble, cropping to take the place of a single crop in the wetter ones. In central Thailand nearly all the rice is produced on flooded land; the fact of annual flooding is predictable, but not its timing or depth. Irrigation has so far been primarily concerned with diminishing the variability of the flooding (I.B.R.D., 1959: 38-9; Trescott, 1968) The same channels which ensure a widespread distribution of flood water at more controlled peak levels also provide some off-season water at lower levels. The expansion of irrigation has therefore produced complex effects, especially where channels are not adequately maintained. In the south and in the north, where rainfall is higher and more continuous, irrigation—where it has been introduced, often by local effort—is able to produce relatively stable water levels and double cropping (Graham, 1924). In the Northeast irrigation is mainly concerned with storage of seasonally concentrated local rainfall (Platenius, 1963; Chira, 1964). The appropriate response to irrigation therefore differs in different provinces.[11]

The combined effect of pressure on rice prices and of greatly improved transport and irrigation might be expected to be a diversion of land and effort from rice growing to other crops, combined with an increase in the total area of land under cultivation. It is not difficult to show that both these results have occurred. The significance of these results is, however, a more complex matter. It is important to find out whether the extension of the area under cultivation has merely continued the old trend of increasing total output but lower output per *rai*. We also need to know whether the shift from rice to other crops is a merely nominal gain—a substitution of other crops for rice, which has an artificially low value—or whether it leads to real and permanently higher incomes because of improvements in productivity. To answer these questions we must look at the principal crops in detail.

(b) *Overall developments*. First, however, we can consider the overall effects as shown in Table 3.8. Compared with the situation before World War II there had already by 1950 been a considerable diversion of land and of effort from rice to other crops. This is perhaps best indicated by the output figures given in the International Bank Mission Report, comparing an average pre-war year with 1950 (I.B.R.D., 1959: 271). During this period—in which external trade was first largely cut off by the Japanese occupation and later dominated by the Combined Siam Rice Commission and international allocation of rice—the figures show an expansion of just over 50 per cent in the output of paddy. Corresponding increases for other crops are 975 per cent for cotton, 850 per cent for sesame, 800 per cent for groundnuts, 575 per cent for maize, 160 per cent for copra, 140 per cent for rubber, 90 per cent for soya beans and 75 per cent for tobacco. Some of

---

[11] This casts some doubt on standardised yield procedures, which assume a uniform relation between irrigation and the yield of land in all regions; see Hsieh and Ruttan, 1967: 317-20; also Trescott, 1968.

Table 3.8 Area planted in millions of *rai* of principal agricultural crops, 1950-65

Year	Rice[a]	Rubber	Maize	Kenaf	Tobacco[b]	Oil seeds[c]	Cassava[d]	Garden crops[e]	Fruits[f]	All non-rice crops	All crops	Population in millions	Area per head in *rai*
1950	34·63	2·11	0·23	0·03	0·19	1·21	0·08	n.a.	n.a.	4·70	39·33	19·64	2·00
1951	37·25	2·20	0·26	0·04	0·26	1·35	0·08	n.a.	n.a.	5·18	42·43	20·22	2·10
1952	33·55	2·30	0·28	0·07	0·27	1·38	0·09	n.a.	n.a.	5·32	38·87	20·83	1·87
1953	38·58	2·40	0·30	0·06	0·34	1·39	0·09	n.a.	n.a.	5·56	44·14	21·46	2·06
1954	34·73	2·50	0·33	0·04	0·34	1·57	0·09	n.a.	n.a.	5·92	40·65	22·10	1·84
1955	36·06	2·60	0·35	0·05	0·35	1·60	0·09	n.a.	n.a.	6·12	42·18	22·78	1·85
1956	37·65	2·69	0·51	0·11	0·36	1·71	0·25	n.a.	n.a.	6·69	44·34	23·45	1·89
1957	31·72	2·77	0·61	0·08	0·39	1·92	0·24	0·24	0·44	8·34	40·06	24·15	1·66
1958	35·99	2·85	0·79	0·13	0·38	1·89	0·28	0·27	0·43	8·69	44·68	24·87	1·80
1959	37·91	2·93	1·25	0·28	0·39	1·91	0·39	0·30	0·48	9·80	47·71	25·62	1·86
1960	37·00	3·01	1·78	0·88	0·37	2·24	0·45	0·38	0·68	11·84	48·84	26·39	1·85
1961	38·62	3·08	1·92	1·72	0·26	2·14	0·62	0·56	0·95	12·92	51·54	27·18	1·90
1962	41·62	3·14	2·05	0·71	0·26	2·44	0·77	0·74	0·92	12·63	54·25	28·00	1·94
1963	41·26	3·27	2·61	0·96	0·25	2·53	0·88	0·77	1·09	14·86	56·12	28·84	1·95
1964	40·87	3·30	3·45	1·36	0·52	2·52	0·66	0·73	1·08	15·86	56·73	29·70	1·91
1965	40·49	3·32	3·60	2·40	0·45	2·78	0·64	0·73	1·51	17·95	58·44	30·60	1·91

[a] The figures for rice are for the crop years 1950-1 to 1965-6.

[b] Tobacco figures have been calculated by adding area planted for local varieties of tobacco to area planted of Virginia tobacco.

[c] Oil seeds include castor beans, groundnuts, sesame, and coconuts.

[d] There are no figures available for cassava for the whole kingdom until 1956. Figures before 1956 are for Chon Buri Province.

[e] There are no figures for garden crops until 1957. Garden crops include Chinese kale, cabbage, cauliflower, Chinese cabbage, string beans, eggplant (long type), eggplant (crisp variety), tomatoes, pumpkins, sweet potatoes, potatoes, yam beans and other potatoes.

[f] There are no figures available for fruits until 1957. Fruits include pineapples, watermelons and bananas.

Source: Ministry of Agriculture, *Agricultural Statistics of Thailand, 1965*, pp. 29, 48, 54, 58, 84 and 176; *1955*, p. 68.

the crops that have since become important were not mentioned in the International Bank Mission Report, and after the wartime industrialisation came to an end cotton failed for several years to live up to its wartime beginning. However, it is clear that the expansion in oil-seeds, tobacco, and maize had its origins during the war.

In the pre-war period the expansion in the area of cultivated land had approximately kept pace with population, with the area under rice expanding more rapidly than population and the area under other crops almost stationary. This could be represented as a slow movement out of other crops into rice, but it would be more accurate to regard it as an increase in the area under rice combined with a slight amount of urbanisation. The war period was plainly one of rapid movement out of rice under wartime pressure. Table 3.8 shows that the area per head under rice continued to fall during the period 1950 to 1965 from about 1·75 *rai* at the beginning to 1·40 at the end. During the same period the area under other crops, which had probably been about 0·1 *rai* per head before the war, increased from 0·25 to 0·55 *rai*.

This diversification of the rural economy is much the most obvious change that has occurred in rural Thailand. It has undoubtedly been accompanied by a fairly considerable growth in output per head, but this output is difficult to quantify because of weighting difficulties. It is natural to suppose that the growth is at least partly a result of the diversification; but to demonstrate this is difficult. A part of the growth is obviously the result of the improvements in transport, irrigation, research, and the like. Even if we can show that the growth in output per *rai* is much greater in the new crops than in rice, it would still be possible that if there had been no pressure towards diversification these growth-generating factors would have impinged more on rice, and created the same amount and degree of growth there as has actually occurred in other crops. It does not seem to be possible to disprove this completely, though the analysis by crops and later by regions which follows perhaps makes it seem improbable.

In any event, it is impossible to discuss these questions intelligently on an aggregative basis only. A more detailed consideration both of rice and of the other principal crops is necessary.

4

Analysis of Crops: Rice, Rubber, and Kenaf

Rice

(a) *General.* Rice is very much the most important crop in Thailand. Its contribution to Thailand's exports (36 per cent) and gross domestic product (10 per cent) greatly underrepresents its total importance and we have no separate figures for rice farmers as distinct from farmers in general to show its contribution to employment.[1] Most Thai farmers probably still grow some rice, though to a good many it has now ceased to be the overwhelmingly important source of real income that it was before World War II. Probably the best indication of the importance of rice is Table 3.8, which shows that the area of land under rice was still more than twice as great as the area under all other crops.

To most Thais it would probably still seem a distortion to treat rice as one product in Thai agriculture. Rice-growing is regarded as the Thai farmer's basic way of life. His first obligation is to grow enough rice for his family's needs for the year. For many farmers it is something of a disgrace, as well as a calamity, to have to buy rice. Though the amount of rice sold in rural areas appears to have increased about threefold in the decade 1952-3 to 1962-3 (Silcock, 1967: 231-57), it seems probable that the depression of the internal price of rice as a result of the rice taxes has caused those farmers who grow rice to consume a higher proportion of it themselves. It has almost certainly, however, encouraged the production for sale of other crops in place of rice.

[1] See Table 2.1.

The decline in the output of rice per *rai* up to World War II has been mentioned in chapter 3. The rate of decline slowed down after the war, but it was only in the mid-1950s that the decline itself came to an end. It is striking that in the 1960s there was an improvement in the yield per *rai* in every region. Table 4.1 shows that during the last few years up to 1965 the rice yield per *rai* increased perceptibly in all four regions.[2] Though fluctuations in yield are normal, as a result of climatic factors and pests, the change is large enough, and has continued long enough, to be regarded as a clear reversal of the previous trend.

More detailed study of the table shows some of the characteristics of rice growing in the different regions. The variability of both the planted area and the harvested area in the Central Plain reflects the caprice of the annual flooding, but it is an area of fairly high yields, and is the main rice area of the country. In an average year about 10 per cent of the planted area is damaged, but flood or drought may also prevent planting of some areas. The Northeast's yields are only about two-thirds of those of the Central Plain, and here also a good deal of the planted area (7·5 per cent) is damaged by poor weather conditions. Damage in the South is due to the occasional disastrous flood; in normal years, with regular monsoon rainfall, the damage is small, but yields appear to be below capacity and improving rather slowly. The North has the highest yields and much the greatest rate of advance, and damage here is very slight. The yield is high because of good local irrigation and also good extension work; but probably the main reason is more intensive farming. It is mountainous country with limited rice farming land, and the farms are smaller than elsewhere (Wijeyewardene, 1967: 78; Chapman, 1967).

Thai rice is by no means a homogeneous product, and the rice produced for local use has far more varieties than the rice exported (Usher, 1967: 208-10). Thai consumers are very sensitive to differences in quality, and a typical rice shop in Bangkok, or even in the main provincial centres, would carry a large number of different types of rice varying in type of grain, colour, local origin, etc., which Thai consumers recognise. Rising standards of living

2 The sharp fall in yield per *rai* for the South Region, for the year 1964 only, is reproduced from the Ministry of Agriculture's *Agricultural Statistics of Thailand, 1965*, but this may be an error, for the *Statistical Year Book, 1965*: 163, shows only a very minor fall (to 263 kg per *rai*) in 1964.

Table 4.1 Rice areas and productions by regions, 1947-65

Year	North				Northeast			
	Area planted million rai	Area harvested million rai	Output 000 metric tons	kg/rai	Area planted million rai	Area harvested million rai	Output 000 metric tons	kg/rai
1947	2·02	1·96	545·9	279	11·04	9·96	1,478·3	148
1948	2·03	1·97	531·5	270	11·98	11·54	1,872·5	162
1949	2·04	2·03	526·7	259	11·66	10·53	1,660·1	158
1950	2·30	2·28	526·6	231	12·69	11·67	1,846·3	158
1951	2·34	2·31	556·5	241	14·77	14·41	2,334·8	162
1952	2·30	2·17	554·4	256	11·76	11·56	1,799·6	156
1953	2·37	2·36	680·0	288	15·86	15·66	2,704·7	173
1954	2·35	2·28	654·9	287	12·19	9·81	1,469·6	150
1955	2·42	2·36	745·5	316	14·52	13·29	2,149·5	162
1956	2·36	2·32	798·7	345	15·52	14·53	2,613·4	180
1957	2·42	2·38	822·1	345	10·37	9·46	1,572·4	166
1958	2·46	2·38	719·5	303	13·49	12·28	1,978·0	161
1959	2·56	2·50	795·8	318	15·42	13·58	2,019·8	149
1960	2·62	2·52	781·6	310	14·56	13·87	2,294·6	165
1961	2·58	2·55	873·7	342	15·41	14·13	2,323·0	164
1962	2·57	2·56	854·9	334	17·82	16·43	3,082·1	188
1963	2·62	2·58	909·0	353	16·92	16·16	3,026·0	187
1964	2·67	2·67	986·0	370	15·47	14·42	2,764·0	192
1965	2·68	n.a.	1,057·0	n.a.	15·18	n.a.	2,222·0	n.a.

Year	South				Central Plain			
	Area planted million *rai*	Area harvested million *rai*	Output 000 metric tons	kg/*rai*	Area planted million *rai*	Area harvested million *rai*	Output 000 metric tons	kg/*rai*
1947	2·49	1·99	502·2	253	14·61	13·00	2,980·0	229
1948	2·73	2·39	636·4	266	15·84	14·91	3,794·8	254
1949	2·91	2·80	660·0	235	16·31	15·65	3,837·1	245
1950	2·89	2·74	599·6	219	16·75	16·39	3,809·1	232
1951	2·90	2·70	597·1	221	17·24	16·43	3,827·0	233
1952	2·78	2·64	616·8	234	16·72	15·70	3,631·3	231
1953	2·98	2·88	683·0	237	17·36	16·17	4,171·6	258
1954	3·04	2·94	657·4	223	17·15	13·24	2,927·0	221
1955	2·67	2·59	669·9	259	16·45	15·36	3,768·7	245
1956	2·86	2·69	661·3	246	16·91	16·48	4,223·5	256
1957	2·68	2·19	522·1	238	16·25	12·75	2,653·6	208
1958	2·97	2·74	624·4	228	17·06	14·91	3,731·3	250
1959	2·85	2·67	646·8	242	17·08	14·14	3,307·4	234
1960	2·81	2·70	639·4	237	17·02	16·18	4,119·0	255
1961	2·99	2·92	706·9	242	17·64	15·75	4,273·1	271
1962	3·15	3·04	742·6	244	18·08	16·67	4,599·9	276
1963	3·29	3·25	886·0	272	18·46	17·93	5,348·0	298
1964	3·27	3·20	733·0	229	19·48	17·19	5,157·0	300
1965	3·24	n.a.	874·0	n.a.	19·39	n.a.	5,066·0	n.a.

Sources: Ministry of Agriculture, *Annual Report on 1962 Rice Production in Thailand*, Tables 21-4; *Agricultural Statistics of Thailand, 1965*, Table 12; N.S.O., *Statistical Year Book of Thailand, 1965*, Table 76.

increase the tendency to choose particular types, so that rice movements are usually not entirely a one-way traffic, even though very much the greater part of the movement is simply from surplus to deficit areas. Cross traffic of special grades is also found. In the export trade the main variations in quality are related to the milling process which ideally produces as its main output rice graded as 100 per cent (no broken grains) or 5 per cent (5 per cent broken grains), and then smaller amounts of rice with a higher proportion broken. Still lower grades are the various grades known as broken rice. The grading, whether for local or overseas sales, is a highly skilled process, mainly controlled by Chinese with extensive market contacts.

One important difference which affects both the local and the home trade is that between white and glutinous rice. The main importance of this distinction is that the proportion of glutinous rice exported is much smaller than that of white rice, and that glutinous rice is grown mainly in the north and the northeast (Dept of Rice, 1962). The northern and northeastern Thais eat glutinous rice themselves and grow white rice for export. In these two regions therefore the proportion of white rice grown is partly an indication of the degree to which any province exports rice. This is not, however, a very reliable indicator, because the line dividing those who eat glutinous from those who eat white rice is not very clearly marked. In the north it approximately corresponds to the regional boundary used by the Ministry of Agriculture (including all the seven far northern provinces in the glutinous rice area); in the northeast it runs roughly across the region from Ubon Ratchathani to Khon Kaen (including both in the glutinous area).

(b) *Techniques.* The methods of planting rice also differ, both in the use of water and in the use of land. Different parts of Thailand have different needs for water control if wet rice is to be grown. Dry rice cultivation in Thailand is mainly confined to hill tribes (and a few lowlanders) in the North (Judd, 1964). The Central Plain's greatest need is to reduce the risk of drought and excessive flood. The Chai Nat dam system was intended to regulate natural flooding, which occurs each year, and spread it over a wider area, not to produce off-season water (I.B.R.D., 1959: 38). In the North the task has been to stabilise the main river levels to feed long established local irrigation systems in the valley bottoms (Chapman, 1967). Here works undertaken in the Ping and Wang river basins before World War II have since the war been extended with further works in the Kok and Yom basins (Royal Irrigation Dept, 1964). In the Northeast the main problem was to find suitable irrigation sites, because of difficulties of soil and topography. Pre-war work in the irrigation of fields in valley areas has been continued along the Mekong and in the Mun and Chee basins where the main concentrations of population had developed, but in the early 1950s the political urgency of doing something for the depressed population on the more arid lands led to the construction of many hastily planned tanks for rainwater storage (Chira, 1964). The South Region chiefly needs drainage works, the rainfall being much more adequate than in the rest of Thailand.

Irrigation policy affects the whole economy, not only rice, and will be considered further in chapter 8. Here it is necessary to consider the bearing that irrigation has on other measures for the promotion of rice growing. For this we must first consider the two production methods known as transplanting and broadcast sowing of rice.

Transplanting is generally favoured by Thai farmers, though it is a very labour-intensive method, requiring between five and ten times as much labour for the planting as the broadcast method. Transplanting wastes less seed, so that only about half as much per *rai* is needed. The quality of the rice is normally much better, though a few selected types of seed suitable for broadcast sowing (e.g. one of the Sing Buri varieties) are reported to be little inferior to transplanted rice. It is difficult, however, to match the quality of the rice suitable for transplanting, since the transplanted rice can be planted more carefully to make maximum use of the available space.

There are, however, a number of irrelevant considerations which tend, in long-run planning, to obscure analysis of the best methods. First, the transplanting method is usually used wherever there is sufficient time to complete the initial planting, the transplanting, and the growing of the rice to a reasonable height, before the land is fully flooded. The broadcast method is adopted mainly in the Central Plain, in areas where the flood comes quickly and is apt to be fairly deep. Therefore the varieties of rice which are broadcast are quick-growing ones, or in some instances long-stemmed or 'floating' ones, which can survive deep flooding. These are special varieties of rice, so that it is difficult to get valid comparisons of quality or yield depending on the method only. This would be unimportant if the relation between broadcast sowing and quick flooding was an essential one.

If we could treat the size of the farm as a datum, we could probably say that the yield from transplanting would justify the effort, so long as labour was available at the appropriate time. If, however, mechanisation reduces appreciably the labour requirements in both ploughing and harvesting, and if additional land is available, the size of farm ceases to be a datum that we can use in evaluating transplanting; for then transplanting techniques become the limiting factor on the size of the farm that a given labour force can handle. The yield per *rai* is not the variable that we have to maximise if new land can be opened up at little cost. It is the yield per worker that is important, and transplanting reduces this by limiting the area one man can work.

Next, it is necessary to think in terms of developing new varieties of rice. So long as broadcast rice has to be quick-growing, and perhaps also long-stemmed, it is difficult to give it also other desirable qualities. This is not, however, relevant to a choice of policies if we are considering substitution of broadcast sowing for transplanting in areas not subject to rapid flooding; for in these areas any strain of rice can be broadcast.

Probably the development of high-yielding, high-quality strains, suitable for transplanting and other labour-intensive techniques, is the best policy so long as other policies create a pressure of surplus population in rural areas; but this raises wider questions than can be considered here (Silcock, 1967: 289).

If transplanting is to remain the norm for Thai rice-growing, and the transplanted area in the Central Plain is to be extended, high priority will have to be given to achieving the potential control of the flood level in the plain which was envisaged when the Chai Nat dam was built. This implies not merely completing the ditches and dykes under plans begun in the second period of the First Development Plan (N.E.D.B., 1964-6: 62-6; n.d.). Greater care by the villagers themselves for all the auxiliary channels will be needed if flood water is to be properly dispersed, so that even considerable variations in the volume of water reaching the Chai Nat system will not lead to excessive flooding or shortage anywhere within the irrigated area.

Irrigation is also relevant to the improvement of rice yields by more adequate use of fertiliser (Hsieh and Ruttan, 1967: 330, 333). It has already been indicated that the chief function of irrigation in the Central Plain and the Northeast—the main rice-growing regions of Thailand—is to stabilise water levels and reduce the risks of rice cultivation. The proportion of the value of a given projected yield increase which it is rational to spend on fertiliser to achieve that yield increase depends on the probability of the yield actually being achieved. Better irrigation will therefore not only increase yields directly, but will also make it more profitable to invest in fertiliser, so increasing yields indirectly.

(c) *Price effects.* Uncertainty is not, however, the only factor preventing investment in fertiliser. Another extremely important factor is the rice premium and consequent low price of rice. Taking into account existing transport costs for both rice and fertiliser, existing levels of risk, and above all existing tax levels, it has been estimated by an F.A.O. soil adviser that only 5 per cent of the rice land in the Northeast would yield an adequate profit to justify use of fertiliser.[3]

This can be used as an argument either for subsidising fertiliser for rice growers or for abolishing (or reducing) the rice premium. With the present rice premium, the orders of magnitude in the Northeast are that with normal conditions and optimum use of fertiliser the yield of rice is approximately doubled, but the cost of the fertiliser is equal to anything from two-thirds to the whole of the value of the original crop. The gain does not adequately compensate for the risk and extra work. The rice premium is approximately equal to the farmer's return per ton in this area. If the rice premium were abolished the farmer's income per ton would be approximately doubled and the gain from the additional rice he could produce by fertilising would be about three times the cost of the fertiliser. The same result could be achieved by halving the cost of fertiliser by a subsidy and leaving the rice premium unchanged.[4]

[3] See *A Report on the Thailand Fertilizer Situation and Potential*, prepared by the Private Enterprise Division, United States Operations Mission to Thailand, p. 23.

[4] Present average return to rice farmers = present additional return from applying fertiliser = rice premium = x per ton

Present cost of fertiliser = $\frac{2x}{3}$ per ton of paddy

Ratio of cost of application of fertiliser to return = 1 : 1½

If rice premium were abolished, average return to farmers = additional

Each method would involve considerable complications, which are further discussed in chapter 8. There can, however, be no doubt that, if it were equally effective, the cost of the subsidy would be very much cheaper, and it is astonishing that most of the writers who are ready to recommend abolishing a tax that brings in a tenth of the government's revenue should dismiss such an equivalent as too costly (*Report on the Thailand Fertiliser Situation,* 1966; Usher, 1965).

With existing prices and risks, failure to use fertiliser in the Northeast can hardly be regarded as irrational. In the Central Plain, especially in areas where irrigation has both improved yields and diminished the risk of total loss, there appears to be a substantial element of ignorance and irrationality delaying the application of fertiliser. Dr Moorman's estimate of lands which could benefit from fertiliser in the Central Plain was 60 per cent. The increased possibility of linking subsidised fertiliser to extension work is an additional argument for subsidy rather than tax abolition in this area. It is an area where fertiliser is not necessary for maintenance of the normal fertility of the soil, because of nutrients deposited by the annual flood. Moreover the uncertainty of flood levels and lack of knowledge of modern fertilisers made distrust of artificial improvements of the soil a natural and reasonable attitude until recent times. Deliberate stimulation of change in response to new conditions is therefore specially likely to achieve results there.

(d) *Double cropping.* One of the original objectives of the Thai irrigation system was to promote double cropping of rice over much of the Central Plain (Ingram, 1955: 82-3; I.B.R.D., 1959: 6-7).

---

return from applying fertiliser = 2x per ton

Cost of fertiliser $= \dfrac{2x}{3}$ per ton of paddy cost: return ratio $= 1 : 3$

If rice premium retained but fertiliser subsidised by 50 per cent

additional return from applying fertiliser = x. Cost of fertiliser $= \dfrac{x}{3}$

to farmer, $\dfrac{x}{3}$ to government

Cost: return ratio to farmer $= 1 : 3$

Cost to government of abolishing rice premium = x per ton of all paddy exported as rice

Cost to government of subsidising fertiliser $= \frac{1}{2}$ cost of fertiliser wasted

$+ \dfrac{x}{3}$ per *additional* ton of paddy produced.

This was envisaged by the distinguished Dutch engineer, Van der Heide, who advised the Thai government at the beginning of the twentieth century. The International Bank Mission Report also envisaged widespread double cropping in this area, but not as a result of the Chai Nat dam alone. A considerably higher dam, such as Van der Heide recommended, might have made this possible by giving adequate storage. With the existing Chai Nat dam the object was merely some stabilisation in the first stage; double cropping on any considerable scale could follow only after the Nan and the Ping were controlled by high dams in the mountain areas.

Now that the Phumiphon dam is in use some sections of the Thai government, particularly the Ministry of the Interior, are anxious to promote as much double cropping as possible. The Department of Rice, however, believes that the same resources could produce more rice if they could be concentrated on the main crop.[5] The additional supplies of water would, by themselves, encourage more cultivation of off-season crops of vegetables. These use less water than rice and villagers could experiment themselves without the diversion of any considerable government resources.

Double cropping uses certain scarce factors that are also required elsewhere. The number of trained extension workers and scientists with a knowledge of rice growing is not yet sufficient for all the research needed to establish suitable Thai strains and control the main pests; there are shortages of rice officers in the districts. Yields can be improved by organising suitable farmers' groups, arranging demonstrations, and distributing supplies. The bottleneck is partly personnel, and partly supplies of improved seed, fertiliser, pesticide, etc. Double cropping can only rarely use personnel in otherwise free time; it makes heavy demands on research and fertiliser supplies. Moreover while the water supply is limited and the officials overburdened the area of double cropping is necessarily a small part of the whole, and this creates special difficulties. Pests from a much wider area tend to concentrate on the harvest of this one small area, so demanding more time and effort for protection of the crop.

All this suggests that much double cropping may at present waste scarce resources. Appropriate policy is, however, difficult to determine because social returns differ markedly from private ones. The

[5] Information based on interview with Dr Sala Dasananda, Director General of the Rice Department. See also Bacon, 1964.

F

rice premium keeps returns to the individual rice farmer well below those to Thailand as a whole. In addition double cropping is gradually introducing a new cycle of cultivation that will become more important as the irrigation channels become better administered and new dams are built.

Probably less emphasis should be given to double cropping, though some should be retained as a means of exploring new techniques. The Ministry of the Interior, now the chief promoter of this activity, might at present divert some attention to improving local government efforts to secure the co-operation of villagers in protecting and maintaining distribution channels in the irrigation areas.

(e) *Industrial linkage.* Rice is not merely much the most important crop of Thailand. It also has a significant effect on industrial employment and familiarity with mechanical methods. Nearly all the rice is now milled by machinery (Usher, 1967: 211-14), and the sacks in which it is exported are mostly manufactured in Thailand, from Thai materials.[6] Both of these are developments since World War II.

Before World War II the rice sold in the towns or exported was milled in cheap and efficient steam mills that used the rice chaff as fuel. Rice consumed on the farm was mainly hand-milled. Decentralisation of milling came about first as a result of wartime disruption of communications and later restrictions on the movement of rice. Once mills were available in country areas some milling of rice for neighbouring farms' home consumption could take place. If a farmer did not keep pigs and use his own bran, and if his farm was near a mill, his milling would cost him nothing, or virtually nothing; for the miller's profit is often no more than the bran which is removed from the rice. The combination of this practice of milling for home consumption with the availability of light petrol engines made it possible to set up small rice mills in the villages themselves. The petrol driven mill is slightly more expensive than the steam mill, but when established in one's own village or a nearby village it can save many hours of family labour.

[6] Some 40 million sacks a year are now produced in Thailand, mainly from Thai kenaf. This is more than enough for Thai rice exports; but of course rice is also sold internally in sacks and there are other demands for sacks in addition; a protected market can be provided for a slightly larger output. See N.E.D.B., 1966: 10; 1967: 168.

Table 4.2 Number of rice mills and their milling capacity and number of
          tambons in each province, 1964

	North	Northeast	South	Central	Whole kingdom
5 *kwien* and below					
Number	1,244	648	1,071	555	3,518
Total capacity	2,802	1,528	2,201	1,429	7,960
5-30 *kwien*					
Number	223	430	282	1,244	2,179
Total capacity	2,223	3,920	2,552	17,736	26,431
Over 30 *kwien*					
Number	33	85	25	227	370
Total capacity	2,317	5,665	3,408	25,596	36,986
All sizes					
Number	1,500	1,163	1,378	2,026	6,067
Total capacity	7,342	11,113	8,161	44,761	71,377
Tambons	1,048	1,273	886	1,715	4,922

Source: Paper read to the British Chamber of Commerce luncheon on 7
April 1964 by Mr Lee Sheng-Yi of Kriang Rit Co. Ltd; U.S.O.M./N.S.O.,
Changwat-Amphur Statistical Directory, 1965.

Table 4.2 shows the total number of rice mills by region and
capacity. Most of the mills of under 30 *kwien* capacity per day are
probably in country areas or small towns. The number of *tambons*
(groups of seven to twelve villages) in each region is given for
comparison. Probably most villages, other than remote mountain
ones, would have a small rice-mill in their own *tambon.*

It seems probable that these rice-mills, together with buses and
motor-cycles, have not merely increased the villagers' awareness of
mechanical possibilities. The greatly increased labour time made
available to each family has probably encouraged the cultivation of
supplementary crops as a source of cash income.

The transport of rice in sacks made of jute had, of course, been
established for many decades before World War II. What was new
in the post-war period was the development of a new industry to
make these sacks, and the recognition that a Thai material, kenaf,
could be used for the purpose (see pp. 77-8 for further discussion
of rice sacks).

(f) *Subsistence cultivation.* The rice sector of the economy of Thailand probably comes nearer than any other to being a subsistence
sector, or a traditional sector, of the economy. It is worth while to
inquire how far this affects the capacity of this sector to develop

and adopt modern methods. To what extent is a Thai rice farmer dominated by traditional and customary modes of behaviour and unable to respond to motives of rational self-interest?

The rationality of subsistence farmers appears to be a topic which generates extreme views. Some economists are so impressed with the rationality of peasants' comments on their use of time that they will argue that a subsistence farmer's attitude to choice, to alternatives and substitutions, is as rational as that of any operator on a commodity market (e.g. Muscat, 1966: 92-3). At the other extreme it is argued that there are large sectors of the economies of less developed countries to which 'Western' concepts of economics do not apply.[7]

There is, of course, nothing surprising in the fact that—within the sphere of behaviour in which they are expected to adjust to the facts of their situation—men in a traditional society behave in ways which can be described in terms of marginal maximising adjustment. In Western society we do not expect every individual to have consciously in his mind the whole production possibility equations and indifference equations in terms of which he behaves. We assume that he develops techniques of learning, short cuts by which he reacts to observations, automatic indications that he is departing from his objectives and the like, all of which enable him in practice to approach the adaptation to multiple goals which we describe him as achieving. People in the West use techniques of budgeting and of watching one or more cash balances, they build up highly sophisticated systems of feeling about value, in the short run and in the long run, described in terms like 'dear' and 'worth', and sophisticated codes of personal conduct described in terms like 'afford'. To anyone who did not share our money-oriented cultural background many of these methods of reacting would seem at first quite irrational. Later, if sufficient contact could be established to explain the psychological and heuristic significance of these techniques they would no doubt seem incredibly ingenious. Yet a sophisticated observer of this kind might well find that our techniques led us to behave irrationally in situations of inflation or rapid change of income, and also that we were relatively insensitive, for example, to interactions in small groups.

In interpreting the rationality of behaviour of subsistence farmers, within the sometimes very wide area in which conduct is not

---

[7] The most distinguished exponent of this view was J. H. Boeke (1953).

prescribed, we should neither be surprised that basic concepts of maximisation and substitution apply nor neglect the fact that techniques of adaptation may become inappropriate if relevant conditions change, and may for a time lead to irrational behaviour.

The fact that we call a non-monetary society traditional does not mean that we expect all the adaptive behaviour, which in our own society is usually guided by acquired monetary techniques, to be eliminated in favour of rigidly prescribed behaviour. It does, however, mean that some areas of behaviour, which in our society are adaptive, in response to monetary or other numerical indications, are in that society prescribed by tradition and custom. Some such traditions are explicable in political terms of the maintenance of a particular group's authority, or in sociological terms of fulfilling some function in maintaining the society's cohesion or continuity; but some are analogous to what Joan Robinson (1956: ch. 2) refers to as the 'rules of the game' under capitalism—particular pieces of conventional wisdom, carrying certain social sanctions, which exist to protect individuals against situations in which the short-run interest is particularly likely to be in conflict with the long-term one. Most societies have traditional practices the function of which seems to be to maintain capital (Firth, 1966).

In relation to Thai rice-growing we must inquire whether the area of traditional behaviour is large, and restrictive of development, or not, and whether, within the area of adaptive behaviour, there is evidence that inappropriate rules of thumb are hampering adjustments.

There is a good deal of evidence that Thai social custom is unusually permissive in its relation to all economic life, and that this is an important part of Thai tradition, as reported in the famous inscription of King Ramkamhaeng (thirteenth century) (Puey: 1956).

> During the reign of Ramkamhaeng, this kingdom of Sukhothai is good: in the water there are fish, in the fields there is rice. The King does not levy tolls. People take oxen to trade, ride on horses to sell. Whoever wishes to trade in elephants can do so; whoever wishes to trade in silver or in gold can do so.

Even where there are fairly definite legal or customary rules governing economic life, the Thais (whose name in their own language means 'free') think of their freedom primarily in terms of not being bound by extensive obligations in their economic life. The emphasis on sovereignty, in relation to their neighbours' experiences under colonialism, is largely a twentieth-century phenomenon.

For example, Thais are less constrained than almost any peasant people in buying or selling land (Wijeyewardene, 1967: 75-80); their geographical and (until recently) social mobility is relatively high (Caldwell, 1967). Though they have a fairly clear conceptual picture of capital, as distinct from income, there is less moral disapproval of capital-consumption than in most capitalist countries.

Probably there were more customary practices governing rice cultivation a century ago than there are today, for some of the royal ceremonies relate to rice cultivation and suggest a more defined political and social pattern than at present (Wales, 1931). The preoccupation of the royal family with modernisation has probably further loosened a tradition which was never markedly custom-bound.

Three respects may be suggested in which tradition limits present economic freedom: the attitude that irrigation is the business of those in authority; the firm belief that transplanting should be done when time permits; and the devotion to peasant ownership of land. The first is a survival from absolute monarchy and the god king.[8] Men could be ordered to work on the irrigation systems which were part of the basic structure of the state; but they ought not to have to pay for water any more than for sunlight. The belief in transplanting is probably a piece of conventional wisdom designed to maintain quality; it would be reinforced by the fact that transplanting is normally a task undertaken co-operatively, on a basis of exchanging days of labour between families (Sharp *et al.*, 1953: 154; Wijeyewardene, 1965); and it would be a rational social attitude so long as the area planted per family was limited by labour requirements in ploughing and harvesting. To call the third feature of Thai society—the preference for peasant ownership—a tradition may seem peculiar. It is certainly a widely held preference in peasant societies, though not many have such abundance of land as Thailand and have therefore been able to turn the preference

___

[8] Wittfogel (1957) explains the original relation of Khmer absolutism to irrigation. In Thai society, especially under the Bangkok dynasty, the central position of irrigation and of the god-king survived as conceptions but were modified towards the paternal form of kingship that was embodied in older Thai traditions. Irrigation became 'the royal bounty of water'.

into reality. In parts of Thailand, however, this preference may be a political obstacle to development. This is discussed further in chapter 8.

When we turn to the rationality of Thai farmers within the region of optional, or adaptive behaviour, it seems clear that a preference for growing one's own rice, even where this restricts income-earning opportunities, is still strong among Thai farmers, and is probably a survival from a time when transport was far less adequate, and it was wise to trust only inessentials to the risks of trade. Still more important, however, is a characteristic of any non-market economy, even so flexible an economy as that of rural Thailand. Those who are not constantly comparing prices are likely to take a little longer to find numerical facts a sufficient reason for changing established practices. Their techniques are not essentially different but they are less fluent in using them (Freedman, 1961). Even in Thailand it appears to be a fact that, when it becomes rational to use exchange, more people gradually come to use it, and as they use it more their response to relevant prices becomes more rapid and less marked by excessive caution. Supplementary crops are becoming an increasingly important part of Thai farmers' income, and this is likely not only to accelerate the adoption of new practices that become profitable but to prepare the way for market specialisation.

Rubber

(a) *General.* The growth of the rubber industry mentioned in chapter 3 has continued since World War II. There appears to have been some planting during the Japanese occupation though the figures are unreliable and the increase in output during the early 1950s may have been a delayed result of planting from 1939 to 1941 which was under-recorded (N.S.O., 1953). The Korean War brought a great boom in rubber planting which produced a large increase in exports in the late 1950s, and up to 1962. Since 1962 production appears to have gone on rising slowly, so that new planting must have continued into the late 1950s (Ministry of Agriculture, 1961-5).

It must be emphasised that it is extremely difficult to obtain reliable figures on the rubber industry. All output figures, except in the Agricultural Census year 1962-3, are based on exports, and the reasons for the unreliability of these have been discussed in chapter 2. For rubber the Ministry of Agriculture figures of area planted are obviously unreliable. Over the period from World War II until 1964 the figures for mature area exactly correspond to those for total area seven years earlier (Ministry of Agriculture, 1961-5). This could only be valid if no rubber trees were ever destroyed. This was a period in which at least some of the larger holdings cut out rubber trees for replanting and in 1962 many thousands of *rai* were damaged or destroyed by a hurricane. It is clear that an attempt is made to secure a return of new planting only, and that is used as a basis for area figures. Nor can an independent figure be obtained from Dr Niwat Tulyayon's research for the Bangkok Bank cited in Silcock, 1967: t. 10.1. For, since Dr Niwat's figures tally in aggregate with the ministry figures they must either be based on local inquiry into the returns submitted to Bangkok or must contain omissions which have been adjusted by difference to the ministry figures.

To make matters worse the Census of Agriculture does not give an area figure for rubber (N.S.O., 1963). For all tree crops it uses a count (or estimate) of the number of trees. This is probably the best method for fruit trees which are often grown singly or in clumps; even for coconuts it may be the best. Rubber, however, is almost always grown over a defined area, while the number of trees (as distinct from the number of tappable trees) is almost a meaningless concept on small-holdings because of self-seeding and selective cutting out of trees. So far as it goes the census total figure tallies reasonably well with the corresponding area figure for the ministry, though the output figure is rather too small for the published exports for 1962 and 1963. The main problem is that the census suggests a rather different regional distribution of the industry from that suggested by Dr Niwat's figures.

Table 4.3 compares the Census of Agriculture tree figures with Dr Niwat's figures for total area planted, with a column showing the corresponding numbers of total trees and tappable trees if the census averages for the whole kingdom were applied to Dr Niwat's figures.

It is apparent that Dr Niwat's figures (based on Ministry of Agriculture figures) give a greater predominance to the four provinces of the extreme south—Songkhla, Pattani, Yala and Narathiwat—than does the census. Dr Niwat credits them with nearly two-thirds of the country's rubber area, the census with barely half.

Dr Niwat's figures conform more nearly to what is usually said in rubber trade circles in the southern area about the distribution of the industry.[9] The following points are relevant. This is an area

Table 4.3 Comparison of Dr Niwat Tulyayon's figures for rubber area by *changwats* with Census of Agriculture tree count, 1962

Changwats	Area under rubber (Dr Niwat) 000 *rai*	Number of tappable rubber trees census 000	Total number of rubber trees census 000	Adjusted number of tappable rubber trees[a] 000	Adjusted total number of rubber trees[a] 000
Phuket	80·8	1,805	5,215	2,644	8,255
Ranong	5·7	60	622	187	582
Phang-nga	88·2	1,732	10,515	2,886	9,011
Trang	274·0	13,445	36,792	8,965	27,995
Nakhon Si Thammaret	182·5	10,662	38,415	5,971	18,646
Surat Thani	39·7	2,970	19,415	1,299	4,056
Krabi	67·4	1,842	12,541	2,205	6,886
Chumphon	4·6	37	1,162	151	470
Songkhla	415·7	13,985	42,069	13,602	42,472
Satun	61·9	1,722	5,690	2,025	6,324
Phathalung	40·4	3,671	14,153	1,322	4,128
Yala	400·8	9,113	23,452	13,114	40,950
Pattani	310·0	5,407	13,177	10,143	31,673
Narathiwat	533·5	15,415	28,023	17,456	54,508
S.E. *changwats*	164·6	5,523	21,387	5,386	16,817
Whole kingdom	2,670·7	87,389	272,888	87,389	272,865

[a] Calculated on the assumptions that the number of tappable trees and the total number of trees for each *changwat* can be derived by multiplying the area by the whole-kingdom average of tappable and total trees per *rai* respectively. These averages are calculated from the census tree count and the Ministry of Agriculture area figure for the whole kingdom. These columns are intended only for comparison with columns two and three respectively to show the difference in distribution of the rubber trees implied by two different assumptions. The figures are rounded and do not add up to the totals given.

Source: Dr Niwat Tulyayon, private communication; Ministry of Agriculture, *Census of Agriculture, 1963, Whole Kingdom* volume and volumes for separate *changwats*.

[9] On a field trip to the South Region in 1964 I was frequently told by rubber traders that most of the rubber was planted in the four southern provinces.

in which government control is not very effective. Communist guerillas collect regular tolls, and there is known to be a great deal of illegal planting. Probably a fairly high proportion of the planting is recent and this might lead to a higher percentage of immature than of mature trees. It seems likely, however, that, vague though the ministry's information may be, its estimates could very well be better than anything that could be derived from a census taken under such conditions.

(b) *Factors affecting development.* Most of those growing rubber still identify themselves as a separate Malay-speaking community. Most of those trading in rubber still consider themselves Chinese. This was relatively unimportant so long as pre-war technical conditions remained. Illegal tenure of land, petty corruption of land officials and (from 1934 on) irregular dealing in export rights may have accentuated political difficulties, but had little effect on the economy. Post-war technical changes have made these problems significant for the economy.

As we have seen, Thailand's bargaining power in the 1930s enabled it to benefit, like Indonesia in the 1920s, from the profitability of peasant production under high prices maintained by international restriction. After World War II, however, the intensive wartime development of synthetic rubber had reduced costs to a point at which unimproved natural rubber could not (in the long run) compete (McHale, 1961: 23-31; Gamba, 1956). It could, however, compete by scientific cultivation, using improved high-yielding strains and effective bud-grafting. This does not necessarily involve plantation methods with their heavy overhead expenses; Malaysia has developed effective techniques for government assistance in the initial stages of group settlement schemes, which may well become fully competitive with any plantation production (Fisk, 1963). Such schemes do, however, require better co-operation between government and settlers than Thailand can at present achieve in its southern areas.

The large areas of illegally planted rubber and the involvement of senior members of the bureaucracy in various irregular relations with Chinese rubber dealers add to the difficulty of reorganising the industry. Malaysia has been actively fostering replanting by small rubber growers since 1952 but Thailand did not introduce a scheme until 1960.

Since then a real effort has been made to foster replanting, without too inquisitive an attitude to the past. Naturally, it is difficult to obtain information about the extent of irregular title and its influence on the replanting program. Success has not been striking. The total area replanted, year by year, from 1961 to 1965, as shown in Table 4.4, is related to different estimates of total area, by province, in Table 4.5. Estimate 1 is that given by Dr Niwat; estimate 2 is based on the total area in the whole kingdom under rubber (as given by the Ministry of Agriculture and Dr Niwat) divided among *changwats* on the assumption that *tappable* trees per *rai* are the same in all *changwats*; estimate 3 is based on the same total area but divided on the assumption that total trees per *rai* are the same in all *changwats*. We do not know enough about the area under rubber to say definitely what proportion has been replanted so far; on the original ministry figures it is only about 6 per cent. The table brings out the importance of more

Table 4.4 Rubber growing *changwats*: areas approved for replanting, 1961-5

Changwat	Areas approved for replanting in *rai*[a]						Area receiving hurricane relief from replanting fund 1962 (*rai*)
	1961	1962	1963	1964	1965	Total	
Phuket	893	994	1,019	947	576	4,429	31
Ranong	299	104	8	47	52	510	—
Phang-nga	575	623	1,324	2,657	1,544	6,723	1,322
Trang	3,162	2,193	1,708	1,800	3,149	12,012	109
Nakhon Si Thammaret	1,329	1,631	5,762	8,541	3,699	20,926	39,240
Surat Thani	131	1,208	1,697	5,458	1,508	10,002	9,722
Krabi	1,256	1,692	640	1,340	1,248	6,176	219
Chumphon	—	—	140	41	163	344	—
Songkhla	5,115	7,025	5,547	5,182	5,950	30,819	12
Satun	1,057	972	783	1,051	766	4,629	—
Phathalung	332	352	425	788	983	2,880	490
Yala	2,430	3,435	3,064	3,194	2,436	14,559	—
Pattani	2,280	1,780	1,653	1,699	1,545	8,957	—
Narathiwat	2,897	4,749	4,967	6,206	7,861	26,680	2
S.E. *changwats*	2,695	5,423	3,117	2,574	2,688	16,522	
Whole kingdom	24,454	32,179	31,845	41,525	34,167	165,968	51,154

[a] Figures are rounded and do not add up to rounded totals given.

Source: Replanting figures supplied by the Rubber Division of the Department of Agriculture.

Table 4.5 Total approvals for replanting of rubber, 1961-5, by *changwats*, expressed as a percentage of different estimates of area planted in 1962

Changwats	Total area approved for replanting 1961-5 *rai*	Total area under rubber estimate 1 000 *rai*	Percentage of total area approved for replanting	Total area under rubber estimate 2 000 *rai*	Percentage of total area approved for replanting	Total area under rubber estimate 3 000 *rai*[a]	Percentage of total area approved for replanting
Phuket	4,429	80·8	5·5	55·2	8·0	51·0	8·7
Ranong	510	5·7	9·0	1·8	28·3	6·1	8·4
Phang-nga	6,723	88·2	7·6	52·9	12·7	102·9	6·5
Trang	12,012	274·0	4·4	410·9	2·9	360·1	3·3
Nakhon Si Thammaret	20,926	182·5	11·5	325·8	6·4	376·0	5·6
Surat Thani	10,002	39·7	25·2	90·8	11·0	190·0	5·3
Krabi	6,176	67·4	9·2	56·3	11·0	122·7	5·0
Chumphon	344	4·6	7·5	1·1	31·3	11·4	3·0
Songkhla	30,819	415·7	7·4	427·4	7·2	411·8	7·5
Satun	4,629	61·9	7·5	52·6	8·8	55·7	8·3
Phathalung	2,880	40·4	7·1	112·2	2·6	138·5	2·1
Yala	14,559	400·8	3·6	278·5	5·2	229·5	6·3
Pattani	8,957	310·0	2·9	165·3	5·4	129·0	6·9
Narathiwat	26,680	533·5	5·0	471·1	5·7	274·3	9·7
S.E. *changwats*	16,522	164·6	10·0	168·8	9·8	209·3	7·9
Whole kingdom	165,968	2,670·7	6·2	2,670·7	6·2	2,670·7	6·2

[a] Because of rounding the figures do not add up to the totals given.

Source: Tables 4.3 and 4.

accurate area figures for any judgment of success or failure. It is apparent that without it we can neither assess what has been achieved nor even compare performance in different provinces.

It is difficult to see how Thailand can increase adequately the planting of its rubber land with modern high-yielding material. Some Thai opinion now favours encouragement of relatively large plantations—probably owned by syndicates comprising Thai political protectors and Malaysian Chinese capitalists (from among the merchants now exporting rubber). Technically this might be the best solution, but it would raise serious political difficulties. In principle the Thai government is aware of the importance of its rubber industry and has attempted to improve techniques by research. In practice the rubber areas are far from Bangkok and it is always difficult to recruit good staff or keep them in the remote southern areas.

Thailand cannot yet match Malaysia—probably not even Indonesia—in its research or technical competence in spite of some United Nations and Colombo Plan assistance. There are reasonably well-staffed research institutes at Kor Hong and at Thanto, but these are far behind the Rubber Research Institute of Malaysia; there are small budwood nurseries in most provinces and the government has its own Rubber Industry Organisation at Nabon which is intended to act as a demonstration centre, but has standards of tapping and weed control no better than those of any reasonably run Malaysian commercial plantation.

Kenaf and Jute

Some kenaf, jute, and other hard-fibre plants were grown for local trade in the traditional economy of Thailand (McFarland, 1944: 514). The fibre was used chiefly for rope. Kenaf, now overwhelmingly the most important of the fibre crops, is listed by McFarland only as a product of Phetchabun province, as late as 1941; though by 1959 kenaf was no longer even a minor crop of that province, having moved mainly to the east—where it has spread over the whole Northeast Region—and to the west and north.

Kenaf is an inferior substitute for jute, making poor rope and much rougher sacking. Its advantage in Thailand is that it grows in drier conditions, and is adequate for rice sacks, for which Thailand can give a protected market. The motives for promoting kenaf growing in Thailand were the desire for industrialisation, and the quest for crops suitable for the climate and soil of the Northeast; kenaf was also assisted by an opportune failure of the jute crop in Pakistan at a time when the Thai industry was ready to respond to high prices.

Thailand was as unrealistic in its first impulse to industrialisation —Pridi's National Economic Plan—as most other development countries (Pridi, 1947). Pridi was a brilliant young lawyer with no knowledge of either technology or administration. The bureaucracy's first actual efforts were much better, beginning with local techniques and resources and systematically acquiring new technical and managerial knowledge (Ministry of Industry, 1959). The choice of gunny-bags was a sound one: a large market for rice sacks could be protected, and a new raw material crop could be fostered; existing techniques were not excessively complicated, and had been adapted to Indian conditions; moreover textiles are a useful introduction to industrialisation. In Thailand it could be anticipated also that other textile factories might develop later e.g. for cotton and silk once factory processes were acclimatised.

Kenaf was first reported as a commercial crop in 1947. By 1957, 10,000 tons were exported. Some kenaf was used— at first mixed with jute—in the government-owned gunny-sack factories, of which one was established in 1949, a second in 1952 and a third in 1953. Some government promotion of kenaf as a suitable crop for the Northeast had begun before the International Bank Mission arrived, and the Mission recommended additional work in this field (I.B.R.D., 1959: 75). By the time of Chaiyong Chuchart's study in 1959 it had spread right across the Northeast, and in 1960 the furthest province, Ubon Ratchathani had become the leading producer (N.E.D.B., n.d.: App. p. 4).

The expansion of the total area under kenaf up to 1965 can be seen from Table 3.8. In Table 4.6 area figures are given from 1960 to 1965 for all provinces in the Northeast and for the rest of the kingdom by regions.

Kenaf expansion was no doubt helped by the disorganisation of the world jute market after the raw jute production of Pakistan was politically separated from the Calcutta factories by the partition of India. But the event which really established the industry was the failure of the Pakistan jute crop which produced high prices in 1960 and still higher prices in 1961. The average wholesale price of kenaf in 1961 was 3·61 *baht* per kilogram and the

Table 4.6 Area under kenaf by *changwats* in the Northeast region and by regions for all Thailand, 1960 to 1965

(000 *rai*)

Changwats	1960ᵃ	1961	1962	1963	1964	1965
Kalasin	72·0	166·4	106·2	71·5	63·4	86·0
Khon Kaen	78·0	105·5	96·8	126·2	299·4	499·3
Chaiyaphum	92·0	218·3	110·0	158·6	178·3	379·0
Nakhon Phanom	1·0	32·4	12·0	11·3	10·1	30·8
Nakhon Ratchasima	95·0	200·2	58·2	120·4	169·6	260·3
Buri Ram	13·0	146·3	94·0	48·0	63·5	89·0
Maha Sarakham	153·0	353·0	121·9	211·8	216·4	427·6
Roi Et	40·0	46·3	12·1	27·4	38·6	78·4
Loei	1·0	1·0	0·8	0·7	6·4	25·9
Si Sa Ket	83·0	99·9	34·5	31·2	58·2	94·9
Sakan Nakhon	8·0	8·9	3·3	1·3	1·1	4·9
Surin	0·4	2·0	11·9	6·7	26·4	65·8
Nong Khai	0·2	25·0	2·3	5·0	2·5	4·7
Udon Thani	2·0	33·5	21·3	23·3	38·2	79·6
Ubon Ratchathani	218·0	193·1	6·5	81·5	165·4	240·0
Northeast	857·0	1,631·8	691·8	924·9	1,337·5	2,366·3
North	n.a.	22·8	5·2	11·7	1·4	2·2
Central	n.a.	65·8	14·8	20·9	26·2	32·2
South	n.a.	—	0·06	0·06		0·2
Whole kingdom		1,720·4	711·8	957·5	1,365·1	2,400·0

ᵃ The figures for 1960 include area under jute and ramie. In 1961 there were 48,000 *rai* under jute and 4,000 *rai* under ramie; 27,000 *rai* of jute was in Ubon Ratchathani and 1,000 *rai* of ramie in Buri Ram. This inclusion of other hard fibres in the 1960 figures is unlikely to cause an error of more than 10 per cent in any *changwat*.

Source: N.E.D.B., *The Government of Thailand: The Northeast Development Plan, 1962-1966*, Table 3 of Appendix; Ministry of Agriculture, *Crop Reports*, 1961-5.

total production was a record 339·3 thousand tons (Ministry of Agriculture, 1964: 84).

Kenaf exhibits both the strengths and the weaknesses of Thai agriculture. Relatively little government encouragement was needed, once the profitability of the crop could be demonstrated. Though some Thai farmers are conservative many will adopt new ways when a few do so successfully. Some three-quarters learnt about kenaf by imitating their neighbours (Chaiyong *et al.*, 1961). Two problems rapidly emerged. First, kenaf rapidly exhausts the soil, and in several provinces farmers have had to move into new areas to find unexhausted land. This process clearly cannot long continue.

It is imperative for the government to undertake more research into the possible use of fertiliser in kenaf growing (U.S.O.M., 1966: 24-6). This is being done. Programs of fertiliser use can be developed to restore the soil, but in view of uncertainties both of climate and of price there are still differences of opinion over whether fertilisers could become an economic proposition in most kenaf areas.

Moreover, though kenaf demands less moisture than jute for growing, the retting (fibre-extraction) process requires deep, clear water to avoid discolouration, and supplies of water, particularly in remoter areas, are often not adequate (Platenius, 1963).

Improving the retting also raises problems that are being further investigated. Farmers can either be helped to develop relatively simple water storage techniques or taught to ribbon the kenaf and take it for mechanical retting in central factories. The former, less capital-intensive, method seems more suited to increasing farmers' incomes; but where kenaf is subsidiary to rice, labour time for harvesting and retting may be the bottleneck. Too little is at present known about either local rainfall and soil conditions or the extent of local specialisation in kenaf to settle the policy issue.

Kenaf seems unlikely to capture much of the world jute market, except in years of exceptional disruption. However, there is a small but fairly steady international demand for kenaf mainly from Europe and Japan (Dept of Customs, 1966, 1967; N.S.O., 1965: t. 155). Research may discover new special uses for it,[10] but on the whole use of natural fibres in packing will probably diminish. Thailand can create a protected market through its own factories and through packaging its own exported rice and its internal shipments of sugar etc., in kenaf sacks. The government factories now supply virtually all Thailand's needs (N.E.D.B., 1966, 1967). Yet even at the maximum this is only likely to absorb 10 per cent of the local output of kenaf. Export markets will be needed, and this requires continued attention to improvement of quality.

Unlike kenaf, jute is grown mainly in the Central Plain; this reflects its greater demand for water. Recently Thai jute output has increased but is only 5 per cent of that of kenaf. Jute requires land

---

[10] It is currently being studied in the U.S.A. as a raw material for paper.

that could be used for rice growing. Even with the present rice premium there are few places where it is profitable, and with a free market in rice it would probably hardly be grown at all.

In all the crops considered in this chapter, location is hardly a significant economic problem. Rice is grown everywhere in Thailand, though the main areas are the Central Plain and the Northeast. Rubber and kenaf are grown almost throughout the areas where the climate is suitable—rubber in the South and Southeast, where rainfall exceeds 2,000 mm, kenaf in the Northeast where conditions are too dry for alternative crops. These three crops have been considered first mainly because their problems can be tackled on a national level. Most of the interesting problems of the other crops of Thailand relate to location, and to these we now turn.

5

Analysis of Crops: Other Crops

It is neither possible nor desirable in a short book on agricultural development to discuss in detail the development of each individual crop. In this chapter we consider maize, which has now become the second most important crop in Thailand, but which was not considered in the previous chapter because it has special characteristics in common with two other export crops, mung-beans and cassava. There is a brief discussion of the sugar industry as it was before the reorganisation now taking place (Wu, 1967): this is a relatively minor product, and heavily dependent on changing international conditions, but its historical importance to Thailand justifies a brief separate treatment (Ingram, 1955: 10). Vegetables and fruit are not discussed crop by crop, but an analysis is given of some interesting features of the growth and location of these crops. Finally there are brief analyses of some of the problems influencing the development of Thailand's livestock industry and also its forestry.

The importance of the concentration or the dispersion of Thailand's different crops as an influence on the development of the rural sector tends to be neglected partly because the *changwat* material is available only in Thai,[1] and partly because it has obvious shortcomings in reliability. Yet without some acquaintance with this detail one can easily form entirely erroneous ideas about

[1] Ministry of Agriculture *Crop Reports, Changwat* Series and Crop Series, printed from 1961; the latest available in 1968 is for 1965. Arabic figures are used but all titles and notes are in Thai for 1961 and 1962. Some of the titles are in English from 1963 and more from 1964, but the table of contents is in Thai only.

Thai rural development. Confusion is increased by the fact that one area of new concentration at the northern end of the Central Plain overlaps three of Thailand's four administrative regions, while the economically and geographically distinct southeastern and southwestern areas are administratively part of the Central Plain. Neither national nor regional figures give a clear picture of what is happening.

Maize

Maize is in many ways the most dramatic of all the 'miracle crops' that have developed since World War II to transform Thailand's rural economy. This crop was widely grown for domestic trade in Thailand even before the war. Output of maize has risen nearly two hundredfold, from the pre-war average of 5,000 tons to the present figure of over a million. Table 5.1 shows the rise in area and output by regions, 1950-65. Like kenaf, maize was partly fostered by government initiative as a crop for the relatively dry Northeast Region (I.B.R.D., 1959: 74-5; Brown, 1963: 8-9). Unlike kenaf, it has not remained there, but has become heavily concentrated in a relatively small corner of the Central Plain, adjacent to the Northeast.

Brief attention must be given to some statistical difficulties concerning maize. The most obvious is the fact that two of the four leading maize provinces, Nakhon Sawan and Phetchabun, are treated as northern provinces in the *Statistical Year Book* and the Development Plan, and as Central provinces in the agricultural statistics. The more widely available regional statistics thus give the impression that maize output is dispersed over the country, whereas in fact about 90 per cent of Thailand's maize is grown in a single block of land near the junction between the North, Central, and Northeast Regions. This block includes parts of Lop Buri and Saraburi (Central), Nakhon Ratchasima (Northeast) and Phetchabun and Nakhon Sawan (North).

Thai statistics do not adequately distinguish between the 'sweet' maize used for human consumption and the 'hard' variety exported as stock feed. The Ministry of Agriculture collects separate figures at the provincial level, but does not publish them separately. According to Gajewski (1965), who presumably had access to working papers, the Census of Agriculture published figures only for the hard variety. The sweet variety, being the traditional crop,

Table 5.1   Maize: area planted, output, and yield per *rai* planted for each region, 1950-65

Year	North Region			Northeast Region			Central Plain Region			South Region		
	Area planted 000 *rai*	Output 000 tons	Yield per *rai* planted kg	Area planted 000 *rai*	Output 000 tons	Yield per *rai* planted kg	Area planted 000 *rai*	Output 000 tons	Yield per *rai* planted kg	Area planted 000 *rai*	Output 000 tons	Yield per *rai* planted kg
1950	23	1·5	65	82	11·1	135	100	12·9	129	21	1·4	67
1951	12	1·2	100	138	21·6	157	100	17·8	178	9	1·0	111
1952	11	1·2	109	156	25·7	165	107	17·2	161	6	0·7	117
1953	11	1·2	109	151	24·5	162	118	22·4	190	18	3·0	167
1954	11	1·6	146	152	29·6	195	150	28·2	188	19	2·8	147
1955	21	2·7	129	160	33·2	208	152	29·3	193	14	2·3	164
1956	24	5·7	238	210	49·4	235	257	55·8	217	23	3·9	170
1957	28	6·8	243	237	55·8	235	316	69·6	220	25	4·8	192
1958	44	10·6	241	326	78·8	242	369	85·1	231	54	11·8	219
1959	66	16·6	252	440	112·3	255	653	167·0	256	89	21·3	239
1960	85	24·8	292	506	154·2	305	1,075	332·3	309	119	32·7	275
1961	15	4·2	280	329	75·6	230	1,530	507·5	332	42	11·0	262
1962	23	6·2	270	277	68·0	246	1,724	584·8	339	26	6·4	246
1963	29	7·3	252	247	64·4	261	2,307	778·7	338	29	7·3	252
1964	48	12·0	250	253	63·4	251	3,113	851·8	274	36	7·9	219
1965	84	20·7	246	296	69·2	233	3,160	916·6	290	66	14·7	223

Source: Ministry of Agriculture, *Agricultural Statistics of Thailand, 1965*, Table 17.

is more likely to be grown as a supplementary crop by rice farmers —mainly for their own use and local sale—than by specialists.

It would be useful to know about the relative proportions of the two varieties, because the recent rise in yields is partly due to the substitution of the hard for the sweet variety; and because very little of the sweet variety is exported.

For one important province, Nakhon Sawan, we have more detailed evidence of the switch to the hard variety as production expanded. Nakhon Sawan was one of the provinces where maize growers were interviewed by Chaiyong Chuchart, G. R. Sitton, and Arkhom Soothiphan in 1960 and questioned about the 1959 crop (Chaiyong *et al.*, 1962). In the Nakhon Sawan 1964 *Annual Report* (pp. 133-208) the detailed district by district agricultural figures as submitted to the ministry are also published. In 1959, when Nakhon Sawan's maize area harvested was 52·8 thousand *rai*—4·2 per cent of the total for Thailand—82 per cent of the farmers interviewed were growing sweet maize. By 1964 Nakhon Sawan was harvesting 976·5 thousand *rai*, 28·9 per cent of the national total, and zero returns were made by every district for sweet maize, every farm apparently having switched to the hard variety. The extent of the change must be very great, though it is hardly credible that it can really be as great as this.

The introduction of the Guatemala type of hard maize was one of the contributions made by American advisers to the economy of the Northeast (Brown, 1963: 25). Table 5.2 shows that in 1951, when the American aid program began, five of the first seven maize producing provinces were in the Northeast. Ten years later, however, only one Northeastern province remained in the first seven. By 1965 there was only one Northeastern province in the first ten.

This development took place in three stages. Up to 1955 the area planted in both the Northeast and the Central Plain expanded. From 1956 to 1959 the expansion of the area under maize in the Central Plain accelerated as a result of increasing development of Thai overseas markets and improved transport links with Bangkok. After 1959 there was additional, very rapid growth as international demand—especially from Japan—impinged on the Thai market; but this growth was concentrated in an extremely limited area. This is brought out in Table 5.3. Between 1959 and 1964 the area under maize increased by about 175 per cent. The increase in area

Table 5.2 Ten leading provinces by output of maize, 1951, 1961, 1964, and 1965

Province	Region	1951[a] Area harvested 000 *rai*	Output tons	Province	Region	1961[b] Area harvested 000 *rai*	Output tons
Nakhon Ratchasima	NE	48·9	8,786·2	Saraburi	C	396·4	138,736·2
Nakhon Sawan	C(N)	21·3	3,450·9	Lop Buri	C	414·3	132,576·0
Khon Kaen	NE	12·9	2,298·6	Nakhon Sawan	C(N)	350·5	131,422·5
Maha Sarakham	NE	6·9	2,077·8	Nakhon Ratchasima	NE	111·1	27,776·5
Saraburi	C	12·2	1,973·8	Phitsanulok	C(N)	50·0	17,494·1
Sakon Nakhon	NE	7·8	1,724·0	Phichit	C(N)	38·9	12,448·3
Ubon Ratchathani	NE	11·4	1,314·9	Prachin Buri	C	38·9	11,679·9
Uttaradit	C(N)	4·1	1,224·3	Sukothai	C(N)	34·0	10,194·0
Suphan Buri	C	5·9	1,060·2	Ubon Ratchathani	NE	33·3	8,311·5
Phitsanulok	C(N)	5·3	1,049·8	Surin	NE	21·5	5,375·0
				Nong Khai	NE	21·5	5,375·0

Province	Region	1964[c] Area harvested 000 rai	Output tons	Province	Region	1965[d] Area harvested 000 rai	Output tons
Lop Buri	C	974·0	292,196·7	Lop Buri	C	972·3	340,305·0
Nakhon Sawan	C(N)	976·5	244,133·0	Nakhon Sawan	C(N)	966·9	241,716·0
Saraburi	C	454·9	136,476·6	Saraburi	C	346·6	103,992·0
Phetchabun	C(N)	133·8	40,141·2	Phetchabun	C(N)	154·3	46,290·0
Nakhon Ratchasima	NE	148·5	37,127·0	Phichit	C(N)	143·0	44,330·0
Phitsanulok	C(N)	147·5	36,872·8	Nakhon Ratchasima	NE	152·8	38,212·0
Phichit	C(N)	107·0	32,112·6	Phitsanulok	C(N)	147·6	36,905·0
Sukothai	C(N)	67·3	20,182·2	Sukothai	C(N)	102·0	30,667·2
Kamphaeng Phet	C(N)	62·8	15,701·0	Kamphaeng Phet	C(N)	70·3	21,090·3
Si Sa Ket	NE	25·1	7,514·4	Nan	N	26·2	7,322·8

Note: NE = Northeast, C(N) = North Central Plain, and C = Central Plain.
Sources: [a] N.S.O., *Statistical Year Book, 1953*, vol. II, pp. 270-9.
[b] Ministry of Agriculture, *Statistics of the Planting of Field Crops and Vegetables* (Crop Series), 1961, pp. 1-3.
[c] Ibid., 1964, pp. 1-3.
[d] Ibid., 1965, pp. 1-4.

Table 5.3 Increase in area under maize, 1959-64

District	Area under maize in 1959 000 *rai*	Area under maize in 1964 000 *rai*	Increase in area 000 *rai*	Increase as percentage of 1959 area	Percentage of total increase
Nakhon Sawan	53	977	924	1,744	42
Lop Buri	86	973	887	1,031	40
Rest of Central Plain[a]	514	1,163	649	126	30
Rest of Thailand	596	336	—260	—44	—12
All Thailand	1,249	3,449	2,200	176	100

[a] Central Plain as given by Ministry of Agriculture, i.e. including all the administrative North Region except the seven far north provinces.

Sources: 'Crop Reports', 1959, mimeo., in Thai; Ministry of Agriculture, *Statistics of the Planting of Field Crops and Vegetables* (Crop Series), 1964, pp. 1-4.

was 2,200 thousand *rai*; but the increase in Nakhon Sawan and Lop Buri provinces was 1,811 thousand *rai*, just over 80 per cent of the total.[2] Indeed nearly a third of the total increase in the kingdom was produced by a quarter of the area of Nakhon Sawan alone—the two southernmost districts Takhli and Phayuha Khiri (*Annual Report*, 1964: 133, 140, 160). Similar details are not available for Lop Buri province.

Why was the development of maize-growing so concentrated during these five years in an area which did not enjoy special government developmental effort? Part of it was probably due to better land and water transport associated with the Chai Nat dam, part to migration of population from the Northeast and the more congested areas in the Central Plain (Nakhon Sawan *Annual Report*, 1964: 278; Dept of Labour, 1965).[3] Maize is not the only crop which has developed on a large scale in recent years within a closely limited area. This will appear in the remainder of this chapter. However, the reasons for this concentration are best deferred for consideration in the regional chapters (6 and 7).

We must next face the question whether maize output expanded as a result of the rice taxes, i.e. at the expense of a rice expansion

[2] Just over 80 per cent of the net increase, just over 70 per cent of the gross increase, for many *changwats* decreased their area during the period.

[3] Note that the immigration to Nakhon Sawan has been going on for many years, but the *Annual Report* refers specifically to much recent immigration.

which might have been more profitable for Thailand. The concentration of the increase in two provinces where rice output has also increased strikingly at first seems to suggest that this is an unreal problem. However, the immigration, the improved transport, and the new irrigation works, might have improved rice output even more.

We may consider the land in Nakhon Sawan and Lop Buri provinces which grew maize and might have grown rice. Ignoring, first, the fact that maize is an 'upland crop',[4] we can compare the gross yield per *rai* of rice and maize in these areas. Table 5.4 compares average yields of paddy and unmilled maize in these two provinces and in the whole kingdom, and also compares the value, in export income, of the yield of one *rai*, at 1964 international values. Relative international values of rice have since risen in comparison to maize, but provincial yield figures are not available more recently than 1964.

Table 5.4 Comparisons of export proceeds from one *rai* of land in rice and in maize: Nakhon Sawan, Lop Buri, and whole kingdom, 1964

	Average yield per *rai* kg	Milled rice equivalent	Export price *baht* per ton	Export proceeds *baht* per *rai*
Rice (paddy)				
Nakhon Sawan	276	179·40	2,287	410·3
Lop Buri	303	196·95	2,287	450·4
Whole kingdom	257	167·05	2,287	382·0
Maize				
Nakhon Sawan	250		1,207	301·7
Lop Buri	300		1,207	362·0
Whole kingdom	276		1,207	333·0

Sources: Ministry of Agriculture, *Agricultural Statistics of Thailand, 1965; Statistics of the Planting of Field Crops and Vegetables* (Crop Series), 1964.

It can be seen from this table that, if land of average yield in either crop could be transferred from maize to rice this would bring Thailand some 30 per cent additional export income from that land; the reason the rice farmers do not transfer is that owing to the rice premium their personal income would be much less. The difference in gross yield, however, may not be sufficient to

[4] This term is used in Thailand to describe all crops not grown in flooded areas.

show any significant loss as a result of the rice premium. Up-to-date comparisons of expenses on rice and maize growing are lacking; but for 1957 the studies in Nakhon Ratchasima by Chaiyong Chuchart and Suphan Tosoonthorn show average costs per *rai*, for all yields, of 210·44 *baht* for rice and 120·76 for maize. Moreover, it is significant that the demand for labour-days per *rai* for rice is over five in soil preparation and four and a half in harvesting, whereas for maize it is four in soil preparation and one and a half in harvesting (Chaiyong and Suphan, 1957: 30, 36, 46, 52). This suggests that the same resources, if transferred from maize to rice, might not be able to meet peak demands unless the area were reduced quite substantially.

It must also be emphasised that maize uses much less water per *rai*, and in those areas partly dependent on irrigation increased need for water per *rai* for rice might reduce the area that could be opened up if rice were grown instead of maize, even if labour were not a bottleneck. All this suggests that while the rice premium may cause some loss of export income by fostering maize growing where otherwise rice would be grown, it is unlikely that this had any significant effect up to 1964.

One qualification of this statement may be suggested. If the high yields in maize were brought about by the use of fertiliser we should make allowance for a similar rise in yields if abolition of rice premiums made fertiliser equally profitable on rice (U.S.O.M., 1966: 100-12). In fact fertiliser is not extensively used in these two provinces; and the greater prevalence of subsistence farming in rice suggests that we could not reasonably assume similar reactions in rice and in maize, even if fertiliser were used on the maize.

On the other hand the table does indicate that if a large-scale program of subsidising fertiliser was undertaken by the government, leaving the rice premium unchanged, there might be substantial loss of export income in this area if the fertiliser was used on maize instead of on rice. As soon as Thailand can count on an efficient production and marketing system there will probably be some areas in these provinces where rice would be a better crop than maize (see chapter 8).

More important policy problems relate to marketing and quality (Lee, 1963: 120-33). The maize marketing system, though built up rather rapidly, is very competitive and gives the Thai farmer a good fraction of the price paid by the overseas importer (Somsri,

1959: 18). Arguments for control on the ground that wholesalers make losses when they sell forward are not convincing. Thailand must, however, face monopsonistic buying, particularly by Japan. The most natural way to deal with this is by widening the range of countries buying Thai maize. At present this is made difficult by high moisture content which prevents shipment to distant markets, for example in Europe. In time, specialised wholesalers will probably emerge, with relatively large resources devoted to maize only. At that stage it may become profitable to break the monopsony by installing maize drying machinery.

These appear to be merely problems of over-rapid growth. It would be dangerous at present to introduce controls which could easily become instruments of patronage and personal gain (Muscat, 1966a: 122-3).

The hard variety of maize may well be one of the best prospects for Thai rural development. If Asian standards of living rise the demand for livestock will increase both in Thailand and in other Asian countries; moreover modern technology involving special feed for animals is likely to replace traditional feeds even if there is no change in the demand for livestock. In the long run, also, Thailand's own livestock industry may cease to be monopolised by politicians and begin to expand, so increasing the local demand for maize. Thailand might even become a considerable exporter of meat products (Muscat, 1966a: 117-25; Silcock, 1967: 255-6; N.E.D.B., 1964: 61).

Other Export Crops: Mung-beans, Cassava, and Sugar-cane

Two other export crops which have recently increased in importance are mung-beans and cassava. Neither of these has received any direct government promotion, and for both the recent expansion has been localised. Table 5.5 shows the expansion in the area under mung-beans by region. During the 1950s the yield per *rai* also increased, from just over 100 kg to the pre-war average of 150 and then to 175.

As the table shows the mung-bean area expanded everywhere after World War II up to 1950.[5] During the 1950s the area planted

[5] This was probably simply a recovery of earlier conditions for an export crop; but mung-bean planting is not shown separately in pre-war figures, where it is listed under 'peas' along with other crops collectively known as *thua* in Thai.

Table 5.5 Mung-beans: area planted, output, and yield per *rai* by regions, 1949-65

Year	North Region			Northeast Region			Central Plain Region			South Region		
	Area planted 000 *rai*	Output 000 tons	Yield per *rai* planted kg	Area planted 000 *rai*	Output 000 tons	Yield per *rai* planted kg	Area planted 000 *rai*	Output 000 tons	Yield per *rai* planted kg	Area planted 000 *rai*	Output 000 tons	Yield per *rai* planted kg
1949	2·9	0·3	103	16·1	1·3	81	213·5	20·4	96	1·1	0·1	91
1950	3·4	0·3	88	21·9	2·4	110	227·1	28·9	127	1·5	0·1	67
1951	2·8	0·2	71	24·7	3·0	121	176·2	22·6	128	1·5	0·1	67
1952	6·7	0·4	59	33·9	3·1	91	162·7	20·0	123	0·8	0·1	125
1953	4·2	0·4	95	25·9	3·0	116	149·7	22·1	148	2·1	0·3	143
1954	1·3	0·1	77	45·7	6·9	151	149·1	20·9	140	0·9	0·1	111
1955	1·3	0·1	77	47·9	7·4	154	163·9	26·4	161	2·7	0·3	111
1956	1·5	0·2	133	49·2	7·8	158	162·9	28·9	177	2·9	0·3	103
1957	2·6	0·3	115	54·2	9·1	168	175·5	31·0	177	4·9	0·8	163
1958	3·1	0·4	129	50·5	8·2	162	197·3	32·7	166	1·6	0·2	125
1959	6·3	1·0	159	50·6	7·8	154	231·1	37·0	160	0·5	0·1	200
1960	10·2	1·7	167	55·1	8·9	162	261·0	49·7	190	0·4	0·1	250
1961	4·0	0·7	175	32·7	5·7	174	189·9	33·8	178	1·9	0·3	158
1962	10·5	1·6	152	27·0	4·6	170	269·6	47·0	174	2·9	0·5	172
1963	17·9	3·1	173	20·3	3·3	163	586·0	108·8	186	5·4	0·8	148
1964	12·5	2·1	168	24·2	3·6	149	568·4	100·6	177	26·9	3·9	145
1965	14·9	2·3	154	23·5	4·4	187	707·0	117·2	166	7·6	0·9	118

Source: Ministry of Agriculture, *Agricultural Statistics of Thailand, 1965*, Table 19.

ceased to expand in the Central Plain, but the increasing development of the Northeast led to some expansion there. Mung-beans fell back to the 1950 level in the Northeast during the kenaf boom in the early 1960s, but from 1959 the area planted in the Central Plain expanded rapidly. Virtually the whole increase since 1959 in Thailand's mung-bean area has been due to the expansion by just over 475 thousand *rai*—over 200 per cent—within the Central Plain. The crop reports, however, make it clear that about two-thirds of this expansion occurred in the one province of Nakhon Sawan and most of the rest in provinces a little further north—Phichit and Phitsanulok—which were also being opened up by increased immigration following improvements in transport. The rapid increase in area did not lead to any falling off in yield, though the substantial increase in yield per *rai* achieved in the 1950s was not repeated.

The cassava crop is just about as highly concentrated as the mung-bean crop. Rather more than half of it is grown in the southeastern province of Chon Buri, and much of the rest in the neighbouring southeastern provinces. Unlike mung-beans, however, cassava (as a commercial crop) has been concentrated in one province at least since World War II. The early statistics record only the production of Chon Buri; elsewhere a little was grown but in Chon Buri the roots were manufactured into tapioca flour for export. Because statistics for production in the rest of Thailand are not available before 1956 we do not know how heavily production was concentrated in Chon Buri before that time. Between World War II and 1956 production in Chon Buri province had declined. It seems likely that it declined even more in the rest of Thailand. McFarland (1954: 645-6) tells us that cassava was introduced to south Thailand from Malaya by the Chinese, but he does not mention the southeast. Consumption of tapioca flour expanded considerably in Southeast Asia during the war, and the immediate post-war period. The processing of tapioca in factories was probably introduced to Chon Buri during the wartime period of industrialisation.

Table 5.6 shows the increase in the area under cassava in Chon Buri and elsewhere. At the beginning of the expansion Chon Buri held and even increased its relative share, which was based on availability of processing plants. In 1963-5 expansion in other centres was offset by contraction in Chon Buri. Improved

Table 5.6 Cassava: area planted and production for Chon Buri and Thailand, 1956-65

	Chon Buri	Rest of Thailand	Total
Area planted, 000 *rai*			
1956	55	190	245
1957	n.a.	n.a.	240
1958	n.a.	n.a.	276
1959	255	136	391
1960	n.a.	n.a.	447
1961	424	197	621
1962	528	239	767
1963	598	277	875
1964	374	282	656
1965	301	336	637
Production, 000 tons			
1956	88·2	67·0	155·2
1957	n.a.	n.a.	163·8
1958	n.a.	n.a.	190·9
1959	299·0	125·5	424·5
1960	n.a.	n.a.	479·0
1961	498·5	178·1	676·6
1962	621·1	193·1	814·2
1963	584·4	243·1	827·5
1964	351·3	259·0	610·3
1965	294·6	283·6	578·2

Sources: Ministry of Agriculture, *Agricultural Statistics of Thailand, 1958*, Table 19; 1965, Table 20; *Statistics of the Planting of Field Crops and Vegetables* (Crop Series), 1961-4.

transport made possible expansion further afield, particularly in Nakhon Ratchasima. Cassava flour is now being exported as an industrial starch on a considerable scale, mainly to the United States and Japan, and there appears to be scope for further expansion.

Chon Buri is also Thailand's main producer of sugar-cane. There are several different and incompatible figures on sugar-cane production, so that it is hazardous to give detailed output figures (Wu, 1967; Gajewski, 1965; *Crop Reports*, 1961-64; N.S.O., 1963). Processing of sugar for local use was initiated as one of the industrialisation measures adopted in the period immediately before World War II (Wu, 1967: Dept of Industrial Promotion, 1959:

App. p. 17). One of the centres was in Chon Buri, another in Kanchanaburi in the West Sub-region.

During the period from 1959 to 1964 the industry was expanding and the relative share of Chon Buri was increasing. At first the expansion appears to have been simply a response to favourable prices. After 1961, however, the government intervened to ban the import of sugar and to impose a levy on sugar sold internally, the proceeds of which were used to foster exports (Wu, 1967; Corden, 1967: 162-3). A great expansion of supply followed in all the main centres in Thailand, and this, combined with a fall in the international price led to abandonment of the support scheme in 1966. Efforts are now being made to establish an industry producing on a more stable basis for the Thai market.

Unfortunately the scheme at present being suggested is one in which costs of manufacture are to be cut by heavy capital investment, and the growers in each area bound to the millers of that area. Area control and production control are envisaged, in accordance with a forecast of total demand in the Thai market. Having regard to the past experience of Thailand it is virtually certain that any such tightly knit control would be used to give a politically protected producing syndicate profits, both through monopoly at the expense of the consumers, and probably also through monopsony at the expense of the cane growers.

Since 1964 there has been a decline in Chon Buri's relative share of the market and even in its absolute output of sugar. The *Report and Project for Rationalisation and Modernisation of the Sugar Industry* attributes the decline to the superior productivity of cane growing in the Central Region, especially in Ratchaburi, Kanchanaburi, and Prachuap Khiri Khan (Wu, 1967: 58-60). If there is any such superiority it does not appear in the crop reports up to 1965.

Summary of Export Crops

The foregoing analysis has shown that for three important export crops, and one which had a relatively brief career as a subsidised export, the increase in production was confined to a fairly narrowly circumscribed area, even though the crops themselves had, up till then, been fairly well distributed. The pattern is clearest for maize and mung-beans; cassava was already fairly well localised before the expansion began.

Another feature of the growth process is that there was first a considerable increase in output per *rai*, and later a rapid expansion of area planted, in the growth centre selected, accompanied by some fall in the yield per *rai*, though not enough to offset the previous increase. It might be expected that the increase in output per *rai* would be clearly localised, but that once higher yields had been achieved they would spread over the country. This has not happened for any of the crops considered here; it is the expansion of area which is localised, while the rise in yields—though not diffused uniformly over the whole country—is far less confined to one place.

This suggests that, at the present time, when the infrastructure for development is being improved over most of the country, we should not look to diffusion of new techniques as the explanation for growth of all crops but should recognise that at least for some the critical factor is localised in one area. It may be possible to make some progress towards isolating such factors when we come to consider the particular areas. Before that, we must attend to a rather large group of crops grown wholly or mainly for use within Thailand.

Crops for Sale in the Thai Market

Two important crops produced for sale within Thailand are tobacco and cotton. Tobacco is still sold to the government monopoly, or can be sold privately (unmanufactured) on payment of excise duty. The official figures show no significant increase either in the area planted or in the yield. Because of the excise duty the area figures are probably more unreliable than other area figures. The monopoly has increased its sales and other consumption may also have increased. Cotton growing has been extended for increased local manufacture, but the yield per *rai* has changed little. More interesting are the fruit and vegetables grown for local consumption.

For most of the crops the ministry figures are not considered sufficiently reliable to be used as a basis for national income calculations. Regional statistics are available for about seven years for the principal fruits and vegetables, and from 1961 to 1965 these figures are available by provinces. Regional figures for chillies, onions, and garlic go back to 1952 and these too are available by provinces from 1961 to 1965. All these figures show a great increase in output per *rai*, though in several instances this is not sustained in 1964-5, the last figures available. These figures are not very reliable, but it seems excessively cautious to estimate production (as the National Income Office does) on the basis of a constant intake per head (Prot, 1967: 111). Unless the amount of error is almost incredibly large there must have clearly have been a very substantial increase in output. Table 5.7 shows the figures for output of twelve of the more important of these crops over a period of nine years. If we compare for each crop the average output for 1957-9 with the average output for 1963-5 virtually all the food crops have at least doubled. During this period the population has increased by about 50 per cent but the gross domestic product has almost doubled. It is fairly probable that coverage of these crops has improved over the period, but the figures as they stand do not seem impossible, except perhaps for tobacco.

Table 5.7 Output of selected crops produced mainly for local consumption, 1957-65

(000 tons)

	1957	1958	1959	1960	1961	1962	1963	1964	1965
Chillies	8·8	11·0	12·6	25·5	27·4	36·8	40·1	32·1	35·6
Onions	8·8	14·8	14·2	39·3	41·3	49·7	36·6	33·7	31·9
Garlic	12·4	14·9	18·5	28·2	33·9	43·2	35·9	34·3	29·5
Pineapples	91·3	123·2	148·6	256·3	450·1	320·8	288·8	260·4	300·8
Watermelons	19·6	22·7	30·4	121·4	116·9	118·0	185·5	171·3	194·5
Bananas[a]	325·5	267·7	357·0	425·1	645·6	652·5	796·0	743·0	1,243·1
String beans	7·5	7·7	8·8	n.a.	22·6	36·8	34·9	33·7	33·4
Eggplant[b]	31·2	34·6	35·7	n.a.	50·1	48·8	62·7	49·2	47·4
Sweet potatoes	66·5	82·8	106·8	n.a.	129·9	147·6	164·9	148·6	156·1
Pumpkin	13·4	13·1	16·8	n.a.	41·0	60·6	96·3	63·7	70·5
Cotton	36·5	34·7	37·4	45·5	38·3	41·3	48·6	49·1	59·8
Tobacco									
Virginia	7·0	8·8	8·0	8·8	8·7	8·6	8·6	8·9	7·6
Local vars.	59·0	56·8	59·1	65·3	39·7	39·3	38·0	53·9	67·9

[a] Includes all types of bananas.
[b] Includes both long and crisp eggplant.
Source: Ministry of Agriculture, *Agricultural Statistics of Thailand, 1958* and *1965*.

Travelling in the country in Thailand certainly gives the impression that fruit and vegetable production has increased. Of course

H

it is easier to notice areas which appear to have been recently planted to these crops than it would be to notice that other crops had taken their place; but field inquiries (discussed in more detail in chapters 6 and 7) indicated that in almost every village visited the area under vegetables for consumption within Thailand had recently increased. This includes both vegetables that can be dried, such as chillies and onions, and miscellaneous truck crops such as eggplant, sweet potatoes, and Chinese cabbage.

It is of some interest to break down the increase in output into increase in area and improvement in yield per *rai*. The increase in area is probably mainly due to improved transport, but an additional cause is probably the continuing pressure of the rice premium, with perhaps a further stimulus from improved irrigation. Better transport would increase the areas within easy reach of an urban market. The rice premium causes a direct shift to vegetable cultivation instead of rice, and an indirect increase in demand through substituting cash agriculture for subsistence agriculture. Irrigation makes possible off-season crops in the rice fields, and vegetables need less irrigation water than a second crop of rice.

Some of the forces making for change would seem likely to increase the concentration of production of these domestic crops and others to reduce it. Road transport and improved availability of freight cars on the railways are making Thailand more of a national market, so that any *changwat* with marked technical advantages could outstrip its rivals more easily than in the past. On the other hand crops with a location mainly determined by the market can now move further from the main market, Bangkok.

An attempt was made to investigate the relative strength of the forces making for concentration and for dispersion for several of these domestic crops. An index of concentration was calculated by expressing the output of the three leading *changwats* as a percentage of the output for the whole country, and examining how this behaved over the period (1961-5) for which *changwat* figures are available.

Area, output per *rai*, and the index of regional specialisation are set out in Table 5.8 for three groups of crops; first, chillies, onions, and garlic, a group of vegetable crops which can be sold either fresh or dried with little difference in value; next, for a group of easily transportable fruits, bananas, pineapples, and watermelons; and lastly, for cotton and tobacco, the two raw materials grown for

Table 5.8 Selected crops: area harvested, yield per *rai* and index of regional specialisation, 1957-65

Year	Chillies Area 000 *rai*	Chillies Output per *rai* kg	Chillies Index of R.S.	Onions[a] Area 000 *rai*	Onions[a] Output per *rai* kg	Onions[a] Index of R.S.	Garlic Area 000 *rai*	Garlic Output per *rai* kg	Garlic Index of R.S.	Bananas[b] Area 000 *rai*	Bananas[b] Output per *rai* kg	Bananas[b] Index of R.S.
1957	64·4	137	n.a.	36·8	242	n.a.	47·8	259	n.a.	283	1,150	n.a.
1958	71·2	154	n.a.	42·1	354	n.a.	56·6	267	n.a.	265	1,010	n.a.
1959	75·6	167	n.a.	43·3	328	n.a.	66·6	279	n.a.	308	1,159	n.a.
1960	142·9	178	n.a.	84·7	464	n.a.	82·4	342	n.a.	n.a.	n.a.	n.a.
1961	148·5	185	29	79·7	518	58	102·4	331	67	578	1,116	35
1962	177·3	208	28	99·7	499	63	144·5	299	57	599	1,089	16
1963	170·6	235	20	93·3	393	43	115·0	312	57	733	1,086	14
1964	152·1	211	18	93·4	361	38	109·4	313	53	715	1,039	16
1965	155·6	229	16	96·0	332	36	94·9	311	54	1,103	1,127	n.a.

Year	Pineapples Area 000 *rai*	Pineapples Output per *rai* kg	Pineapples Index of R.S.	Watermelons Area 000 *rai*	Watermelons Output per *rai* kg	Watermelons Index of R.S.	Cotton Area 000 *rai*	Cotton Output per *rai* kg	Cotton Index of R.S.	Tobacco[c] Area 000 *rai*	Tobacco[c] Output per *rai* kg	Tobacco[c] Index of R.S.
1957	101	904	n.a.	48	408	n.a.	256	142	n.a.	381	173	n.a.
1958	100	1,232	n.a.	48	473	n.a.	253	137	n.a.	378	174	n.a.
1959	106	1,402	n.a.	60	507	n.a.	298	125	n.a.	384	175	n.a.
1960	n.a.	n.a.	n.a.	n.a.	n.a.	n.a.	343	133	n.a.	365	203	n.a.
1961	252	1,788	54	104	1,123	40	330	116	65	254	191	58
1962	185	1,737	41	110	1,072	25	361	116	58	255	188	63
1963	188	1,537	38	153	1,212	39	435	112	68	251	186	43
1964	183	1,425	42	150	1,143	19	413	119	65	320	196	38
1965	219	1,323	52	160	1,215	27	453	132	60	438	174	36

[a] Includes onions and shallots. About 90 per cent of production is shallots.
[b] Includes four varieties of bananas.
[c] Includes both Virginia and local varieties. About 85 per cent of production is local varieties.

Sources: Ministry of Agriculture, *Agricultural Statistics of Thailand, 1958 and 1965*; *Crop Reports* (Crop Series), 1961-5; and 'Crop Report', 1959, mimeo.

use in Thailand. It will be seen that for the first group there has been a moderate expansion in area accompanied by first a rise then a fall in yield. Localisation has fallen quite markedly with the loss of part of the market by the West Sub-region, which previously enjoyed transport advantages to Bangkok by canal.[6] The fruits all show a fairly good increase in the area harvested, with a downward tendency in their yield; for pineapples only—probably because of low prices—the total output fell. These fruits all show a fairly high degree of local specialisation, though all three can grow virtually anywhere in Thailand; but there is a trend toward more dispersion. For cotton there is no clear trend in localisation. Production is strongly concentrated in the border area between the Northeast and the North. Tobacco also shows no clear trend.

The index of localisation is not a particularly adequate measure, and detailed field inquiries could no doubt produce clearer information about the tendencies to specialisation and dispersion in the rural sector. The opening up of the country by new transport is clearly leading to many rapid changes in the pattern of crops, which can only be very inadequately shown in this chapter. The table does show, however, that there is not the same tendency in crops for sale in Thailand as there is in export crops for development to be highly localised in a limited area.

There are so many vegetable crops that have increased in area harvested and yield that it was not considered worthwhile to calculate indices of localisation for them. However, Table 5.9 shows the increase in area and yield of a miscellaneous group of them. It is obvious that for these vegetables the main component in the expansion has been an increase—as much as threefold or more—in the area harvested. For several of the crops, however, such as string beans and pumpkins, there has also been a considerable increase in the yield per *rai*.

The government, on the whole, does little to further expansion of these crops for Thai consumption, apart from helping to combat pests which reach a plague level. Private merchants in the district capitals have, however, actively promoted the use of fertilisers and insecticides. There can be little doubt that almost every farmer planting vegetables is aware of the possibility of using chemicals to increase yields and control pests. Experimentation in trying differ-

---

[6] The Damnoen Saduak and Phasicharoen canals enable produce from this region to come directly to Bangkok.

Table 5.9 Selected vegetables: area harvested, output, and yield per *rai*, 1957-65 (area in 000 *rai*, output in 000 metric tons, yield per *rai* in kg)

| | String beans | | | Eggplant[a] | | | Sweet Potatoes | | | Pumpkin | | |
	Area	Output	Yield per *rai*	Area	Output	Yield per *rai*	Area	Output	Yield per *rai*	Area	Output	Yield per *rai*
1957	30	7·5	250	39	31·2	800	52	66·5	1,279	22	13·4	609
1958	33	7·7	235	48	34·6	720	57	82·8	1,453	24	13·1	548
1959	35	8·8	251	48	35·7	744	67	106·8	1,594	25	16·8	672
1960	n.a.	n.a.	n.a.	n.a.	n.a.	n.a.	n.a.	n.a.	n.a.	n.a.	n.a.	n.a.
1961	68	22·6	305	80	50·1	626	104	129·9	1,252	54	41·0	760
1962	112	36·8	329	91	48·8	537	125	147·6	1,184	90	60·6	670
1963	99	34·9	352	108	62·7	581	132	164·9	1,251	92	96·3	1,044
1964	94	33·7	358	105	49·2	469	134	148·6	1,112	67	63·7	946
1965	90	33·4	369	102	47·4	465	134	156·1	1,166	74	70·5	948

| | Tomatoes | | | Cabbage | | | Cauliflower | | | Chinese Cabbage | | |
	Area	Output	Yield per *rai*	Area	Output	Yield per *rai*	Area	Output	Yield per *rai*	Area	Output	Yield per *rai*
1957	5	2·3	460	13	11·1	854	5	4·6	920	20	7·9	395
1958	6	2·7	458	14	16·6	1,186	6	5·1	842	19	9·8	502
1959	7	4·0	571	15	16·1	1,104	7	6·0	900	21	10·5	501
1960	n.a.	n.a.	n.a.	n.a.	n.a.	n.a.	n.a.	n.a.	n.a.	n.a.	n.a.	n.a.
1961	16	10·8	657	31	36·2	1,171	17	14·4	855	58	27·7	476
1962	16	9·0	559	33	37·7	1,136	28	23·8	836	68	36·5	536
1963	19	11·5	601	50	59·8	1,202	24	21·5	897	60	42·6	703
1964	28	13·5	476	48	56·6	1,182	26	24·7	950	63	44·4	701
1965	28	11·9	429	42	47·6	1,146	19	18·3	949	71	55·6	786

[a] Includes two types of eggplant.

Sources: Ministry of Agriculture, *Agricultural Statistics of Thailand, 1958, 1964,* and *1965; Crop Reports* (Crop Series), 1961-5 and 'Crop Report' 1959, mimeo.

ent brands on different crops is a topic of conversation in villages, and this probably increases awareness and receptivity to similar possibilities with rice.

The pattern of development of agriculture as between different areas, and the evidence of imitation of technical changes, merit much more study than they have received. Any such study would need to go beyond the doubtful figures issued by the Ministry of Agriculture.

Livestock Production

Both cultural and climatic factors in Thailand might reasonably favour expansion of livestock. Though strict Buddhism prohibits killing of animals, ordinary Thais are not expected to do without meat, and non-Buddhists do the slaughtering. The Northeast—the area with the lowest rural incomes, and the one which most needs development—is traditionally an exporter of cattle, buffaloes, and elephants to other regions; and the International Bank Mission recommended expansion of livestock production in this area (I.B.R.D., 1959: 19).

Disease control has made good progress, and the breeds of cattle, pigs, and poultry have been improved throughout much of the country. Compared with several larger departments the Livestock Department's allocation under the Plan is generous (N.E.D.B., 1964: 61). Yet after a good beginning in the period after World War II the growth in livestock production has slowed down, as shown in Table 5.10.

This is mainly the result of a tight control over the sale of meat products in the important Bangkok market, organised—like most of the other cartels—by Chinese businessmen in co-operation with powerful Thai politicians (Muscat, 1966: 117-25; Silcock, 1967: 256). This control is supplemented by controls, when necessary, over the export of pigs or cattle.

The alleged purpose of the control is to prevent speculation by Chinese middlemen forcing up prices. Attacks on the control in the Bangkok press usually criticise it on the ground that it forces up the price of meat in Bangkok. It is interesting that both the F.A.O. and Muscat, who quotes extensively from the F.A.O. report, complain that the monopoly keeps the price unreasonably low, giving inadequate returns to farmers (Muscat, 1966: 117-25).

Table 5.10 Number of buffaloes, cattle, and pigs slaughtered in Bangkok, 1947-65

Year	Buffaloes	Cattle	Pigs
1947	1,695	15,421	181,749
1948	330	17,298	289,748
1949	221	29,353	335,192
1950	2,000	29,453	394,141
1951	4,977	26,316	365,390
1952	9,482	21,880	343,270
1953	11,864	21,190	394,828
1954	15,542	25,531	383,888
1955	17,248	20,047	361,285
1956	15,275	16,988	386,020
1957	14,456	14,663	412,867
1958	15,446	10,654	316,911
1959	15,921	28,741	462,405
1960	35,096	48,402	613,134
1961	35,369	40,926	553,122
1962	36,522	52,590	506,232
1963	35,656	62,326	546,002
1964	42,395	50,999	558,614
1965	43,116	56,933	614,485

Source: Ministry of Agriculture, *Agricultural Statistics of Thailand, 1965*, Table 62.

It seems probable that the monopsonistic aspect of the Meat Traders' Federation is more important than the monopolistic aspect. Nor need we suppose that this monopsony and monopoly owes its existence only to the politicians who derive a substantial revenue from it. The meat trade is not one that functions smoothly under free competition in many countries. The fact that publicity given to speculative and monopolistic activity was used to justify a form of semi-government interference, profitable to some powerful men, does not mean that such activity did not exist, or that left to itself this particular market would run smoothly and avoid collusion. There are real problems, in the Thai situation, of organising any parts of the economy where substantial government intervention is necessary, and the meat trade is probably one of these. Free exports, with active measures to maintain competition among exporters, may be the best available solution for meat, as it may for sugar; but we cannot pretend that many countries are content to leave these particular industries uncontrolled and to let the farmers and the public face the resulting instability, as well as receive the probable higher gains. These matters are considered further in chapter 9.

Forestry Products

Another rural industry in which the difficulty of organising competition under an overall government control has led to substantial abuses is the forestry industry, particularly the cutting of teak. Teak has become a scarce timber, commanding good prices, but it is difficult to control felling in such a way that forests are not overcut (Puey and Suparb, 1955: 60-2). Before World War II, as we have seen in chapter 3, foreign firms had timber concessions and were required to observe certain rules and pay royalty to the government. The Thais wanted to transfer the profits to Thai nationals after the war, but the government at first was nervous about American attitudes to government enterprise and there were no private Thai capitalists available to cut and control the forest areas.

During World War II the government had established a Thai company to take over the foreign teak concessions (Meth, 1963: 9). At the end of the war some of these concessions were renewed for a limited period and later all foreign firms were amalgamated; the aim, finally achieved in the late 1950s, was Thai ownership of all leases. But the post-war uncertainty was damaging to the industry, and much illegal cutting took place, reducing the stands of teak and inflicting damage on Thailand's productivity from which it has not even yet recovered (N.E.D.B., 1967: 134-5, 138).

An attempt was made to offer concessions to Thais who could exploit them. For example Kasetsart University was given a forest concession as a means of giving it an independent income. However, the main agency which took over from the foreign firms was the Forest Industry Organisation. The greatest problems are to prevent overcutting and to secure a substantial share of the income from teak for public purposes.

The first problem (of conservation) is now being solved more comprehensively and with better control over illegal cutting than in the immediate post-war period (Krit, 1957). The second is still far from solution. Usher (1967: 225-7) has shown that the structure of the industry divides up the government's revenue from teak into four different accounts: royalties, export duties, business tax, and profits of a public corporation all reckoned in different ways, and making it possible for considerable leakage to occur without detection.

His analysis of the cost structure of teak processing compared with the export price of teak shows that the total yield per cubic metre to the government should be 2,500 *baht*, at 1965 prices. The total export of teak in 1965 was 45,000 metric tons. Thus, even assuming substantial underestimation of costs by Usher, the revenue accruing to government from teak in 1965 should be about 90 million *baht*.

The income from forestry shown in the budget documents (Office of the Prime Minister, 1967: vol. II, pt II, pp. 7-30) is as follows (million *baht*)

From teak		Partly from teak		From other timber	
Teak export		Forest duties	53	Other export	
duty	10·5	Profits of Forest		duty	4
Teak royalty	7	Industry		Other royalty	50
		Organisation	18	Sale of forest	
		Sawmill duty		produce	14
		(approx.)	40		
Total	17·5		111		68

Probably a negligible proportion of the 'forest duties' item and not more than a third of the sawmill duty are derived from teak. This suggests the government is getting between 30 and 45 million *baht* from teak, depending on the proportion of the Forest Industry Organisation's profits that come from this one timber. Half or more of the potential revenue is failing to reach the government treasury.

As a result of the damage to the teak industry caused by post-war overcutting attention has partly shifted to other timbers. Unlike teak, most of these need to create an international demand and companies have been established to process them into plywood and other timber products. Here, because the government controls the raw material and some of these factories are subsidiaries of government concerns, it is possible to fix a monopoly price, at least internally, based on control of the raw material, and to absorb the profits in inflated costs by using the factories as sources of patronage to political clients.

It appears, therefore, that the forests are of less importance to the public revenue of Thailand than to the organisation of its political life. Yet the wider awareness of the forests as a whole and of conservation problems, in the last decade, has had one important effect on agriculture proper. The government now clearly sees its available land as limited and recognises the importance of higher yields (Silcock, 1967: 297; N.E.D.B., 1964, nos. 1 and 2).

6

Regional Analysis: Central and North Central

For any analysis of development it is desirable to have some idea of the factors influencing the level of aggregate demand. If growth is to be rapid the arrangements of an economy must be such that new supplies of equipment and skill are being made available by using existing resources which are being withheld from consumption. Moreover these new supplies must be reasonably well adapted to what will be required as growth takes place. It is well known that no free market system or planning system yet available to us allows constant full employment of resources and adaptation to changing requirements without some central steering of the economy of a country, adjusting to excessive or inadequate pressures in money, the capital market, and the international exchanges. In the less developed countries the influence of prestige and imitation tends to produce similar central steering of the economy when in fact overall pressures at the centre can hardly achieve the intended results. Movement between different parts of the economy, whether of persons or of goods, is relatively sluggish, and often attention needs to be directed to corrective action in a particular region. There may well be evidence of inflationary pressure in one region while another is stagnating mainly because of an inadequate level of local demand. Products may be too specialised and costs of movement too high for these different pressures to adjust themselves automatically.

Of course the less developed countries tend to be short of both statistical information and administrative talent, and making adjustments regionally is even more costly in terms of these scarce resources than making them nationally. It is not to be expected that more will normally be possible than an *ad hoc* response to evidence in a particular region; but recognition that the strategic policy measures for applying pressure are in fact often not national but regional may change the focus of interest and make action more effective.

In dealing with the Thai rural economy there are a number of different regions on which we have information, and a number of different regions which have clearly distinguishable characteristics which suggest that special development influences may apply to them. Since statistics are collected for practical purposes, including economic development as an important objective, we should expect the division into regions to correspond to what is required for policy, and in general it does. There are, however, certain problems posed by the way the data are organised.

Ideally what we should require would be separate regional figures for gross regional product, regional balance of payments, regional private and government consumption, and regional capital formation. Of these, regional balance of payments figures could hardly be expected in any country except one geographically divided by stretches of sea or foreign territory, where collection of interregional trade figures would be almost a necessary by-product of customs administration. Thailand is exceptionally fortunate in having, for the years 1960-3, regional figures for gross domestic product (N.E.D.B., 1965), and also a household expenditure survey classified regionally for 1962-3 (N.S.O., 1962-3). We can gain some information about government consumption and government and private fixed capital formation from the regional income figures if we compare them with the national figures and make certain standardising assumptions. However, without full regional capital formation figures we cannot estimate a regional balance of payments by difference.

There are some differences between the regions used in the collection of the different kinds of information, which complicate the problem. The regional gross domestic product figures divide the country into the four standard administrative regions with the number of provinces as shown, North (16), Northeast (15), South (14) and Central (26). The Household Expenditure Survey divides the Central Region into three, and the additional information is so useful for work on the rural economy that for most purposes it is not desirable to aggregate the three subdivisions; they are Central ($17\frac{1}{2}$), East (7) and Bangkok-Thon Buri ($1\frac{1}{2}$). The other three regions are divided in the same way as in the regional gross domestic product figures. The Ministry of Agriculture figures make a useful division of the North region, including only seven *changwats* in their North figure (Ministry of Agriculture, 1965: Introduction). Unfortunately they include the southern half of the region in the Central Region; and the southern half is not merely completely different from the northern, but perhaps the most interesting part of the whole country from the point of view of development. It is not separately identified in either set of statistics, and such figures as we have must be built up from provincial figures. For this chapter we have called it the North Central Region.

For some purposes it is also desirable to isolate as a sub-region the six *changwats* in the southwest corner of the Central Region. These are not geographically part of the Central Plain, their productivity—for historical reasons—is higher and their type of agriculture differs considerably from that of the Central Plain. When discussing them separately we shall call them the West Sub-region.

The procedure adopted in these two regional chapters is to give first an overall picture of gross regional product and gross regional consumption and fixed capital formation in Table 6.1. In this table it is not possible to show any of the sub-regions. A few general comments, on a comparative basis, will be made. In the remainder of the present chapter a few points will first be made about the Central Region as a whole. Thereafter the analysis will be broken up into four sections: Inner Central Plain, West Sub-region, North Central Region, and East Sub-region. In each of these such statistics as are available about the sub-region's domestic product, expenditure, etc. will be given but no attempt will be made to give even rough estimates of the entire set of figures. These could be estimated officially with as much accuracy as the full regional figures, with no great difficulty if they were required. Comments will be made on the implications of the figures available, when taken in combination with other information available about the sub-region.

In addition, rather more detailed studies will be made of *changwats* visited in the Central Region during the period of field

Table 6.1 Regional accounts (estimated) for Thailand
(in *baht*)

	Northeast 1962	North 1963	South 1963	Central[e] 1962	Whole kingdom[f] 1962	1962-3	1963
1 Gross domestic product	11,368	9,959	9,348	33,705	63,129		57,650
2 Private consumption expenditure (total)[a]	10,323	7,462	6,447	17,971	47,151	42,203	50,315
a Towns	1,787	1,652	1,491	8,888	n.a.	13,813	n.a.
b Villages	8,536	5,810	4,956	9,085	n.a.	28,385	n.a.
3 Gross capital formation[b]	n.a.	n.a.	n.a.	n.a.	11,639		14,962
a Government construction	187	394	348	1,143	1,981		2,639
b Private construction	351	253	191	1,803	4,001		5,054
4 Government consumption expenditure (total)[c]	n.a.	n.a.	n.a.	n.a.	5,833		6,022
a Public admin. and defence	395	374	258	2,035	3,202		3,336
b Education and research	338	214	157	547	1,447		1,486
c Medical and health	24	45	31	116	213		248
5 Total expenditure (For provinces the sum of 2 + 3a + 3b + 4a + 4b + 4c; for whole kingdom the sum of 2 + 3 + 4)	11,618	8,742	7,432	23,615	64,623		71,299
6 Balance[d] (GDP (1)— total expenditure (5))	−250	1,217	1,916	10,090	−1,494		−3,649

[a] The *per capita* figures from the *Whole Kingdom* volume of the *Household Expenditure Survey* are multiplied by an estimate of the appropriate population in 1962 or 1963 according to the survey date. Figures for municipal areas are available for 1962 and 1963 and it is assumed that sanitary areas in the same region have increased by the same proportion since 1960. Village populations are estimated by difference, using regional totals and town totals. The figures differ significantly from those on p. 243 of *Thailand: Social and Economic Studies in Development*, both because a figure for total consumption had to be estimated for the different regions, and because for some the volume had not yet been published. An arithmetical error has also been detected in that table. The figure for aggregate expenditure in villages in that table should have been 5,100, not 5,900.

[b] Income from government construction in the regional gross domestic product figures is multiplied by 1·45; income from private construction is

work mentioned in chapter 1, and comments will be given on developments in the particular village which I visited in such *changwats*.

Table 6.1 is an attempt to bring together, from different sources, such information as is available about gross regional product, consumption, and capital formation in the years 1962 and 1963. Clearly the fact that the Household Expenditure Survey was taken in different years in different regions, and used weights based on the 1960 population census, introduces some distortion as between areas where the relative size of the population is changing. We should probably allow for some minor upward adjustment of private consumption expenditure, especially in the towns; however, the figures are clearly fairly rough (N.S.O., 1964).

One thing that is apparent from the table, apart from considerable differences in urban, and also in rural, expenditure between different regions, is the fact that there is some margin for a favourable regional balance of payments and regional capital formation (other than in construction) in the Central Region, and to some extent in the North and South. In the Northeast there is none. If there is any capital formation it is financed by an unfavourable balance with the rest of Thailand. This will be discussed further in chapter 7. Here it must be emphasised that these are gross figures, and that the rice premium accrues in Bangkok, even on rice produced in the Northeast, so that an 'unfavourable balance' will have to be interpreted in a special sense.

---

multiplied by 1·15. These ratios are derived from the national income figures for the whole kingdom. No regional figures are available for other items of gross capital formation. These are probably the main components in the balance in line 6.

c Probably most of government consumption other than in the Central Region is covered in the three sub-headings given.

d In principle the balance should give the sum of all other capital formation plus all other government consumption plus the favourable balance of payments. However, regional private consumption is clearly understated.

e Including Bangkok-Thon Buri and East Region also.

f The column 1962-3 is an aggregation of the *Household Expenditure Survey* figures, merely as a rough comparison with the figures from the national accounts for 1962 and 1963.

Sources: N.S.O., *Statistical Year Book, 1965*; N.E.D.B., *National Income Statistics*, 1964 ed., mimeo., Jan. 1966 and *Regional Gross Domestic Product*, 1963.

Inner Central Plain

We turn next to the Inner Central Plain, excluding the sub-region to the east and also excluding, as best we may (since this is a study of agricultural development), the Metropolitan Area, comprising the greater part of the provinces of both Phra Nakhon and Thon Buri. The relevant statistics concerning the rural sector in this region are set out in Tables 6.2 and 6.3.

Table 6.2 Inner Central Plain and West Sub-region family income and expenditure statistics, 1963

	Villages	Towns	Two towns in the West Sub-region	
			Kanchanaburi	Samut Sakhon
Average income per family per annum in *baht*	8,616	13,080	14,535	13,862
Average outlay per family per annum in *baht*	8,717	11,486	12,783	12,474
Average income as % of national average income	118	101	113	108
% of families with annual money incomes				
Under 3,000 *baht*	27	11	n.a.	n.a.
3,000-6,000 *baht*	33	19	n.a.	n.a.
6,000-12,000 *baht*	28	41	n.a.	n.a.
12,000 *baht* and over	12	29	n.a.	n.a.

Sources: N.S.O., *Household Expenditure Survey, 1963, Whole Kingdom* volume, pp. 31 and 68; *Central Region* volume, pp. 18, 19, 49, and 52.

The regional gross domestic product figures do not allow us to eliminate the metropolitan incomes, but we can use the Central volume of the Household Expenditure Survey, which shows that the general pattern in the Inner Central Plain and the West Sub-region is that rural incomes per head are higher than elsewhere in Thailand, but urban incomes rank below the South and the East.

The character of the agriculture in the West Sub-region—the mostly highly capital-intensive market gardens and orchards in Thailand—suggests that this may contribute something to the high rural income. This will be discussed later. The Inner Central Plain itself, broadly the flood-plain of the Chao Phaya River, is very largely a monoculture area, growing only rice, over quite considerable areas. After the flood subsides, most of the land becomes parched and will not grow off-season crops except where irrigation is possible.

Mechanisation—mainly by irrigation pumps and large hired tractors—and improved seed selection have been increasing the yield per *rai* and it is higher than in other regions except the far north, where farms are much smaller. Irrigation is making it possible in some places to grow off-season crops, but over much of the area the channels are not yet well enough maintained (N.E.D.B., 1964: 2; 1966: 22).

This is the area where the incidence of tenancy is highest (Wijeyewardene, 1967: 79; N.E.D.B., 1967: 123). It is an area over most of which commercial rice growing spread at least fifty years ago, and there is now little vacant land available, except in two provinces, Saraburi and Lop Buri. Differences in the amount of land held per family have had time to be accentuated, and merchants who had secured a steady source of supply by selling consumer goods on credit and buying the growing crop, have in some cases gained possession of land. The provinces with the largest average holdings, Pathum Thani and Ayuthaya, are both among the most long-settled areas.

In spite of their proximity to Bangkok, many villages in this area have transport no better than—and indeed probably much worse than—average villages throughout Thailand. Perhaps the main reason is a lack of any sense of urgency; the rice crop can be transported economically by water, and there are main roads to the *changwat* capitals, so that the burden of administration with inadequate mechanical transport falls on district officials, who have little influence. Subsidiary roads in this area do not open up new land, as in more remote areas of Thailand; for (with the exception of the northern and western fringes of the plain) nearly all the land has been occupied for a good many years. Moreover there are severe difficulties in building the roads with local funds and by local initiative. Because of the annual flood, roads must be built up high, with many bridges, and maintenance cost is also expensive. Moreover valuable land must often be bought, since there is not enough waste land available for the roadway. (In the more remote parts of Thailand a buffalo cart track over unused land can usually be used most of the way.)

J

Table 6.3 Agricultural data: Inner Central Plain, 1964

| | Metropolitan | | Adjacent | | | | | | | | | | |
	Phra Nakhon	Thon Buri	Samut Prakhan	Nontha-buri	Pathum Thani	Nakhon Pathom	Ayu-thaya	Sara-buri	Ang Thong	Other Sing Buri	Suphan Buri	Chai Nat	Lop Buri
Area, m rai	0·7	0·3	0·6	0·4	0·9	1·4	1·6	1·9	0·6	0·5	3·3	1·6	4·1
% area under crops	76	69	67	84	87	76	90	51	81	84	55	53	30
Area under crops m rai	0·5	0·2	0·4	0·3	0·8	1·0	1·4	0·9	0·5	0·4	1·8	0·9	1·2
% crop land irrigated	97	96	95	95	94	68	85	22	87	96	67	67	43
% crop land under rice[a]	90	56	83	81	85	76	51	62	78	75	79	86	36
Output of rice, 000 metric tons	190	44	131	55	161	223	178	180	78	112	456	340	133
Population, 000	1,577	559	235	196	190	370	479	304	198	154	491	245	336
% agricultural population	11	23	55	61	67	77	54	67	73	76	79	82	71
Agricultural population, 000	173	129	129	120	127	285	259	203	144	117	388	201	238
Av. area agricultural holdings, rai	26	13	25	19	42	24	32	31	20	23	29	27	28

Other leading crops,
area harvested,
000 rai[b]

Maize	5	7	8	455	17	5 974
Namlawa bananas	4	5	3	3		4
Other bananas		1	1			
Cassava			6			
Watermelons			3	10		
Sugar-cane				3	44	
Mung-beans			4	22	3	17
Groundnuts				3	3	

[a] Area planted figures were not available. These percentages were calculated from the area harvested.
Sources: U.S.O.M./N.S.O., *Changwat-Amphur Statistical Directory, 1965; Statistical Year Book, 1965;* Ministry of Agriculture, *Crop Reports,* 1964.
[b] Only the area under the two leading crops in each *Changwat* is recorded here.

Although cost-benefit studies have not been undertaken, it seems probable that in spite of the difficulties mentioned above, many feeder roads in the Inner Central Plain area would justify their building cost. Because of the relatively close proximity to Bangkok, a good road to a village opens up a great many possibilities of casual employment, lowers the cost of living and facilitates diversification of the economy. There are, however, institutional reasons why such roads might not be actively encouraged in face of the special difficulties in the Inner Central Plain. Positions of monopsony based on control of access, payment of rent in kind, or land ownership are likely to be threatened by competition if transport improves.[1] No doubt the value of land would rise, and the wealthier villagers may well have a rational interest in improved access to Bangkok; but a position of influence and security may well seem more attractive to people whose world is mainly their village.

Though the metropolitan area should be excluded from the Inner Central Plain, its influence on the economy of the region cannot be ignored. There are industrial sites in the *changwats* of Phra Nakhon (Bangkok) and Thon Buri, outside the municipal area, and also in neighbouring *changwats*. This—and some long-distance suburban development—keeps the agricultural population relatively low as a proportion of the total in Nonthaburi, Samut Prakan, and Pathum Thani. The industries may lead to some diversion of savings (through the banks) from the rural areas. They certainly act as a magnet for unskilled labour.

There is some opposition both from local landowners and from the government to migration away from the Inner Central Plain.[2] Rural employers of labour fear the effect of freer movement in raising rural wages; the government, on the other hand, has little sympathy with rural employers, but does not like farmers leaving the country, because ideologically it favours the small independent farmer. Nevertheless there is already opportunity for the size of

[1] Facts about local monopsony are difficult to obtain. My usual experience was that both in the Central Plain and in the South the majority of people would deny any credit ties or other monopsony, but a few—clearly well-informed and willing—would say that it was very widespread, and that I was not being told the truth. I am certainly inclined to believe that patron-client relations which are effectively binding exist between the wholesalers and the farmers in the more remote villages.

[2] In Department of Labour, 1965, Information Document No. 7, ch. 3 and 6, migration is treated mainly as a symptom of hardship or disaster.

the farm that one family can operate to increase. Ploughing with hired tractors has become fairly general, though harvesting is mainly done by traditional methods. As mechanisation and irrigation improve, the size of the typical family farm can be expected to rise to 30-40 *rai*, with part of the area growing an off-season crop, possibly of rice in the areas with the best water supply, but more commonly of some crop using less water. Yet there is no vacant land to provide larger farms. If they are to develop, migration out of the region—which is at present the main source of migrants to the capital and also to the North Central Sub-region —will have to be increased (Caldwell, 1967: 42-3).

As already indicated, there is probably a tendency for capital to move out of the rural areas in the Inner Central Plain to the metropolis and the highly capital-intensive new industries. Larger farms with more mechanisation will need more capital, and probably methods to secure an inflow of capital will be needed. Present plans to lend mainly through the new Agricultural Bank may, for ideological reasons, tend to bolster the position of small farmers, some of whom should probably be encouraged to sell their land.

The provinces visited in the Inner Central Plain were Lop Buri, Sing Buri, and Ang Thong, and Table 6.4 gives figures of rice production and production of the other leading crops during recent years for these three provinces. Lop Buri is on the northern edge of the Inner Central Plain, and parts of the province which lacked transport and irrigation were previously unoccupied; Sing Buri is within the area which was already largely settled at the beginning of the period—transport improvements have not made new areas accessible, but irrigation has had rather more effect here than in Ang Thong; most of Ang Thong is technically irrigated, but the condition of the channels is not such that irrigation is fully effective.

The figures reflect this situation. For rice there have been increases in both area and yield per *rai* in all three *changwats*, with some setback in 1964. The increase in area is greatest in Lop Buri, while both Lop Buri and Sing Buri show considerable increases in yield; Ang Thong has achieved less in both respects. The striking difference is in supplementary crops. Lop Buri's more than tenfold increase in maize has brought maize into the position of leading crop, and mung-beans have also increased more than tenfold, though the change in yield may not be significant. On the other hand irrigation does not appear to have brought any net benefit in

Table 6.4 Leading crops in *changwats* Lop Buri, Sing Buri, and Ang Thong, 1959 and 1961-5

	Rice				Maize			Mung-beans			Groundnuts		Cotton	
	Lop Buri	Sing Buri	Ang Thong	Price[a] bt/kg	Lop Buri	Ang Thong	Price[a] bt/kg	Lop Buri	Ang Thong	Price[a] bt/kg	Sing Buri	Price[a] bt/kg	Lop Buri	Price[a] bt/kg
1959														
Area harvested, 000 *rai*	305	279	325	0·85	86	10	1·00	7	8	2·02	1	3·18	24	3·68
Yield/*rai*	230	183	168		300	270		150	195		190		120	
Output, 000 metric tons	70	51	55		26	3		1	1		0·2		3	
1961														
Area harvested, 000 *rai*	498	352	361	1·10	414	4	1·12	26	7	2·32	2	3·31	45	4·38
Yield/*rai*	285	292	217		300	300		150	210		250		100	
Output, 000 metric tons	142	103	78		124	2		2	1		0·4		5	
1962														
Area harvested, 000 *rai*	538	361	376	0·96	475	2	1·01	17	2	3·03	1	3·61	35	3·67
Yield/*rai*	288	313	274		350	300		150	210		250		100	
Output, 000 metric tons	155	113	103		166	0·7		3	0·4		0·2		4	
1963														
Area harvested, 000 *rai*	567	364	425	0·77	504	2	1·06	26	1	2·53	1	3·67	45	3·35
Yield/*rai*	384	338	285		350	250		180	200		250		45	
Output, 000 metric tons	218	123	121		177	0·4		5	0·2		0·3		2	
1964														
Area harvested, 000 *rai*	439	333	388	0·83	974	3	1·08	17	4	2·30	3	4·60	13	2·80
Yield/*rai*	303	337	202		300	250		150	150		200		200	
Output, 000 metric tons	133	112	78		292	0·8		3	0·7		0·7		3	
1965														
Area harvested, 000 *rai*	n.a.	n.a.	n.a.		972	3	1·22	70	3	2·10	3	4·10	6	4·08
Yield/*rai*	n.a.	n.a.	n.a.		350	250		170	160		200		70	
Output, 000 metric tons	n.a.	n.a.	n.a.		340	0·8		12	0·6		0·7		0·4	

[a] Bangkok wholesale prices. Price for rice is for paddy.

Sources: N.S.O., *Statistical Year Books, 1963 and 1965; Agricultural Statistics of Thailand, 1965; Annual Reports of Rice Production,* 1961 and 1962; Ministry of Agriculture, *Statistics of the Planting of Upland and Garden Crops,* 1959, mimeo. (*Changwat* Series), 1961, 1962, 1963, and 1964.

either area or yield in supplementary crops in the other two provinces, either through increased area or through higher yields.

No village was visited in Lop Buri, the itinerary allowing time only for collecting information in the *changwat* capital; in both Sing Buri and Ang Thong the villages visited had no access by road. In Sing Buri the village—Singh in Bangrajan district—was only half a kilometre from an irrigation road, and was strung out along a river which—at least since the building of the Chai Nat dam—was always navigable. In one respect it was not a normal Sing Buri village; for a new area of land had been cleared between an irrigation channel and the river, and successfully developed as orchards. This was largely due to the fact that one of the deputy district officers had his own orchard in the village, and was keen on spreading the study of agriculture and of modern methods among the villagers.

Pump irrigation had become common, knapsack sprays were used to destroy pests, experiments had been made with chemical weed-killers, and tractors were used in the rice fields. A small mechanical cultivator for orchards was being tried out at the time of my visit. Double cropping of rice was being tried out for the first time over part of the irrigated area.

In spite of this comparative success there was a good deal of discouragement that the improvements resulting from irrigation had been comparatively minor. Apparently propaganda related to the Chai Nat dam had raised excessive expectations.

In the Ang Thong village—Huey Khanlaen in Wisetchaichan district—there was a much keener sense of disappointment over the results of irrigation. This village, though long settled, and even having its own junior secondary school, was a most isolated one. Powered boats could reach it along its stream at the height of the annual flood. Trucks could reach it across the rice fields for two or three months of the dry season. At other times no mechanical transport could reach it.

The village grew virtually only rice. One or two holdings grew vegetables, using irrigation pumps in deep ponds, in the dry season. The slight improvement in the off-season water level was helping both the accessibility of the village and the chance of off-season crops, but there had been little recent innovation in methods except for the use of tractors—mainly hired—for ploughing.

It was virtually the only single-crop village that I visited. Perhaps by chance, it conformed very closely to the image held by Thai politicians and the public concerning the rice trade. A small group of Sino-Thais controlled the rice-mill and most of the transport and credit, and also owned a good deal of the land. It was striking that public opinion in the village was hostile to the current high price of rice; those who approved it did not express this view openly. It appeared that most of the rice farmers had prior obligations to deliver all their surplus rice, and were net buyers of rice, having to supplement the rice they produced for themselves by earning cash as casual labour in the off season. Some of their obligations were for rent paid in kind, some had sold most of their crop for current needs in advance.

West Sub-region

We have seen in Table 6.2 that income per family in two of the towns of the West Sub-region is some 10 per cent higher than in all the towns of this sub-region and the Inner Central Plain combined. Since the two towns selected do not appear to be as prosperous as several other towns in the same area, we may perhaps infer that at least urban incomes in the West Sub-region, like those in the East Sub-region, are higher than in the Centre.[3]

There are no income figures for the sub-region, and we can only conjecture about rural incomes from the general figures available about holdings and crops. These are given in Tables 6.5 and 6.6. The tables in themselves do not show high rural incomes: rice occupies about the same relative area in the West as in the Inner Central Plain; the average holding is 19 *rai* against 27, and the average yield of paddy, at around 290 kilograms per *rai* for the six provinces, is roughly the same. The difference lies in the crops grown in the non-rice areas. These are not (for the most part) upland crops like maize and mung-beans, but garden crops like chillies and radishes which yield gross and net incomes per *rai* far higher than paddy.[4] Moreover the West Sub-region has highly

[3] This is based on personal visits to Kanchanaburi and five other towns in the West Sub-region. On the basis of casual impressions the towns in the West Sub-region seem rather busier than those in the East, but such judgments are little more than guesses.

[4] This is shown in the 'other leading crops' column of the table. For most garden crops one or other of these provinces is the largest producer in the kingdom.

Table 6.5 Agricultural data: West Sub-region, 1964

	Kanchana-buri	Phetcha-buri	Prachuap Khiri Khan	Ratcha-buri	Samut Songkhram	Samut Sakhon
Area, m *rai*	12	4	4	3	0·3	0·5
% area under crops	5	14	14	27	53	63
Area under crops, m *rai*	0·6	0·6	0·6	0·9	0·1	0·3
% of crop land irrigated	33	69	10	61	88	90
% crop land under rice[a]	43	76	4	63	13	61
Output of rice, 000 metric tons	53	128	7	131	6	82
Population, 000	233	238	152	411	162	166
% agricultural population	83	68	70	66	56	52
Agricultural population, 000	194	162	107	271	91	86
Average area of agricultural holdings, *rai*	22	22	25	20	10	26
Other leading crops, area harvested, 000 *rai*[b]						
Sugar-cane	44	n.a.	39	37		
Cotton	19	n.a.				
Maize		n.a.	20			10
Short chillies		n.a.		37		19
Long chillies		n.a.			3	
Chinese radish		n.a.			2	

[a] Area planted figures were not available. These percentages were calculated from the area harvested.
[b] Only the area under the two leading crops in each *changwat* is recorded here.
Sources: U.S.O.M./N.S.O., *Changwat-Amphur Statistical Directory* and *Statistical Year Book of Thailand, 1965*; Ministry of Agriculture, *Crop Reports* (*Changwat* Series), 1964.

capital intensive and efficient methods of producing some of the most profitable crops such as chillies and pineapples. Normally, of course, the area of these more profitable crops that one family can work is much smaller; but the degree of mechanisation in the West Sub-region is reflected in the fact that the average holding is only one-third smaller than in the Inner Central Plain in spite of the high proportion of such crops.

Table 6.6 Area harvested and output of selected crops in the West Sub-region, 1961-5

(Area in 000 *rai*, output in 000 metric tons)

Crop	1961 Area	1961 Output	1962 Area	1962 Output	1963 Area	1963 Output	1964 Area	1964 Output	1965 Area	1965 Output
Rice	1,002	236	1,160	305	1,437	413	1,468	405	n.a.	n.a.
Sugar-cane	71	322	99	489	113	545	127[a]	575[a]	113	476
Long chillies	29	6	43	10	29	8	22[a]	4[a]	20	4
Short chillies	28	8	55	12	45	11	63[a]	14[a]	48	11
Maize	39	12	46	14	42	13	47[a]	12[a]	76	20
Pineapples	25	57	24	56	27	52	24[a]	43[a]	46	81
Namlawa bananas	43	47	64	68	63	72	43[a]	46[a]	118	125
Shallots	n.a.	n.a.	n.a.	n.a.	28	13	31[a]	10[a]	28	9
Groundnuts	15	2	14	2	12	3	16[a]	4[a]	20	4
Cotton	22	3	18	3	23	3	19[a]	3[a]	21	4
Total area harvested of above crops	1,274		1,523		1,819		1,862[a]		490[b]	
Total area harvested all crops	1,363		2,043		2,189		1,845[a]		907[b]	

[a] The figures for Phetchaburi for other crops than rice are not available. Below are the estimates (calculated by averaging the figures for 1963 and 1965) which were used in arriving at the total

	Area	Output
Sugar-cane	15	82
Long chillies	1	0·3
Short chillies	2	0·3
Maize	9	3
Pineapples	2	2
Namlawa bananas	28	68
Shallots	1	0·3
Groundnuts	1	1
Cotton	6	1

[b] Figures for rice not available.

Sources: Ministry of Agriculture, *Crop Reports*, 1961-5.

The area is one in which many of the farmers are Sino-Thai, and there appears to be a great deal of capital investment in fertilisers, agricultural machinery, and chemicals to control pests and weeds. The source of this is partly the farmers' own profits and partly the highly progressive merchants of Ratchaburi and the neighbouring maritime provinces.

Table 6.7 Basic data and leading crops in *changwat* Ratchaburi,[a] 1959-65

		1959	1960	1961	1962	1963	1964	1965
Rice	Bangkok wholesale price, *bt*/kg paddy	0·85	0·91	1·10	0·96	0·77	0·83	1·21
	Area planted, 000 *rai*	n.a.	n.a.	594·1	606·2	n.a.	n.a.	n.a.
	Area harvested, 000 *rai*	494·4	496·8	399·0	466·4	553·1	541·7	n.a.
	Yield, kg per *rai*	228	218	223	233	270	242	n.a.
	Output, 000 metric tons	112·9	108·3	89·1	108·9	149·3	130·9	n.a.
Sugar-cane	Bangkok wholesale price, *bt*/kg	114·28	108·46	110·18	121·90	130·00	100·00	102·55
	Area planted, 000 *rai*	10·6	n.a.	14·1	32·7	43·8	37·2	19·8
	Area harvested, 000 *rai*	10·6	n.a.	14·0	32·5	43·3	37:2	19·6
	Yield, kg per *rai*	4,500	n.a.	4,500	4,500	4,500	4,500	5,000
	Output, 000 metric tons	47·8	n.a.	63·0	146·1	194·8	167·3	98·2
Short chillies	Bangkok wholesale price, *bt*/kg	7·20	8·48	6·29	6·45	4·66	6·83	6·35
	Area planted, 000 *rai*	11·6	n.a.	19·3	41·9	35·2	37·0	24·4
	Area harvested, 000 *rai*	11·5	n.a.	18·8	41·7	35·1	37·0	24·4
	Yield, kg per *rai*	200	n.a.	200	200	250	230	230
	Output, 000 metric tons	2·26	n.a.	3·8	8·3	8·8	8·5	5·6

[a] Agricultural population 1960, 000, 271·7; area, km², 5,118; cultivated area, 27%; crop land irrigated, 61%.
Other non-rice crops > 1% harvested area in 1964, 000 *rai*:
  Shallot 19·9, banana (*namlawa*) 15·9, mung-bean 15·1, other bananas 14·5, Chinese cabbage 8·7, pumpkin 8·2, maize 8·1, cassava 6·9, taro 6·8, watermelon 4·9, Chinese radish 4·6, groundnuts 4·2, long chillies 4·1, castor bean 3·2, cabbage 3·0, cauliflower 2·7, Chinese kale 2·5, garlic 2·3.
Sources: Statistical Year Books, 1963, 1965; U.S.O.M./N.S.O., *Changwat-Amphur Statistical Directory*, 1965; Ministry of Agriculture, *Agricultural Statistics of Thailand, 1964; Annual Reports on Rice Production,* 1961, 1962; 'Statistics of the Planting of Upland and Garden Crops', 1959, mimeo. (*Changwat* Series), 1961, 1962, 1963, 1964.

Within this Sub-region I visited the province of Ratchaburi, and basic data for Ratchaburi are given in Table 6.7. The yield figures for chillies are certainly understated. Chilli-growers make incomes which are high enough to be liable for income tax, and true yields are normally concealed. The same probably applies to most of the vegetable-garden crops. Yet on the basis of stated yields Ratchaburi is the leading province in the kingdom in the production of many of the vegetable crops for local consumption, such as shallots, taro, and Chinese radish.

Ratchaburi has played a leading role in its own special type of agricultural development for many decades. It seems likely that Chinese farmers were established there as early as the reign of King Taksin (1767-82):[5] his reign was a period of substantial immigration of Chinese, as well as of attempts to develop this area. Later the cutting of the Phasicharoen and Damnoen Saduak canals brought this fertile area within easy reach of Bangkok by the then prevailing method of transport by water.

The Klawng River, though smaller than the Chao Phya, gives a more continuous supply of water through the year in its delta region; even the fairly distant canals are dry for little more than a month.[6] Here Chinese farmers developed a system of almost continuous cultivation of chillies, onions, etc., using a Chinese wooden pump based on the endless chain principle.

The village which I visited, Donmottanoi, was one of many Christian Sino-Thai villages in the District of Damnoen Saduak. The village was accessible by road but I approached it by canal and was able to see the market gardens which are fertilised, watered, and protected against pests by mechanical sprayers from powered boats traversing the farms in a system of canals, in which the level is maintained by water pumps from the main canals. Much of the land in this area has been developed and is looked after by the church, which rents it out to farmers. Without the need to buy land, farmers can focus more attention on buying equipment. The contrast of a landlord interested in development and long-term revenue with the landlords in Huey Khanlaen was striking.

Most of the farmers grow two or three vegetable crops together in the same piece of ground, but judging by the crop reports published it appears that the yield per *rai* for one crop is reported in

[5] Skinner, 1957, pp. 13 and 386 n., suggests that Chinese settlement may be even earlier than Taksin's reign.

[6] Information from my visit to Donmottanoi.

respect of the whole area, so that true yields may be up to three times as high. With irrigation they are able to cultivate almost continuously, cropping several times a year.

The main innovations in the village were experiments with new chemicals and with new mechanical methods of distributing them. A Market Gardeners' Association had just been formed, mainly for obtaining fertiliser and other assistance from the government.

If this village was typical of the area, the financing and promotion of development there is efficiently organised. Land is developed and provided, for a cash rent, by the church; working capital—for fertilisers etc.—is supplied by merchants who are also interested in maximum development. This leaves the farmers themselves free to invest savings in productive equipment, as most of them do.

North Central Region

The area here described as the North Central Region is not treated as a part of the Central Region except in the Agricultural Statistics. The fact that it is aggregated with the very different far northern area for purposes of calculating gross domestic product and regional expenditure greatly reduces the usefulness of these figures, since there is little interaction between the two sub-regions and their agricultural problems are totally different. There are, however, marked differences also between this North Central Sub-region and the rest of the Central Plain, except perhaps that it has much in common with two of the northernmost *changwats* of the Central Region, Lop Buri and Chai Nat. Its recent development has been as different from that of most of the Inner Central Plain as from that of the Far North.

This area immediately north of the Central Plain is one of the most interesting areas of economic development in Thailand. As already indicated, sensational growth has occurred in the southern end of Nakhon Sawan Province; this is land most of which did not derive much irrigation advantage from the Chai Nat dam, but which benefited from the development of transport and trade in the neighbourhood. There has been even greater proportional development—though starting from a smaller base—in some of the provinces further north. In Phitsanulok rice production doubled, maize production trebled, mung-bean production increased more than fourfold and there was also a growth in the output of jute between 1961 and 1965 (*Crop Reports*, 1961-5).

Table 6.8 Agricultural data: North Central Region, 1964

	Kamphaeng Phet	Tak	Nakhon Sawan	Phichit	Phitsanulok	Phetchabun	Sukothai	Uttaradit	Uthai Thani
Area, m *rai*	6	10	6	3	6	7	4	5	4
% area under crops	15	2	41	57	19	13	23	11	14
Area under crops, m *rai*	0·8	0·2	2·5	1·6	1·1	0·9	1·0	0·5	0·6
% crop land irrigated	23	57	51	79	41	52	48	28	58
% crop land under rice[a]	30	62	60	70	49	45	49	50	87
Output of rice, 000 metric tons	71	34	414	344	169	245	153	87	128
Population, 000	173	168	648	389	352	320	316	260	146
% agricultural population	86	75	80	80	81	85	86	86	83
Agricultural population, 000	149	126	518	311	285	272	272	224	121
Average area agricultural holding, *rai*	20	10	30	32	23	18	21	14	28
Other leading crops, area harvested, 000 *rai*[b]									
Maize	63		977	107	147	134			
Lady finger bananas	11								
Namlawa bananas		3							6
Soya beans		2					92		
Mung-beans			319	39		28		21	
Castor beans					52				
Cotton							181		
Sugar-cane								24	
Groundnuts									4

[a] Area planted figures were not available. These percentages were calculated from the area harvested.
[b] Only the area under the two leading crops in each *changwat* is recorded here.

Sources: U.S.O.M./N.S.O, *Changwat-Amphur Statistical Directory and Statistical Year Book of Thailand, 1965;* Ministry of Agriculture, *Crop Reports,* (*Changwat* Series), 1964.

There have been large increases in the area cultivated. However, taking the sub-region as a whole, yields per *rai* have been maintained rather than increased. The growth of the rice output along with that of other crops, and the absence of detailed studies, makes it uncertain how far the increased area planted to other crops and the occasional higher yields arise from complete specialisation on a commercial upland crop. New land has been taken up and there has probably been some new specialisation, but the extent of it has not yet been determined.

Farmers have poured into this region, taking up new land, perhaps in anticipation of more irrigation but more immediately because of better transport. The building of the Chai Nat and Phumiphon dams has led to considerable improvements in road transport; and water transport has improved with the stabilisation of the water level, making regular boat services throughout the year an economic proposition. This is certainly important in Nakhon Sawan Province where river junctions and lakes make water transport essential. It may also be significant in Phichit and Uthai Thani. In Phetchabun the new strategic highway to Lomsak is the main development influence.

In general we may say that development here has not followed lines foreseen by the government; yet it has probably been stimulated almost incidentally by rural development work undertaken for other purposes. Table 6.8 shows the agricultural situation in the sub-region in 1964.

It is a matter of some importance to examine more closely the causes of development in this area. First, although we have not adequate information to analyse the whole income flow, it is obvious that there is a great deal of capital being invested in opening up new land. Next, it is clear that a strong trade demand for export crops exists in the area, so that farmers can take up new land with some security that they can dispose of their crops in a competitive market. Finally there was accessible vacant land available.

Clearly, in most of the area new transport has been a key factor. The time sequence suggests that transport alone might have been enough to cause a good deal of growth. More freight cars on the railways in the early 1950s, and a simultaneous rationalising of the system of official corruption, lowered the margins on goods for export from the north and northeast generally (I.B.R.D., 1959:

124-5; Skinner, 1957: 345 ff). Then came the improvement of the main road, associated with the building of the Chai Nat dam (completed 1956) and the thoroughgoing change in government policy toward main highway development. Improvements in water transport followed the completion of the dam; and the main agricultural development began in 1959.

New transport developments have, however, been found in many parts of Thailand, and the dramatic increase in the area planted in the North Central Region—which owes relatively little directly to irrigation, for the percentage of crop land irrigated in the most rapidly growing areas is only about 50 per cent, much lower than in many areas which have developed much less—suggests that a further explanation is needed. This may well be the active business enterprise of traders attracted into the area by other influences. Such an explanation seems particularly relevant in Nakhon Sawan, the *changwat* which I visited in this region.

Like other *changwats*, Nakhon Sawan produces an annual report from time to time. These reports are difficult to obtain in Bangkok and impossible to order on a regular basis; they are produced only in Thai; and normally contain no useful statistics which do not appear elsewhere. Fortunately in 1964 the annual report contains over seventy pages of agricultural statistics by districts (Nakhon Sawan *Annual Report*, 1964: 278, 306-8). These are not particularly reliable—there are arithmetical errors and in some instances serious obscurities—but they give a good general picture of the place where the growth occurred. Table 6.9 shows the area and population by district and the areas harvested of the most important crops in 1964.

It is apparent from the table that the district of greatest expansion of the new crops is Takhli and the adjacent district of Phayuha Khiri. In 1959 the total area in Nakhon Sawan *changwat* under the various crops was: maize 52·8, mung-beans 22·4, groundnuts 43·7, and castor beans 15·7 thousand *rai*, so that there would have been a tenfold increase for maize and mung-beans and a 50 per cent increase for castor beans even if the whole area under each crop had been concentrated in these two districts in 1959.

The town of Takhli had developed into an important junction and trading centre because of its favourable situation at the junction of the main road and railway, even before the district was selected as one of the chief American air bases. Very probably the

Table 6.9 Analyses of area under maize, mung-beans, groundnuts and castor beans by district, Nakhon Sawan Province

District	Population 1960 000	Area under agriculture 1962-3 000 rai	Area under maize 1964 000 rai	Area under mung-beans 1964 000 rai	Area under ground-nuts 1964 000 rai	Area under castor beans 1964 000 rai
Muang	119·8	242·7	72·2	4·3	2·0	0·9
Krok Phra	26·9	115·9	31·0	12·0	3·1	1·8
Chumsaeng	62·6	245·0	58·0	10·0	1·8	0·1
Nong Bua	39·3	185·3	8·3	1·8	0·5	0·5
Banphot Phisai	84·8	359·6	48·0	18·5	5·0	1·2
Takhli	104·8	409·7[a]	446·7[a]	173·0[a]	24·5[a]	18·1[a]
Tha Tako	57·3	299·7	17·3	2·3	1·0	2·8
King Phaisali	30·7	165·6	37·0	4·0	1·0	1·0
Phayuha Khiri	53·6	218·2[a]	193·5[a]	78·0[a]	2·0[a]	5·0[a]
Lat Yao	67·9	267·6	70·5	15·0	3·0	2·0
Total	647·7	2,509·3	982·5	318·9	43·9	33·4

[a] The total area under agriculture in 1962-3 is based on the Census of Agriculture figures. The area under maize, mung-beans, groundnuts and castor beans in 1964 is based on Ministry of Agriculture returns. It is probable that this fact in itself would lead to some inconsistency. However, it is by no means impossible that the area under these four crops in these two districts could have at least doubled in a year and a half. The discrepancy is not greater than could be explained by mere lapse of time. However, the Takhli District Officer, while noting the great expansion, apparently uses a census figure for upland crops; compare pp. 140 and 278 of Nakhon Sawan *Annual Report.*

Sources: U.S.O.M./N.S.O., *Changwat-Amphur Statistical Directory*, p. 15; *Nakhon Sawan Annual Report*, 1964, pp. 133-208; N.S.O., *Census of Agriculture, 1963, Nakhon Sawan.*

rapid growth of this important trading centre was the catalyst that turned a generally favourable situation for growth into a focus of really dramatic growth for a large and expanding area of new land. The presence of large numbers of Americans with money to spend must certainly have attracted many keen entrepreneurs to move to the district, and money spent in the district must have helped to provide farmers with the means to expand their operations.

The village in which I stayed in Nakhon Sawan *changwat* was Khok Maw in Chumsaeng district, in the north of the *changwat* and many kilometres from the area of most rapid growth. It was a

K

village on a river bank, with no road access, and was a convenient point from which to observe some of the effects of the main irrigation works. The greater stability of the river level had substantially improved water transport over the past eight years. Itinerant traders visited the village often by boat and had promoted an interest in weed-killers, fertilisers, and insecticides. Not many of the farmers could yet afford irrigation pumps; there were, however, a few hand-operated appliances, such as hand-pumps and knapsack sprays.

Visiting traders may have stimulated the change to upland crops, such as tobacco, chillies, and some maize, which had taken place in the past few years. Another influence, however, was the more stable water level. Several of the farms had previously relied on the annual flooding of the river. The construction of the Phumiphon dam had diminished the peak level of flooding, and this left many of the farmers without water. A local plan for pump irrigation from the river was under discussion, but in the meantime several farmers had switched to upland crops.

East Sub-region

The Household Expenditure Survey groups together as the East Region a rather miscellaneous, but generally prosperous, group of seven *changwats* stretching southeast from the head of the Gulf, near the metropolis, along the coast of the Gulf of Thailand. In terms of family income this area differs only slightly from the Inner Central Plain, the villages being a little less prosperous, the towns a little more so (N.S.O., 1962-3: *Whole Kingdom* vol. and pp. 31-2).

In its agricultural characteristics the sub-region varies more than most areas of similar size in Thailand. Nakhon Nayok, Chachoengsao and most of Prachin Buri hardly merit being separated from the Inner Central Plain, which they resemble in almost every respect. There is a high proportion of irrigation in the first two, the lower proportion in Prachin Buri being due to the dry eastern end, very sparsely populated, near the Cambodian border.

In the south, Chanthaburi and Trat are characterised by the heaviest rainfall in Thailand and their rather sparse population, apart from the coastal fishermen, cultivates mainly rubber and other tree crops in addition to rice for its own consumption. The northern part of Chanthaburi, however, is affected by the proximity

Table 6.10 Agricultural data: East Sub-region, 1964

	Chan-tha-buri	Chac-hoeng-sao	Chon Buri	Pra-chin Buri	Trat	Nakhon Nayok	Rayong
Area, m *rai*	4	3	3	7	2	2	2
% area under crops	15	34	37	16	17	46	33
Area under crops, m *rai*	0·6	1·2	1·0	1·2	0·3	0·7	0·7
% crop land irrigated	8	80	33	44	1	51	15
% crop land under rice[a]	23	92	34	68	20	97	19
Output of rice, 000 metric tons	38	289	105	135	19	131	26
Population, 000	158	323	392	335	66	154	148
% agricultural population	77	68	60	77	77	74	77
Agricultural population, 000	122	219	235	259	51	114	114
Average area agricultural holdings, *rai*	26	33	27	33	32	40	29
Other leading crops, area harvested, 000 *rai*[b]							
Groundnuts	18	8		9			
Cassava	16	17	373	7	16		46
Sugar-cane			332				11
Namlawa bananas					4	3	
Maize						3	

[a] Area planted figures were not available. These percentages were calculated from the area harvested.

[b] Only the area under the two leading crops in each *changwat* is recorded here.

Sources: U.S.O.M./N.S.O., *Changwat-Amphur Statistical Directory* and *Statistical Year Book, 1965*; Ministry of Agriculture, *Crop Reports* (*Changwat* Series), 1964.

of Chon Buri and has a similar agriculture, cultivating cassava and sugar-cane.

It is the central part of the East Sub-region, the *changwats* of Chon Buri and Rayong, which are of special interest as a growth centre. Table 6.10 gives the main agricultural characteristics of the East Sub-region, from which it is apparent that these two provinces are primarily producers of cassava and sugar-cane. Chon Buri is indeed Thailand's leading producer of both these crops. It is also an area in which the last few years have seen quite dramatic growth, though not comparable in rate of expansion or in scale to that in the North Central Region.

In 1959 the one *changwat* of Chon Buri produced about two-thirds of Thailand's cassava. In the next three years its production doubled, until it produced some three-quarters of the country's whole crop. Since 1962 production in Chon Buri has fallen back, and in 1965 it was back to about the 1959 level, but output had expanded in the rest of the country. Expansion in sugar-cane came a little later and was greatly assisted by the government's export subsidy scheme. Output approximately doubled during the five years the scheme was in operation, from 1961-6, rising from under 30 per cent to about 45 per cent of the country's output. Table 6.11 shows basic data for Chon Buri *changwat*.

Output of these two crops in Chon Buri is partly due to the rainfall of the area, which is higher than in the Central Plain;[7] this makes cultivation of upland crops easier, but their rapid expansion is probably due to the presence of factories for making starch and refining sugar in Chon Buri town.

The growth of this town is also probably due to a combination of transport facilities and the attraction of enterprise and capital into the area by outside influences. The highway to the southeast was improved to a high standard in order to give more convenient access to the seaside resorts along the east coast of the Gulf of Thailand. These resorts were patronised first by the king and the bureaucracy, and later by very large numbers of foreign advisers and United Nations officials. The flow of foreign funds was further increased by the construction of an American air base in the region.[8] The presence of heavy foreign spending appears to attract a flow of capital and enterprise highly favourable to development.

The village which I visited in Chon Buri—Nongproe in Phanat-nikhom district—was one in which a small group of mainly Sino-Thai farmers had cultivated vegetables for many years on the edge of a marsh. Since the vegetables had to be carried five kilometres to the nearest road the work was very laborious. The building of a road some ten years earlier had led to bus services and buyers visiting the village. Cultivation of vegetables spread more widely among the farmers, and this created an awareness of fertilisers and insecticides. The demand for irrigation to improve the water supply,

---

[7] The average rainfall for gauges in the Central Plain (excluding those in the East Sub-region) 1961-4 was 1,247·8 mm; the average for Chon Buri over the same period was 1,448·2 mm.

[8] At Sattahip in Rayong *changwat*.

Table 6.11 Basic data and leading crops in *changwat* Chon Buri,[a] 1959-65

		1959	1960	1961	1962	1963	1964	1965
Rice	Bangkok wholesale price, *bt*/kg	0·85	0·91	1·10	0·96	0·77	0·83	1·21
	Area planted, 000 *rai*	n.a.	n.a.	339·9	337·3	n.a.	n.a.	n.a.
	Area harvested, 000 *rai*	260·0	285·7	339·6	306·8	309·6	348·3	n.a.
	Yield, kg per *rai*	262	274	261	232	228	303	n.a.
	Output, 000 metric tons	68·1	78·3	88·8	71·1	70·7	105·3	n.a.
Cassava	Bangkok wholesale price, *bt*/kg meal	0·87	0·63	0·65	0·86	0·62	0·55	0·70
	Area planted, 000 *rai*	254·7	n.a.	423·9	528·1	597·9	374·1	300·8
	Area harvested, 000 *rai*	254·7	n.a.	423·9	528·1	596·3	373·4	300·6
	Yield, kg per *rai* (meal equivalent)	1,081·9	n.a.	1,176·0	1,176·0	979·0	940·8	980·0
	Output, 000 metric tons (meal equivalent)	299	n.a.	499	595	584	351	294
Sugar-cane	Bangkok wholesale price, *bt*/kg	114·28	108·46	110·18	121·90	130·00	100·00	102·55
	Area planted, 000 *rai*	191·1	n.a.	141·8	130·1	372·1	332·4	293·5
	Area harvested, 000 *rai*	191·1	n.a.	141·8	130·1	372·1	332·2	293·5
	Yield, kg per *rai*	8,600	8,000	8,000	8,000	6,000	6,500	7,000
	Output, 000 metric tons	1,644	1,134	1,134	1,041	2,236	2,159	2,055

[a] Agricultural population, 1960, 000, 235·2; area, km², 4,480; cultivated area, 37%; crop land irrigated, 33%. Other non-rice crops occupying > 1% harvested area in 1964, 000 *rai*: pineapples 18·1, groundnuts 15·9, bananas 9·0.

Source: *Statistical Year Books, 1963, 1965*; U.S.O.M./N.S.O., *Changwat-Amphur Statistical Directory, 1965*; Ministry of Agriculture, *Agricultural Statistics of Thailand, 1964*; *Annual Reports on Rice Production, 1961, 1962*; 'Statistics of the Planting of Upland and Garden Crops', 1959, mimeo. (*Changwat* Series), 1961, 1962, 1963, 1964.

not only for vegetables but for rice, was stimulated by the new market experience, and a dam had been built by local government effort just before I arrived. Ten years after the road arrived the village had recently acquired a rudimentary electricity supply, and even a part-time beauty parlour.

The sequence from highway development to vegetables to experiment with fertiliser, weed-killer, etc., seemed a fairly general one, all over Thailand, visible at different stages in different villages, according to the time the road had been there. For really rapid development, however, an external force attracting a large number of entrepreneurs to compete for new business seemed to be an important, though perhaps not essential, added favourable factor.

7

Regional Analysis: Outer Regions

The outer regions—the Far North, the Northeast, and the South —to which we now turn are not those in which the most striking development has been taking place. They are, however, the regions which have been attracting special attention from the Thai government, because of the problems that trouble them and need much attention if they are to be solved.

It is easy to think of these simply as security problems: the areas most remote from Bangkok might seem to be those most easily threatened, particularly as they are all areas containing appreciable numbers of people whose language and culture differ from that of the Central Thais. Yet if it were not for the economic difficulties it is by no means clear that these would be the areas most at risk. After all, Bangkok is the area containing the highest proportion of Chinese who are culturally and linguistically differentiated from the Thais (Caldwell, 1967: 45-50; Skinner, 1957: 81-3); and no Thai would be likely, in the current situation in Asia, to regard these cultural differences as less important than those that separate Thais from the hill tribes, the Lao-speakers of the Northeast, or the Malay-speakers of the South Region. Moreover parts of the Central Plain—for example Kanchanaburi or Ratchaburi—have historically proved as vulnerable as Thailand's more remote boundaries.[1]

There has been a fair measure of success in tackling the econ-

[1] Visiting either Kanchanaburi or Ratchaburi one constantly sees evidence of past threats of Burmese invasion; see also Ratchaburi *Annual Report*, 1962, pp. 1-2 (in Thai).

omic problems of the North and the Northeast. Some of these problems are, however, intractable, and the measure of success achieved has not produced any dramatic improvement, such as has occurred —largely as an incidental result of some government and some private activities—in parts of the Central Region.

In all three outer regions we are considering measures directed, more or less successfully, to resisting pressures that might make matters worse. In the Far North there are problems of rising population and falling water levels (Chapman, 1967. Also interviews between author and headmen and agricultural officers in Chiang Mai and Chomthong). In the Northeast there are also population pressures, but there is an additional problem of deterioration of the soil (Platenius, 1963; I.B.R.D., 1959: 43). In the South the long-foreseen fall in the price of rubber has—for various reasons —come upon its rubber industry before the plans to meet this threat had matured (Ministry of Agriculture, 1966). In the North and the Northeast these pressures threaten communities that are already worse off than most Thais. In the south there is a decline from a previous high level.

Far North Region

It has been often observed that agriculture in north Thailand differs sharply from that of the Central Plain (Wijeyewardene, 1967: 75-80). The area cultivated per farm is much smaller, cooperative irrigation is almost everywhere a necessity, double cropping is fairly common, but most farmers grow other crops in addition to rice as a source of cash income rather than producing a rice surplus for sale (Chapman, 1967).

Table 7.1 sets out the basic facts about the region. The table shows the very small size of farms, the high incidence of irrigation, except in Nan, the relatively high proportion growing the main off-season crops, and the relatively low output of rice. The rice equivalent of 275 kg of paddy per head is needed by subsistence farmers eating glutinous rice (Chapman, 1967: 4), so that only in Chiang Rai, Chiang Mai, and Lampang do the agricultural households grow a surplus.

The present situation is mainly a result of the topography. Thai farmers, accustomed to subsistence wet-rice farming, occupied these broad upland valleys, where rice land is relatively scarce but

Table 7.1 Agricultural data: Far North Region, 1964

	Chiang Mai	Chiang Rai	Lam-pang	Lamp-hun	Mae Hong Son	Nan	Phrae
Area, m rai.	14·4	11·8	7·8	2·8	8·3	7·3	3·7
% area under crops	6	11	6	10	1	3	9
Area under crops, m rai	0·9	1·3	0·5	0·3	0·1	0·2	0·3
% crop land irrigated	92	76	73	89	79	52	71
% crop land under rice[a]	72	84	77	75	47	·65	66
Output of rice, 000 metric tons	272	470	91	71	15	42	55
Population, 000	798	812	472	250	81	240	299
% agricultural population	70	78	76	78	74	92	79
Agricultural population, 000	559	633	358	195	60	221	237
Average area of agricultural holdings, rai	7·6	11·1	7·4	8·0	7·4	6·2	8·3
Other leading crops, area harvested, 000 rai[b]							
Groundnuts	41			21		·15	57
Tobacco	·40	41	14			·17	51
Garlic		16			2		
Sugar-cane	.		42		2		
Soya beans				16			

[a] Area planted figures were not available. These percentages were calculated from the area harvested.
[b] Only the area under the two leading crops in each changwat is recorded here.
Sources: U.S.O.M./N.S.O., Changwat-Amphur Statistical Directory, Statistical Year Book, 1965; and Ministry of Agriculture, Crop Reports (Changwat Series), 1964.

water is abundant, and fairly soon co-operative irrigation works must have become necessary. Traditionally most of the irrigation systems required were quite small, involving no more than half a dozen villages. Schemes of this size are not too large to be organised mainly by personal contact and consensus, with a minimum of compulsion. Central Authority was necessary only for initiating them and establishing the system of maintenance. The princes who organised the schemes were, however, regarded as their owners, and received a part of the produce (Graham, 1924: Vol. II, p. 34).

The area to which the central government gave most attention, both during the absolute monarchy and subsequently, was the valley of the Ping River, in which the northern capital, Chiang

Mai, is located. Recently good extension work, combined with some protection, has led to a great expansion of cash crops in addition to the main rice crop. For almost every crop, farmers have first reached a wider market and learnt new techniques in the Ping River valley. Then, either by migration or by imitation the practice spread to other areas, some of which have now surpassed Chiang Mai in groundnut production and are not much behind in other crops (Chapman, 1967). Tobacco, particularly the Virginia variety which yields almost double the price of local tobacco, is produced for the government's Tobacco Monopoly. Garlic is protected by a ban on imports. Other new crops are still being successfully tried in the Ping River valley, and this area is also taking the lead in new methods.

Development in the whole of the Far North Region encounters difficulties resulting from rapid population growth. Excessive cutting of the forests has adversely affected the water level in the valley bottoms. First there was the illegal over-exploitation of the teak industry already mentioned in chapter 3. This is now rather better controlled. But another problem has arisen in the *swidden* (slash and burn) agriculture of the hill tribes (Judd, 1964): overcrowding (by the very land-demanding standards of hill-people) has forced them to cut out forest areas and plant again before soil fertility is fully restored. This means that more land is needed in future, and the regeneration is also made less rapid. The forest becomes steadily more denuded.

Population is increasing among the hill tribes both by excess of births over deaths (because of the control of malaria and epidemics) and by migration from disturbed neighbouring countries. There is also an active world demand for opium, the hill tribes' main commercial product (Usher, 1967: 224-30).

Population growth is also involving the lowland Thais in *swidden* cultivation—with or without legal tenure, for normally temporary holdings of this kind are illegal—to supplement the cultivation of cash crops in their valley land (Chapman, 1967). For available rice land, in spite of some double cropping, is becoming inadequate for the rice needs of the population. Population pressure is also being met by migration into the outlying provinces. Migration has filled up most of the available land in Lamphun Province, and population is moving into vacant lands in Chiang Rai, where flood control in the Kok River basin and recent road building along the

Ing River have opened up new areas to this type of cultivation (N.E.D.B., 1964: 49-66; U.S.O.M., 1960b). In this region the population movements from the rest of the north have been augmented by an overflow of population from the northeast (U.S.O.M., 1966).

Chiang Rai is, indeed, becoming the development area of the Far North. In part this is a result of deliberate government policy, for example in the development of irrigation. In part it is an indirect result of strategic road building which has been undertaken because of anxiety about the northern border.

It is necessary to emphasise, however, that in spite of the large area of Chiang Rai the amount of new valley bottom land made available is very limited, and in some stretches such land is already becoming expensive. It will very soon become necessary—even if population growth can ultimately be slowed down—to face the problem of the proper use of the higher lands (Chapman, 1967). This will involve solving three problems.

First it will be necessary to secure fuller facts about soils and configuration: there are large areas which are promising on both grounds, but further research is necessary, and a suitable cropping pattern, with use of fertiliser, to allow continuous cultivation, will have to be found. Next it will be necessary to know more about the economy of the hill tribes. Investigations are being undertaken, but already the government's ambivalent attitude to opium and its attempts to control deforestation have made some of the hill tribes security risks. Any extensive development of upland areas will involve better control over some of the forest, and profitable opportunities must be found for the hill tribes, and techniques discovered to make these acceptable to them. Finally it may be necessary to promote more specialised farming, without the need to grow a subsistence crop of rice as a basis. The area as a whole can grow enough rice for its needs; but the need to provide an upland crop of rice within reach of any other upland crop will be a probably excessive restraint on the development of suitable crop cycles.

At present the typical farming pattern in the Far North includes the aim to grow enough rice for family subsistence as a first priority, with supplementary crops—whether or not there is a surplus of rice for sale—as sources of cash income (Chapman, 1967; Wijeyewardene, 1965). In economic terms the rice crop is

Table 7.2　Basic data and leading crops in *Changwat* Chiang Mai,ᵃ 1959-65

		1959	1960	1961	1962	1963	1964	1965
Riceᵇ	Bangkok wholesale price, *bt*/kg paddy	0·85	0·91	1·10	0·96	0·77	0·83	1·21
	Area planted, 000 *rai*	n.a.	n.a.	642·9	651·8	n.a.	n.a.	n.a.
	Area harvested, 000 *rai*	603·9	614·8	638·6	651·8	616·4	619·8	n.a.
	Yield, kg per *rai*	340	350	369	376	363	439	n.a.
	Output, 000 metric tons	205·4	216·8	235·7	245·1	223·9	272·3	n.a.
Soya beans	Bangkok wholesale price, *bt*/kg	1·93	1·89	2·58	2·43	2·54	2·06	2·68
	Area planted, 000 *rai*	39·4	n.a.	33·7	58·9	41·6	41·6	18·3
	Area harvested, 000 *rai*	39·2	n.a.	33·7	58·9	41·6	41·6	18·1
	Yield, kg per *rai*	165	n.a.	210	210	180	180	200
	Output, 000 metric tons	6·48	n.a.	7·08	12·37	7·48	7·49	3·63
Groundnuts	Bangkok wholesale price, *bt*/kg	3·18	4·19	3·31	3·60	3·67	4·00	4·10
	Area planted, 000 *rai*	38·8	n.a.	34·1	53·0	30·0	40·8	40·1
	Area harvested, 000 *rai*	38·5	n.a.	34·1	53·0	30·0	40·8	39·9
	Yield, kg per *rai*	195	n.a.	210	210	230	250	220
	Output, 000 metric tons	7·53	n.a.	7·16	11·14	6·89	10·21	8·78
Tobaccoᶜ	Bangkok wholesale price, *bt*/kg	7·36	7·43	8·06	6·85	7·32	7·11	5·68
	Area planted, 000 *rai*	61·7	n.a.	39·1	32·98	32·6	39·8	46·4
	Area harvested, 000 *rai*	60·2	n.a.	39·1	32·96	31·4	39·8	46·1
	Yield, kg per *rai*	210	n.a.	300	300	250	300	250
	Output, 000 metric tons	12·62	n.a.	11·7	9·89	7·86	10·21	8·78
Garlic	Bangkok wholesale price, *bt*/kg	4·26	6·97	10·69	6·96	2·61	2·85	6·62
	Area planted, 000 *rai*	14·3	n.a.	26·4	33·27	15·12	21·40	24·58
	Area harvested, 000 *rai*	14·3	n.a.	26·0	33·27	14·88	21·40	23·99
	Yield, kg per *rai*	300	n.a.	350	350	350	350	350
	Output, 000 metric tons	4·30	n.a.	9·11	11·64	5·21	7·49	8·40

^a Agricultural population 1960, 000, 555·2; area, km², 22,993; cultivated area 6%; crop land irrigated 92%. Other non-rice crops occupying > 1% of harvested area 1964, in 000 *rai*: Chinese cabbage 8·3, long chillies 6·7, *namlawa* bananas 5·6, cabbage 4·2, shallot 3·2, string beans 3·2, chillies 2·5.

^b The rice figures for 1959 and 1960 are from the 1963 *Statistical Year Book*. The 1960 figures for the whole kingdom were subsequently. revised upwards but revisions for the separate provinces are not available.

^c Local variety prices. Virginia type tobacco is also grown in Thailand. I did not encounter any in north Thailand, but believe some is grown there; total production of Virginia type, which. is sold to the Tobacco Monopoly, was between 8 and 9 thousand and metric tons in every year, 1959-64, but there is no breakdown available by provinces. Prices of Virginia type tobacco were (*bt*/kg): 1959, 13·60, 1960, 13·04, 1961, 15·33, 1962, 13·73, 1963, 14·64, 1964, 14·22.

Sources: Statistical Year Book, 1963, 1965; U.S.O.M./N.S.O., *Changwat-Amphur Statistical Directory,* 1965; Ministry of Agriculture, *Agricultural Statistics of Thailand, 1965; Annual Reports on Rice Production,* 1961, 1962; 'Statistics of the Planting of Upland and Garden Crops', 1959, mimeo. (*Changwat* Series), 1961, 1962, 1963, 1964, 1965.

probably of diminishing importance. The change to fully commercialised farming is likely to begin in the more prosperous
bottom lands; but it may be desirable to initiate such a change as
part of the preparation for developing the upland area.

The *changwat* I visited in the Far North Region was Chiang
Mai. Particulars of recent development in the leading crops in
Chiang Mai are given in Table 7.2. It is apparent from the table
that, while there is an upward trend in both area harvested and
yield, there is also a great deal of change in the cropping pattern
from year to year. An example is the *namlawa* banana. Ranking of
the crops is based on 1964—the last year for which full information, including rice, was available. In 1964 *namlawa* bananas were
one of the minor crops; in 1965, 58,000 *rai* were planted, making
this fruit crop the leading non-rice crop for the year.

Chiang Mai is chiefly important, however, not for any one
crop, but for the constant experimentation with new methods, the
changes in the crops grown, and the vigour in the extension work
among the lowland farmers. It is impossible to travel through the
area, see the farms and talk to farmers and agricultural officers,
without being aware that this is an area of keen farmers, conscious
of being leaders in their own type of farming.

The village visited, Donghadnak in Chom Thong district, was in
the southern part of the Ping valley, not very far from the boundary
of the *changwat*. The village gave an impression of prosperity,
though it had no special advantages; the farmers interviewed all
appeared to have both interest in, and resources available for,
buying mechanical equipment. Seven out of ten had bought at least
one knapsack spray, small tractor, or irrigation pump in the last
four years. Probably, however, difficulty in conversing in Northern
Thai led to my making contact only with better educated and more
sophisticated farmers—the average area of their holdings was 17·3
rai against about 5+ for the village as a whole.

In this village the farmers all used fertiliser on their off-season
crops.[2] The past two years had seen a great deal of experimentation
with government-recommended fertiliser on the rice fields. Several
farmers were also developing orchards growing *lamyai* fruit (*Eup-
horia longana*) or oranges. Most of the bottom land was double-
cropped with rice, but in several cases supplementary off-season
crops were grown as well.

---

[2] Information derived from questionnaires and interviews.

An interesting recent innovation had been the transformation of an irrigation scheme, initiated some thirty years ago by a local prince and still maintained by corporate labour, into a 'co-operative'—or local irrigation organisation run by the Ministry of the Interior—with paid labour and contributions according to use. The chief effect seemed to have been a considerable increase in agricultural extension work, since the organisation had served as an agency to help with both fertiliser and irrigation advice.

Northeast Region

Such regional income figures as we have indicate that income per head in the Northeast is lower than in any other region in Thailand, and that this is mainly because of low incomes in the villages (N.S.O., 1962-3, N.E. Region, p. 52; *Whole Kingdom* Vol., p. 62). Town incomes are a little higher than the average for all towns in the kingdom. Nevertheless the town figures must be interpreted with some caution. In 1960 only about a twelfth of the population of the Northeast were found in towns, as against a fifth to a sixth in the other regions; and of the 700,000 living in towns, a fifth were in the five largest ones. Separate figures given for Nakhon Ratchasima in the Household Expenditure Survey show that its income level is about 50 per cent higher than the average of Northeastern towns, and the figures may well be dominated by the few large towns which are important market centres, simply because the majority of centres in the Northeast rank as nothing more than villages.

Limited regional gross product figures have been given, in comparison with other regions in Table 6.1. Table 7.3 gives rather more detailed figures, with some breakdown of both income and expenditure.

It is apparent that expenditure considerably exceeds income, indicating either substantial dissaving or a balance of payments deficit or both. There is, however, some reason to believe that 1962 —the only year for which both income and expenditure figures are available—was rather an abnormal year in this respect. The previous year, 1961, was the peak year of the kenaf boom, and many Northeastern Thais must have had windfall profits. It is only reasonable to suppose that some of these were spent in the following year, and indeed the Household Expenditure Survey shows a considerable excess of family expenditure over income in the year.

Table 7.3 Northeast Region: family income and expenditure statistics, 1962

(*baht*)

	Villages		Towns		Whole Region
	Per family	Total	Per family	Total	
Income					
Cash income	2,986	4,104m	13,068	1,707m	5,811m
Income in kind	2,273	3,192m	448	59m	3,251m
Total	5,259	7,296m	13,516	1,766m	9,062m
Income from rice	n.a.	n.a.	n.a.	n.a.	2,930m
Income from other agriculture	n.a.	n.a.	n.a.	n.a.	1,988m
All other income	n.a.	n.a.	n.a.	n.a.	6,450m
Total	n.a.	n.a.	n.a.	n.a.	11,368m
Expenditure					
Income in kind	2,273	3,192m	448	59m	3,251m
Rice	376	528m	1,404	183m	711m
Other food	581	816m	3,736	488m	1,304m
Taxes, gifts, and services	1,357	1,906m	5,197	679m	2,585m
All other	1,383	1,942m	2,822	369m	2,311m
Total	3,697	5,192m	13,159	1,719m	6,911m
Total cash and kind	5,970	8,384m	13,607	1,778m	10,162m
Other expenditures					
Govt and private constructions	n.a.	n.a.	n.a.	n.a.	538m
Govt admin., defence, education, medicine	n.a.	n.a.	n.a.	n.a.	757m
Total known expenditure	n.a.	n.a.	n.a.	n.a.	11,459m

Note: The population figures used were those for 1960 given in the *Whole Kingdom* volume of the *Household Expenditure Survey*.

Sources: N.S.O., *Household Expenditure Survey*, Northeast volume, 1963, Tables 1:0, 1:1 and 6; *Whole Kingdom* volume, Table L; National Income Division of the Office of the N.E.D.B., *Regional Gross Domestic Product*, 1964 ed., Tables 1 and 3 and Table VI.2.

Probably we must also reckon a regular element of balance of payments deficit in the accounts of rice exporting regions, except the Central, because of the rice premium. Income for rice is valued on the basis of the Bangkok price less an appropriate discount to approximate to the farm price. The proceeds of the rice premium accrue as an indirect tax to the central government. Central government spending in the regions tends to create an adverse balance in so far as it is financed from this tax, or indeed from other central revenues of similar type.

The kenaf boom and the rice premium thus suggest explanations of the excess of expenditure over income which do not imply any serious long-term depletion of resources. However, the general pattern is not one in which expansionary influence can easily flourish. A large part of the region's export income is taxed away. Consumption is partly financed by salaries paid from Bangkok, and expenditure on imports exceeds income from exports.

Hardly surprisingly, this region is the one with the largest net loss of population to other regions (Chapman and Allen, 1965). Within the region, however, there is also very substantial migration. This is mainly a movement of people in the southeastern part of the region to its north, northwest, and southwest areas. The *changwats* of migration loss are Ubon Ratchathani, Si Sa Ket, Roi Et, and Maha Sarakham. The others are *changwats* of migration gain, particularly Udon Thani and Nakhon Ratchasima, and to a smaller degree Khon Kaen, Chaiyaphum, Buri Ram, Nong Khai and Sakon Nakhon. The migrant-losing *changwats* are mainly those with the highest proportion of their area cultivated and the highest ratio of population to land. These facts are shown in Table 7.4. More important is the fact that these are areas in which the land suitable for wet rice cultivation has been mostly taken up. In spite of irrigation along the Chi and Mun rivers there is not enough wet rice land for the increasing population (Caldwell, 1967: 48-9). The character of the *changwats* gaining from immigration is more varied, ranging from the modern Nakhon Ratchasima with its many new crops, to Khon Kaen the government-promoted 'development centre' (N.E.D.B., n.d.: 3-5), and Udon Thani with its animal rearing, sugar-cane, and kenaf.

Taking the region as a whole the Northeast is much the largest in the country—with a third of the total population—as well as the poorest. It is the area most open to communist penetration, for both ethnic and geographic reasons, and hence its low productivity is a source of great anxiety to the central government.

For many years the diagnosis of the problem of the Northeast was that it was impoverished because it lacked the flooding brought down each year into the Central Plain, had a rainfall too greatly concentrated in two or three months of the year, and was difficult to irrigate for both topographical and pedological reasons (White *et al.*, 1962: 27 ff; Chira, 1964). This analysis assumed that the Northeasterners were basically subsistence rice farmers and that

L

Table 7.4 Agricultural data: Northeast Region, 1964

	Migration loss changwats				Principal migration gain changwats							Other changwats			
	Maha Sarakhan	Roi Et	Si Sa Ket	Ubon Ratcha-thani	Nakhon Ratcha-sima	Udon Thani	Khon Kaen	Chaiya-phum	Nong-khai	Buri ram	Sakon Nakhon	Kala-sin	Nakhon Phanom	Loei	Surin
Area, m rai	3·6	4·9	5·5	14·2	12·2	10·4	8·4	6·7	4·5	6·7	6·0	4·8	6·1	6·8	5·5
% area under crops	40	45	31	27	26	21	28	17	10	30	20	19	11	4	33
Area under crops, m rai	1·4	2·2	1·7	3·8	3·2	2·2	2·3	1·1	0·5	2·0	1·2	0·9	0·7	0·3	1·8
% crop land irrigated	16	24	18	16	29	35	28	54	16	46	18	21	25	32	21
% cropland under rice[a]	33	50	66	61	50	61	40	63	92	51	83	58	81	51	63
Output of rice, 000 metric tons	80	146	153	331	374	268	184	187	126	188	232	95	113	45	172
Population, 000	499	668	601	1,131	1,095	744	844	486	257	584	427	427	436	211	582
% agricultural population	92	93	94	88	87	86	85	91	79	88	88	93	87	90	91
Agricultural population, 000	459	621	565	995	952	640	717	443	203	514	376	397	380	189	529
Average area of agricultural holdings, rai	24·5	23·1	19·8	23·6	23·6	23·3	21·5	19·7	17·3	26·5	19·4	20·4	12·8	8·1	23·3

Other leading crops

Area harvested

000 rai[b]

											4·8	6·1	6·8	5·5
Kenaf	200	39	58	168	38	299	177	63		63			26
Other hemps		33											
Groundnuts	11												
Maize	149		25			10							
Sugar-cane	145					22	12	42	5				
Namlawa bananas							9						9
Long chillies											11		
Short chillies												13	
Pineapples								9					
Watermelons										6	12		
Tobacco													
Cotton												64	

[a] Area planted figures were not available. These percentages were calculated from the area harvested.

[b] Only the area under the two leading crops in each *changwat* is recorded here.

Sources: U.S.O.M./N.S.O., *Changwat-Amphur Statistical Directory*; N.S.O., *Statistical Year Book*, 1965; Ministry of Agriculture *Crop Reports* (*Changwat* Series), 1964.

unless their rice yields increased they would remain impoverished. The International Bank Mission concentrated on the development of suitable products for the Northeastern climate, but did not really explain the nature of Northeastern backwardness (I.B.R.D., 1959: 7, 36, 75). In the last few years there has been a shift of emphasis, with local studies of migration and marketing problems, more serious attention to new crops, and some expansion in road building.

Probably history rather than geography should be the focus of attention in studying the backwardness of the Northeast (Keyes, 1967). Certainly it is an area of some difficulty but this has been aggravated by historical factors creating an agriculture inappropriate to the climate and terrain, with inadequate assistance from any central authority.

Paradoxically the part of Thailand most accessible to world trade, the Central Plain around Bangkok, is one where wet rice subsistence agriculture is relatively easy; the large Northeastern area, which in a well-knit trading system could profitably produce livestock, fibres, sorghum, and various specialised crops in particular districts, has for some centuries been relatively isolated, lightly administered and hence compelled to produce mainly its own glutinous rice, in relatively small political units, for its own subsistence.

Muscat (1966: 89-91) has argued that within the limits of the Northeastern farmers' economic situation, their cultivation of glutinous rice was a rational choice; but it is not clear whether he regards the preference as still rational in the light of existing information and transport facilities. No doubt some of the alternatives to rice would exhaust the soil more, and some would not pay for the cost of the fertiliser. It may be that Muscat merely means that no other alternatives were known to these farmers, for he explicitly distinguishes between ignorance and irrationality; but the ignorance and the preference for the security of rice are both related to the historical background of small units.

During most of the Ayuthaya dynasty the Thais, threatened by Burmese and Khmers, were too weak to control their kinsmen to their north and northeast and were mainly concerned to limit Khmer influence among Lao speaking people. The stronger Bangkok monarchy began, during the nineteenth century, to extend its control both to the northeast and to the south, but had neither the resources nor the transport system to control them by the central-ised system used in Thailand proper (Vella, 1955: ch. 1). After Khmer influence was pushed back the northeast was ruled through small local states, not integrated into Thailand.

When the French began supporting Khmer claims in this area the Bangkok dynasty was forced to assimilate the northeast as quickly as possible. The building of the railway there was designed to forestall pretexts for French intervention, by ensuring that there was no doubt about Thai sovereignty and administration.

The Thai government, however, was never really interested in the area's economic development. The railway could have pro-moted more economic specialisation if the government had encour-aged it. What actually occurred, however, was an expansion along the railway lines of the same Chinese trading system which had gained control of the rice surplus in the Central Plain (Skinner, 1957: 213-14; Ingram, 1955: 70-4). A limited range of textiles and other consumer goods was supplied, often on credit, and part of the rice crop was bought in advance. The Northeast became a rice exporting area, though in the more distant provinces the output was never sufficient to make the export more than marginal.

There was, of course, some trade between the Northeast Region and the Central Plain in products other than rice—e.g. buffaloes and (from Loei) cotton, but little interest was taken in fostering such trade. When it first became urgent to stimulate economic growth to offset communist pressure, the main emphasis was on irrigation tanks to combat the water shortage which had led to many rice crops being lost in the Northeast.[3] The maintenance of law and order, and improved public health, had increased the population. The river valleys had become overcrowded, and rice farmers had moved out to lands where only an occasional good crop was to be expected. The problem was, in one sense, a shortage of water. Yet, more fundamentally, it was a problem of inadequate specialisation and incorrect land use.

The attitude to the Northeast is now changing. From the begin-ning American advisers attempted to promote both upland crops and a livestock industry; but this emphasis was naturally not very

[3] In the immediate post-war years, when Thailand was mainly seen as a source of rice, an F.A.O. mission was recommended to look into improving rice supplies in the Northeast. The Report of this Committee was presented in 1951. See I.B.R.D., 1959: 44-5.

strong in the immediate post-war years when the rice supply was an important international problem. The International Bank Mission showed a similar concern for crops that would use less water (I.B.R.D., 1959: 44-5). The surprising impact on the economy of the opening of the Friendship Highway between Saraburi and Nakhon Ratchasima in 1958 led to increased interest in the economic effects of roads (U.S.O.M., 1960). Kasetsart University also sponsored economic surveys of the Northeast (Chaiyong *et al.*, 1959, 1961, 1962). There have also been several migration studies, mainly using the new data on birthplace and residence change of the 1960 Population Census (Chapman and Allen, 1965; Caldwell, 1967; Dept of Labour, 1965; I.L.O., 1965).

As a result of these studies much more is now known about the region's economy, and modern extension work is concentrating on promoting new lines appropriate to local resources and marketing possibilities. Often it seems that increased specialisation in kenaf, cattle, sorghum, watermelons, egg-production, etc., would bring an advantage, but the attachment to producing a basic subsistence crop of rice is hard to break and this restricts regional specialisation, partly by limiting the distance that can be moved from available rice land, and by restricting the time that can be spent on supplementary crops. Those crops that need lower rainfall reduce the climatic risk of loss but increase market risks, since the farmer's demand is for rice. Northeastern farmers are accustomed to risk, and put by a rice surplus sufficient for several seasons (U.S.O.M., n.d.; Long *et al.*, 1963). The greater returns from kenaf, groundnuts, etc., would give better protection than rice if farmers in the region were as able to save money income as paddy. Specialisation occurs naturally when large centres of population develop, but more attention might reasonably be given to developing nodal points round which economic specialisation and expansion could take place and to focusing effort on extension work in the immediate neighbourhood of such points.

The Northeastern road network has developed rapidly since the opening of the Friendship Highway. Because the area is large, and road development new, many roads are still dry-weather only; but their effect on market orientation and openness to new methods is very great (U.S.O.M., 1960a and b); and even greater awareness of this might lead to fruitful concentration of effort where maximum change could be achieved.

A useful beginning has been made by the very detailed study of market structure in the Northeast, undertaken by the Agricultural Economics Division of the Ministry of Agriculture (1964). This sets out the trade routes for all types of produce by different districts within the Northeast Region, making use of the roads, the railway, and travel of stock on the hoof. It analyses market prices through the year and the distribution of the consumers' or exporters' *baht* spent among various participants in the market.

This could well lead to helpful policy decisions when it is intended to modify or realign a road, build new feeders, or link two main roads. A few incidental comments are made, crop by crop, about transshipment or performance of some necessary market function at a particular point. However, if a junction or terminus is going to produce growth like that of Banphai in Khon Kaen *changwat*, or of Nakhon Ratchasima, anticipation of local reactions in the aggregate could lead to provision of ancillary extension or assistance services in advance.

Unfortunately the study itself pays little attention to the reciprocal effects from the growth of active centres of exchange. Most of the centres are mentioned quite incidentally.

A full-scale study of the reaction on crop patterns, modernisation and income of the different trade centres that have sprung up —rather on the lines of the Longs' (1963) study in Khon Kaen, but specifically related to growth diffusion—would probably meet an important need.

The two *changwats* visited in the Northeast Region were Roi Et, a central *changwat* in the area of migration loss, and Nakhon Ratchasima, the most active centre of development in the whole region, and an area of migration gain. Basic data about the rural sector in Roi Et are given in Table 7.5.

One thing that stands out from this table is that, in spite of the poor average yield per *rai* of rice and the fact that gross yields from two to five times as high in money value can be obtained from other crops as from rice, it is still overwhelmingly the most important crop in the region. The low productivity means that there is a relatively small surplus for sale beyond the consumption requirements of about 280 kg per inhabitant per year. Kenaf, for example, is one of the relatively important non-rice crops, yet even in the kenaf boom year of 1961 the area under kenaf was only about one-thirtieth of that under rice.

Table 7.5 Basic data and leading crops in *changwat* Roi Et[a], 1959-65

	1959	1960	1961	1962	1963	1964	1965
Rice							
Bangkok wholesale price, *bt*/kg paddy	0·85	0·91	1·10	0·96	0·77	0·83	1·21
Area planted, 000 *rai*	n.a.	n.a.	1,293·0	1,695·7	n.a.	n.a.	n.a.
Area harvested, 000 *rai*	1,452·8	1,587·8	1,115·7	1,438·2	1,434·6	1,109·8	n.a.
Yield, kg per *rai*	102	144	112	136	130	131	n.a.
Output, 000 metric tons	148·8	229·9	125·0	195·9	187·0	145·7	n.a.
Kenaf							
Bangkok wholesale price, *bt*/kg	2·24	3·17	3·61	2·33	2·73	2·75	3·02
Area planted, 000 *rai*	2·1	n.a.	46·3	12·1	27·4	38·6	78·4
Area harvested, 000 *rai*	2·1	n.a.	46·3	12·0	27·4	38·6	78·4
Yield, kg per *rai*	120	n.a.	240	240	250	200	200
Output, 000 metric tons	0·25	n.a.	11·11	2·87	6·85	7·72	15·69
Maize							
Bangkok wholesale price, *bt*/kg	1·00	1·01	1·12	1·01	1·06	1·08	1·22
Area planted, 000 *rai*	19·8	n.a.	9·1	9·5	3·8	4·5	3·0
Area harvested, 000 *rai*	18·3	n.a.	9·1	9·4	3·8	4·5·	3·0
Yield, kg per *rai*	240	n.a.	250	250	240	240	240
Output, 000 metric tons	4·41	n.a.	2·28	2·34	0·91	1·08	0·25

[a] Agricultural population 1960, 000, 621·5, area, km² 7,856, cultivated area 45%, crop land irrigated 24%. Other non-rice crops occupying > 1% harvested area in 1964, 000 *rai*:
Other hemps 32·8, tobacco 11·4, *namlawa* bananas 9·1, other bananas 6·7, groundnuts 5·3, taro 4·0, long chillies 3·8, Chinese cabbage 3·5, cucumbers 3·5, pineapples 3·4, cotton 3·4, shallot 3·3, sweet potato 2·6, sugar-cane 2·3, garlic 2·2, string beans 2·2, short chillies 2·1, sesame 1·9, watermelons 1·9, musk melons 1·9, pumpkin 1·7.

Sources: Statistical Year Books, 1963, 1965; U.S.O.M./N.S.O., *Changwat-Amphur Statistical Directory, 1965;* Ministry of Agriculture, *Agricultural Statistics of Thailand, 1965; Annual Reports on Rice Production,* 1961, 1962; 'Statistics of the Planting of Upland and Garden Crops', 1959, mimeo. (*Changwat* Series), 1961, 1962, 1963, 1964, 1965.

Kenaf is a marginal crop in Roi Et not because the yield is poorer there or the income from rice larger, but simply because of the denser population. The Northeast is a barren area, by no means all planted. There are considerable variations, for climatic reasons, in the area planted to rice, but rice is plainly preferred. It may be that limited amounts of rice land were planted to kenaf in 1961 and 1964, but this is clearly not the rule. In the provinces all round Roi Et, where rural population is less dense, new land is opened up for kenaf; the comparative advantage of kenaf in these other provinces is not greater than in Roi Et, but there is no need there, because empty land is available, to increase the risk of having insufficient rice. The other crops grown all have the appearance of supplementary crops grown to raise a cash income when subsistence needs have been met.

Wang Yao, the village to which I was sent, was in the district of Pontong, one of the areas newly opened to road transport, and less densely settled than most of Roi Et. Hence it was a fairly favourable situation for kenaf and a good many of the farmers were growing it. They were interested in growing more; three, when asked about investing a hypothetical windfall, mentioned planting kenaf or buying land for kenaf. Yet in every case, in spite of a considerably higher income yield from kenaf, enough rice land at least to secure rice for family consumption remained a priority.

In Wang Yao road transport was also an important feature of development. A road was in course of construction and, as is usual in Thailand, trucks were already using the road track, though it was barely passable and often dangerous. The money cost of transport had not yet fallen much, but its cost in time had fallen appreciably, since Wang Yao was ten kilometres from its nearest market centre.

There had been a notable expansion of interest in kenaf growing about four years before my visit and in beans and cucumbers two years later. Increased interest in vegetables had spread from their production for family use and had been accompanied by increased use of insecticides. The increased interest in kenaf had apparently preceded the arrival of road transport at the village. Previously buffalo carts had been used to transport it to the nearest market.

In Wang Yao local traders carried limited stocks of fertiliser and insecticide, but shopkeepers reported that nearly all farmers

Table 7.6 Basic data and leading crops in *changwat* Nakhon Ratchasima,[a] 1959-65

		1959	1960	1961	1962	1963	1964	1965
Rice	Bangkok wholesale price, *bt*/kg paddy	0·85	0·91	1·10	0·96	0·77	0·83	1·21
	Area planted, 000 *rai*	n.a.	n.a.	1,176·1	1,407·5	n.a.	n.a.	n.a.
	Area harvested, 000 *rai*	648·9	395·8	868·1	1,187·9	1,325·9	1,589·9	n.a.
	Yield, kg per *rai*	171	81	188	232	223	235	n.a.
	Output, 000 metric tons	110·8	32·0	163·5	276·1	295·8	373·7	
Kenaf	Bangkok wholesale price, *bt*/kg	2·24	3·17	3·61	2·33	2·73	2·75	3·02
	Area planted, 000 *rai*	34·3	n.a.	200·2	58·16	120·4	169·6	
	Area harvested, 000 *rai*	32·7	n.a.	184·5	55·02	115·0	168·4	
	Yield, kg per *rai*	150	n.a.	200	200	250	254	
	Output, 000 metric tons	4·91	n.a.	36·9	11·0	28·8	42·10	
Maize	Bangkok wholesale price, *bt*/kg	1·00	1·01	1·12	1·01	1·06	1·08	1·22
	Area planted, 000 *rai*	75·3	n.a.	137·0	126·6	136·2	148·7	260·3
	Area harvested, 000 *rai*	74·4	n.a.	111·1	123·8	124·8	148·5	249·6
	Yield, kg per *rai*	300	n.a.	250	250	300	250	200
	Output, 000 metric tons	22·31	n.a.	27·78	30·94	37·43	37·13	49·9
Castor bean	Bangkok wholesale price, *bt*/kg	2·35	2·93	2·60	2·04	2·40	2·40	2·17
	Area planted, 000 *rai*	36·0	n.a.	109·0	99·8	72·87	73·29	74·3
	Area harvested, 000 *rai*	31·6	n.a.	105·7	99·6	72·38	72·08	69·4
	Yield, kg per *rai*	225	n.a.	120	120	200	210	140
	Output, 000 metric tons	7·12	n.a.	12·69	11·95	14·48	15·14	9·7

[a] Agricultural Population 1960, 000, 918·2, area, km² 19,590, cultivated area 26%, crop land irrigated 29%. Other non-rice crops occupying > 1% harvested area 1964, 000 *rai*:
Sugar-cane 46·9, groundnuts 46·7, cassava 42·6, bananas 13·9, short chillies 10·6, long chillies 9·4, cotton 8·7.

Sources: Statistical Year Books, 1963, 1965; U.S.O.M./N.S.O., *Changwat-Amphur Statistical Directory,* 1965; Ministry of Agriculture, *Agricultural Statistics of Thailand,* 1965; *Annual Reports on Rice Production,* 1961, 1962; 'Statistics of the Planting of Upland and Garden Crops', 1959, mimeo. (*Changwat* Series), 1961, 1962, 1963, 1964, 1965.

now travelled regularly to Pontong and usually bought supplies there. There was as yet little interest in modern investment in farming: nearly all the farmers would spend windfalls on livestock or buying land.

The second *changwat* visited in the Northeast was Nakhon Ratchasima, the nearest in the Northeast to Bangkok, and also the most prosperous, mainly as a result of the building by the Americans of the Friendship Highway; this has led to an enormous increase in traffic to and from Bangkok. Rather more than three-quarters of the cultivated land is rice land, but there has been much development of other crops. Kenaf expanded nearly six-fold in the boom year of 1961, fell back to a little over double the previous area and has since expanded again to nearly the 1961 level. Maize and castor beans have both expanded to approximately double the 1959 level, cassava has expanded in the last few years and sugar-cane and groundnuts are also important but more or less stationary crops. Information about the leading crops in Nakhon Ratchasima is given in Table 7.6.

At least a part of the development seems to be a result of the rapid growth of Nakhon Ratchasima City (Korat). There are additional reasons for the rapid growth of Korat, apart from the agricultural development of the surrounding region: Americans from the nearby air-base with plenty of spare cash, and also the development of road transport both northward to Khon Kaen and through to Laos, and eastward to Roi Et and Ubon Ratchathani (Ministry of Agriculture, 1964). The proximity of a rapidly growing city has encouraged enterprise in the surrounding country-side, mainly in the form of stimulating demand for cash income. New crops such as vegetables can be grown.

Nevertheless my subjective impression should be reported that in Korat and its neighbourhood there was some feeling of a relaxation of effort. In a sense growth had become accepted and expected, but there was also a sense that a peak had been passed. This impression may, perhaps, be influenced unduly by the village I visited.

The village of Bankhok is part of the *tambon* of Phlapphla in the district of Chokchai. In the second part of the National Development Plan Chokchai was to have been the starting point for a new national highway to Buri Ram and Ubon Ratchathani, improving the transport system for much of the kenaf country

(N.E.D.B., 1964: map opp. p. 114; n.d.: 25-56). The contractor defaulted leaving the work less than half finished (N.E.D.B., 1966: 43). This must have led to some discouragement in government and business in Chokchai, though it was only once mentioned to me there.

In Bankhok as in Nongproe the effects of new transport had had some time to take effect. The road to the village was ten years old, and a bus service ran from the village itself right to Korat, thirty kilometres away, every day. Everyone in the village went to Korat; four-fifths had visited Bangkok, and more than 10 per cent of the adults went there regularly for part time work. Most of those I interviewed had introduced innovations in recent years: some had begun growing kenaf or cotton, some were beginning to use fertiliser, insecticide, or weed-killer, some had begun growing vegetables on the suggestion of the agricultural officer; there was also a new interest in mechanisation; two farmers had recently begun hiring tractors and two had bought mechanical irrigation pumps.

The village had a government irrigation scheme covering just over half the rice fields, and there was a local co-operative irrigating the rest; both of these had been in operation some seven years. It was difficult to identify the source of different developments. There was certainly no expressed interest in investment among the farmers I interviewed,[4] yet most of them seemed to be responding slowly to the changes that had taken place in their environment some years earlier.

South Region

The South Region is interesting in that it has the highest domestic product and income per head in the kingdom (N.S.O., 1962-3, S. Region and *Whole Kingdom* vols.), but is also the only region in which gross domestic product was falling during the period covered by the regional domestic product figures (N.E.D.B., 1964: 41-4). It is interesting also because the policy problems are peculiarly puzzling: the situation appears to be one in which considerable

---

[4] Interest in investment was assessed by their response to questions about the use of a hypothetical gift of money. Usually my interviewing conditions were fairly informal and relaxed, in the interviewee's home. The interviews in Bankhok took place in more formal conditions in a private room, and may have been less favourable to expression of such interests.

potentialities for growth exist if certain difficulties outside the strictly economic sphere can be overcome, yet the difficulties are intractable because of political and related problems obstructing the more obvious solutions.

There is no difficulty in isolating the main reason for the decline. It is the long-run fall in the price of natural rubber, foreseen many years ago but not adequately forestalled because of the difficulties of achieving adequate planting of high-yielding strains of rubber by the thousands of small growers whose relations with the government have been marked by suspicion and reserve. These difficulties have been discussed in chapter 4.

A comparison of the regional domestic product and expenditure of the South with other regions has already been given in Table 6.1; the more detailed figures in Table 7.7 show that—largely as a result of profits from tin and rubber—excess of income over the visible items of expenditure, of about a billion *baht* in 1963, existed either as an export surplus or as unrecorded capital formation in the South. It seems probable that a good deal of this was an export surplus, building up accumulations invested principally by the banks in developments elsewhere.[5]

If there were good prospects for growth, much of this surplus could be invested in the South, giving rise to further growth. This involves decisions both concerning the method of modernising whatever is retained of the rubber industry and as to the extent to which alternative crops should be fostered. It is difficult to obtain adequate information on which to base decisions. Apart from rubber—concerning which the statistical difficulties have been discussed in chapter 4—some of the important agricultural products in the South are tree fruits the statistics of which are not available even on a regional basis except in the census year. An analysis in terms of the principal crops in the crop reports is seriously misleading unless supplemented by other information which can usually not be given in a statistical form. Table 7.8, however, brings together information about tree crops and field crops for the different Southern *changwats* in the census year 1962-3.

South Thailand is a good deal less dependent on rubber for its agricultural income than Malaysia, even though their economies are moderately similar. The soil is rather more fertile, producing

---

[5] Information based on interviews in banks in the southeast.

Table 7.7 South Region: family income and expenditure statistics, 1963
(*baht*)

| | Villages | | Towns | | Whole |
	Per family	Total	Per family	Total	Region
Income					
Cash income	7,433	3,898m	14,471	1,408m	5,306m
Income in kind	1,630	855m	773	75m	930m
Total	9,063	4,753m	15,244	1,483m	6,236m
Income from rice	n.a.	n.a.	n.a.	n.a.	730m
Income from other					
agriculture	n.a.	n.a.	n.a.	n.a.	2,734m
All other income	n.a.	n.a.	n.a.	n.a.	5,884m
Total income	n.a.	n.a.	n.a.	n.a.	9,348m
Expenditure					
Income in kind	1,630	855m	773	75m	930m
Rice	550	288m	788	77m	365m
Other food	2,132	1,118m	4,926	479m	1,597m
Taxes, gifts, and services	2,747	1,441m	5,287	515m	1,956m
All other	1,884	988m	2,735	266m	1,254m
Total	7,313	3,835m	13,736	1,337m	5,172m
Total cash and kind	8,943	4,690m	14,509	1,412m	6,102m
Other expenditures					
Govt and private					
constructions	n.a.	n.a.	n.a.	n.a.	539m
Govt admin., defence,					
education, medicine	n.a.	n.a.	n.a.	n.a.	446m
Total known	n.a.	n.a.	n.a.	n.a.	7,432m

Note: The population figures used were those from 1960 given in the *Whole Kingdom* volume of the *Household Expenditure Survey*.

Sources: N.S.O., *Household Expenditure Survey*, 1963, *Southern Region*, Tables 1:0, 1:1 and 1:5, *Whole Kingdom* volume, Table L; National Income Division of the Office of the N.E.D.B., *Regional Gross Domestic Product*, 1964 ed., Tables 1, 3, and VI.1.

a fair range of alternative crops, though most of them could not compete with high-yielding rubber even at recent low prices. Moreover the rainfall is more highly concentrated, giving a total of under two hundred tapping days in most Thai areas, as against over two hundred and fifty in Malaysia;[6] this does away with one of rubber's chief advantages as a peasant crop, its yield of an income almost throughout the year.

[6] Information based on local information from farmers and from the Thantho rubber research station.

Table 7.8 South Region: principal field crops and tree crops[a] by province, area planted, and number of trees, 1962-3

Province	Principal field crop	Area planted 000 rai	Second principal field crop	Area planted 000 rai	Principal tree crop	Number of trees 000	Second principal tree crop	Number of trees 000
East Coast								
Chumphon	Pineapples	6·1	*Namlawa* bananas	3·0	Betel nut	2,115	Rambutan	191
Surat Thani	Sugar-cane	11·3	Pineapples	10·2	Betel nut	998	Rambutan	334
Nakhon Si Thammaret	*Namlawa* bananas	15·4	Pineapples	12·5	Betel nut	2,858	Oranges (all kinds)	349
Phathalung	Pineapples	5·3	Other bananas	2·7	Betel nut	772	Oranges (all kinds)	202
Songkhla	*Namlawa* bananas	14·5	Cassava	14·1	Oranges (all kinds)	712	Sugarpalm	528
Pattani	*Namlawa* bananas	2·7	Cassava	2·1	Betel nut	271	Rambutan	165
Narathiwat	Cassava	7·5	Pineapples	6·7	Betel nut	246	Rambutan	154
West Coast								
Ranong	*Namlawa* bananas	0·7	Cassava	0·7	Betel nut	218	Jack fruit	36
Phang-nga	Cassava	1·3	Pineapples	1·1	Betel nut	82	Durian	75
Phuket	Pineapples	7·6	*Namlawa* bananas	1·9	Durian	33	Betel nut	19
Krabi	Cassava	4·0	*Namlawa* bananas	2·6	Betel nut	258	Jack fruit	72
Trang	Other bananas	1·6	*Namlawa* bananas	1·5	Betel nut	566	Oranges (all kinds)	86
Satun	*Namlawa* bananas	1·3	Pineapples	0·6	Betel nut	83	Oranges (all kinds)	53
Interior								
Yala	Other bananas	2·4	*Namlawa* bananas	2·4	Betel nut	150	Oranges (all kinds)	131

[a] Excluding rubber and coconut trees.

Sources: Ministry of Agriculture, *Crop Reports* (*Changwat* Series), 1962; N.S.O., *Census of Agriculture*, 1963, South Region volume.

Hence, though rubber is usually the chief income earner and export of the region, any account of south Thailand's agriculture must pay attention to other crops.

Rice for family use is grown by a high proportion of the rubber growers and other farmers. In Yala and Narathiwat, and even in the crowded and prosperous mining island of Phuket there is some subsistence cultivation of rice. We can, however, say little with confidence about the area under rice (or, for that matter, under other crops) in this region, because the statistics here are the least reliable in the kingdom. Not only is there a great deal of illegal occupation of land;[7] the agricultural staff is also seriously inadequate. It is also profitable to smuggle rice across the southern border into Malaysia where the price is not kept down by an export duty. In the immediate post-war years this was a very important trade; in the 1950s it had dwindled but a good deal was still carried by casual labour which used to cross the border. This movement is no longer permitted and rice smuggling is now believed in the south to be unimportant. However, a good deal of secretiveness still surrounds rice dealings. The general movement of rice is southward, both from other regions into south Thailand and from Nakhon Si Thammaret and Phatalung, rice surplus areas, to the provinces further south. Probably rice will never be more than a subsistence crop in most southern provinces. What other crops are available if the proportion of rubber is to decline?

The potential for other crops is probably quite high. Coconuts were exported from the west coast provinces in the south before rubber became important, and a considerable surplus is still produced there. In 1961, the only year for which *changwat* figures for a few tree crops are available in the crop reports, some 60,000 *rai* were planted with coconuts in the six west coast provinces (*Crop Reports*, 1961). The east coast provinces had, however, become the most important producers, especially Surat Thani which had half the total area of coconuts in the south—over 200,000 *rai* in the one province. One of the industries proposed in the Southern Development Plan was copra production (N.E.D.B., 1964-6: 104). The small province of Phang-nga has increased its production of cassava to become one of the major producers outside the Southeast, and cassava which grows everywhere in the south could be expanded as an export, with processing probably at Trang or Kentang.

---

[7] Information based on local statements from many government officials.

The east coast provinces send fruit to the Bangkok market—pineapples, bananas, and some watermelons are recorded in the crop reports. The Census of Agriculture and the *Changwat-Amphur Statistical Directory* also list a number of tree fruits in these *changwats*—durians and rambutans in Chumphon, Surat Thani, Nakhon Si Thammaret and elsewhere, oranges in Songkhla and other *changwats* (U.S.O.M./N.S.O., 1965). Cultivation of fruit could probably be expanded if rubber became much less profitable.

At present, in spite of the narrowness of the peninsula there is a sharp difference between the economies of the east and the west coast provinces. The east coast economy is Bangkok-oriented. Most trade goes north up the Gulf of Thailand. From the west coast provinces, Ranong, Phang-nga, Phuket, Krabi, Trang, and Satun, virtually all trade has until recently been with the Malaysian port of Penang.[8] Improvement of the main road has led to a trickle of fruit to Bangkok, and this will no doubt increase when the modern highway from Bangkok to the south is finished.[9]

There are still no ports for ocean-going vessels in the south, though several sites on the east coast are believed to be capable of development and one is to be selected on engineering and economic grounds. If the west coast provinces are to continue to produce for export to the west there might be an advantage in developing Kentang, or perhaps Krabi, provided that engineering studies show this to be feasible. The ports may be improved under the Southern Development Plan, but only for coastal traffic (N.E.D.B., 1964-6: 62).

Development of the south has received a good deal of attention, and the army is actively concerned with agricultural progress in the border areas. There has, however, been a great deal of uncertainty about the economic future of the area and frequent changes in the plans. Much has been spent on transport yet most of the key routes remain incomplete. Problems of widespread illegal land tenure and

[8] Satun, though the nearest west coast province to Malaysia, is comparatively little developed, has poor shipping facilities and sends much of its produce through Hadyai and Songkhla to Bangkok.

[9] There have been great and not obviously explicable delays in completing the last thirty kilometres of the highway to the south and to Malaysia. All but this short stretch north of Ranong has now been completed for over five years. This highway is scheduled as part of the Economic Commission for Asia and the Far East's proposed Asian Highway.

M

of influence by Malaysian Chinese merchants over the local bureaucracy need to be tackled with firmness and in a constructive spirit.

The main problem of the south, however, is the choice of a policy toward the rubber industry. The first plan for the south was drawn up before the long-run decline in the price of rubber had become a reality. An increase of 25 per cent in output was planned, and this was easily achieved by 1965. However, a much larger yield per *rai* is needed if the industry is to survive in future, and this will involve capital expenditure which will not be incurred either by estates or by the small rubber growers themselves without official encouragement.

The foregoing survey indicates that alternatives are available, though at some cost to the standard of living of the south. However, most of these will also involve some government action. Some of the policy problems are discussed in chapter 9.

In the South Region I made no detailed village studies, and most of my interviews were with traders, bankers, and officials. I visited seven of the fourteen *changwats*, but did not collect *changwat* annual reports or apply questionnaires. The two *changwats* in which I interviewed farmers were Nakhon Si Thammaret and Phuket, but the interviews were insufficiently standardised to justify separate presentation.

In the Southern *changwats* there was far more scepticism about the Ministry of Agriculture statistics than in other regions, even among agricultural officials themselves, and almost everywhere a tendency to believe that the Census of Agriculture was much more accurate. The main reason given was serious shortages of trained staff in these more remote provinces.

Comparison of Village Data

Most of the village data which I collected by questionnaires, though standardised in several ways, are on too small a scale, with far too many variables, to lead to any statistically interesting comparative results except as part of a wider project. It may, however, be worthwhile to draw some comparisons partly in statistical and partly in descriptive terms.

Table 7.9 sets out some of the characteristics of the villages. Radios per family may be taken as one index of awareness of general news and relevant market information—which is regularly broadcast. This seems to be related, not to general accessibility but to proximity to a large city—Bangkok for Huey Khanlaen, Don-mottanoi, and Nongproe; Nakhon Sawan for Khok Maw—and hence to reception facilities. There is a desire for contact where the instrument to achieve it is effective, even in villages with poor transport and hence infrequent personal travel.

Mechanisation—mainly the use of large hired tractors—has spread over most of the area of the Central Plain. Insecticide and fertiliser have been tried out lately mainly in villages recently introducing vegetable planting, usually as a result of new transport.

It does not, however, seem possible to range the villages in any kind of scale which will correlate well with acceptance of change and modernisation. By almost any criterion Donmottanoi was the most modern of the villages and Nongproe the second, and this was related to their production of vegetables (and ducks in Nong-proe) for the Bangkok market, and their good transport system. By almost any criterion Wang Yao was the most backward, with poor transport in a relatively remote district in a migration-loss *changwat* in the Northeast. Yet the recent arrival of the road had introduced vigorous change in Wang Yao, even though it was change from a low level. Some of the difficulties of arranging the others in any significant order may be illustrated by comparing Singh with Bankhok and Khok Maw with Donghadnak.

Singh was part of a long settled area, where the international rice trade had led to development along the banks of the river, and then as a result of a monoculture economy over many years substantial inequalities of landholding had developed. The majority of the villagers were poor and most of the rice surplus was either paid to landlords as rent or sold in advance to finance consumption. Change from this situation had been initiated fairly recently by local pump-irrigation, made possible by the more stabilised water level in the river, and by the introduction of suitable cash crops, mainly on the initiative of a keen district official who owned some land in the village.

Bankhok had started from a much lower basic level of income. Much of the rice surplus had come to be sold for export, but this led to real hardship because the rice harvest left a smaller margin and was less reliable than in the flood plain of the Chao Phaya River. However, new development had been stimulated rather earlier than in Singh, and the agent of the change was a rapidly growing town not far away. Traders had come more frequently to

Table 7.9 Basic data about villages visited on field trip, 1967

Village	Population	Families	Radios	Village shops	Principal products	Principal innovations	No. of graduates Junior High	No. of graduates Senior High	Modern transport
Nongproe (Chon Buri)	350	80	70	11	Rice Vegetables Ducks	Vegetables Ducks	20	1	Road A
Wang Yao (Roi Et)	1,805	224	30+	3	Rice Kenaf Vegetables Livestock	Kenaf Insecticide	6	0	Road B
Bankhok (Nakhon Ratchasima)	350	70	40+	4ª	Rice Kenaf Kapok	Cash crops Mechanisation	10	3	Road A
Donghadnak (Chiang Mai)	1,730	380	about 200	6	Rice Groundnuts Tobacco Garlic	Fertiliser Mechanisation	4	0	Road A River
Khok Maw (Nakhon Sawan)	464	90	about 90	6	Rice Chillies Tobacco Egg plant	Insecticide Fertiliser	7	1	River
Singh (Sing Buri)	400	73	60	1	Rice Sugar-cane Fruit	Mechanisation Insecticide Fertiliser	10	1	Road C

Huey Khanlaen (Ang Thong)	1,045	188	180	3	Rice	Mechanisation	15	4	None
Donmottanoi (Ratchaburi)	850	146	about 230	7	Chillies Onions Garlic Taro Rice	Mechanisation Improved fertiliser and insecticide	20	4	Road A

[a] Shops in adjacent village only.
A = effective all-weather.
B = dry weather only.
C = dry weather road near, but not reaching.

the village, and the villagers themselves had taken to travelling often to a modern city.

The character of the physical and institutional causes of change had affected the form which development took. In Singh there was a sense that the farmers were improving themselves by co-operation, experiment, and study of new techniques, under the rather paternal guidance of a government official who himself came from a farming family. It was rather a self-conscious attempt to adopt scientific methods, not often well understood, partly out of respect for a successful and sympathetic official.

In Bankhok the modern world had impinged from outside, and the impact had occurred long enough ago for the village to feel backward, though the techniques in use were probably more scientific and certainly more capital intensive than in Singh. Modernisation was being felt as a pressure to keep up rather than as the opening up of new possibilities.

Turning to Khok Maw and Donghadnak, both were in *changwats* where rapid change was taking place and both were relatively far from the focus of this change. In Khok Maw the change was initiated mainly by irrigation, though here its effect had been rather paradoxical. Its impact on the water level for the former main crop, rice, was adverse. The village relied on the peak flood level, and the stabilisation of the water level had meant that it had to rely on rain or pump irrigation. On the other hand irrigation works had so improved its transport system that rapid contact with Chumsaeng, and quite practicable contact by water with Nakhon Sawan, were now a part of the villagers' lives. These affected their awareness of new methods and their consumption horizons. On the other hand, largely because it had no road, the village had little experience of mechanisation.

Donghadnak had built its own road, just over a kilometre long, to join the main highway, and had ceased to use water transport though the river had once been its main means of communication. It was far from Chiang Mai, and the variable level of the river made it unnavigable for part of the year. The main sources of change, however, were the efficient extension services and the keenness of the farmers themselves. Recently the extension services had operated through the irrigation co-operative.

In neither of these villages had a high proportion of the villagers travelled beyond their own *changwat*. Change had come to them from forces bringing new developments to their *changwat* from elsewhere. Isolation had been only partly destroyed because communications were still fairly difficult; but contact both through travel and through trade had been sufficient to change economic life quite markedly.

8

Factors Promoting Growth

In a contact economy such as that of Thailand we must attempt to explain economic development in terms not only of increased factor supplies and of technical change but also of movements of factors into new places, new combinations, new opportunities. Overcoming previous immobility of factors is sometimes the key to development, though new capital or technical progress or both may be necessary to bring this about.

Either an outflow or an inflow of factors may be favourable to growth according to circumstances. These circumstances may have a bearing on the macro-economic or the micro-economic situation; and it is not always true that trusting individuals to follow their own interest will always work to promote growth over the economy as a whole. Steps need to be taken to ensure that growth can sustain itself, and then to attract appropriate factors to mitigate inflationary pressure. When growth has been initiated it may need to be sustained by an inflow of labour, or even enterprise or capital.

(a) *Sources of growth.* Thailand's rural development—in those areas where there has been development—has been due to elements that can be classified along the lines indicated above. First there has been an increase in the supply of factors of production. Naturally, as in all the less developed countries, there has been an increase in the population (Caldwell, 1967: 35). This in itself is only a source of potentially impoverishing growth: it puts a strain on capital supplies and makes difficulties associated with limited supplies of land and minerals more severe. Almost its only advantage, in comparison with a more stable population, is that it promotes more flexibility in the installation of capital or the trying out of new techniques. However, other factors have been increasing more rapidly than population, mainly capital and skills of various kinds, and these have assisted some growth in rural incomes.[1] It is not, of course, only the capital invested in agriculture and other rural occupations, nor only the rural skills and techniques, that have a bearing on rural growth. There is some mobility, at least locally, between rural and urban sectors of the economy, and each has many impacts on the other. However, here we shall consider chiefly the capital and skills that have a direct bearing.

The new public capital formation has mainly contributed through transport and irrigation. Private capital formation has consisted of much private development of land,[2] some fairly considerable investment in mechanical equipment,[3] and a rapidly expanding investment in fertilisers (U.S.O.M., 1966: 31-2), pesticides and chemical weed-killers.[4] There has also been both public and private investment in road, rail, and river transport equipment.

Skills have been formed in the public sector mainly by the expansion and strengthening of Kasetsart University, producing more extension officers, co-operative officers etc., and the sending of students abroad for training in various fields of research relevant to

[1] The growth of capital formation is shown in N.S.O., 1964: Tables 25 onwards, and is discussed in the N.E.D.B.'s National Economic Development Plans. The growth of skills has been under study by the Manpower Division of the N.E.D.B. The best published source showing development over time is the joint Thai-U.S.O.M. study, *Preliminary Assessment of Education and Human Resources in Thailand*, Bangkok, 1963. See also Sundrum and Daroesman, 1960.

[2] Figures from National Income Statistics.

[3] According to the Census of Agriculture, which also certainly underestimated the degree of mechanisation, because of the prevalence of *ad hoc* hiring of tractors, the proportion of all farms using machinery in 1962 was 15 per cent. The proportion of the area would be considerably higher. The rate of gross capital formation in the private sector of agriculture more than doubled between 1956 and 1963, according to National Income Statistics. The Agricultural Statistics show a fourfold expansion in imports of machinery for soil preparation, and a more than threefold expansion in the import of water pumps between 1960 and 1965.

[4] Imports of fungicide and insecticide have increased sevenfold (by weight) in the decade to 1965. See Ministry of Agriculture, 1965, t. 100. The detailed trade returns show that the bulk of this is insecticide and fungicide and not the other items mentioned.

agriculture. In the private sector there has been considerable education of farmers, both by merchants and by one another, in the techniques of planting export crops—maize, kenaf, mung-beans, cassava, sugar-cane—and also vegetables and fruits. Both of these developments were made possible by the very considerable expansion of both primary and secondary education spreading out from the palace in the last quarter of the nineteenth century until at least primary education had reached virtually every village by the 1920s.

The source of the new public capital was partly foreign aid and partly the continuing foreign demand for Thailand's main export product, rice, the export of which was heavily taxed and the proceeds used for public purposes. The resulting low price of rice lowered the Thai cost of living and stimulated the export of other crops where new land could be developed. There may, however, have been difficulties in finding the necessary capital for the production of these export crops over most of Thailand. Kenaf in the Northeast expanded rapidly everywhere at the time of very high prices in 1960-1; but the other export crops have expanded rapidly in relatively limited areas where entrepreneurs with capital are likely to have been attracted on other grounds. It is not possible to say with any confidence that capital, or the enterprise to promote a new export crop, was the bottleneck, but it seems probable (see ch. 6).

The combination of capital equipment and new skills has made possible some new methods: superior varieties through seed selection; mechanised pump irrigation and ploughing; scientific control of some pests and weeds. It is largely these things which have been responsible for the increases in yields per *rai*, where these have occurred.

A fair proportion, however, of the development which has occurred has resulted from a simple transfer of factors of production from areas or products in which they were previously unemployed or underemployed, to new areas or products. In several respects Thailand is unusually well fitted to take advantage of such movements, which may be made possible by new transport systems, education and the like, but do not use appreciably more of any factor of production than before.

(b) *Factors favouring change.* First, a highly commercial attitude to land gives a good deal of flexibility, and avoids many of the

problems which often arise from feudal relics, rigid village struct-
ures, excessive subdivision by inheritance and the like. This commercial attitude, however, did not arise from a functional economic
approach to land by the government. It came about partly because
the original royal grants were grants of quantities of land rather
than specific tracts, and partly because (under pressure of the need
to abolish extra-territorial rights) legal concepts and training were
hurriedly assimilated from the West (Wijeyewardene, 1967; Vella,
1955: 347-8).

Next, although like most traditional systems Thai economic
structure is based on superior-inferior relations, these relations are
reasonably well adapted to rapid change and development. The
Thai patronage system is more flexible than the superior-inferior
relations of many traditional societies (Van Roy, 1967; Evers and
Silcock, 1967; Wilson, 1962: chs. 2, 3; Hanks, 1962: 1247-61).
The mutual and temporary character of client-patron relations
brings them near to a contractual system. From the point of view
of development they are probably less efficient than a modern
credit structure, but they can play a useful role in promoting local
irrigation and other rural development. It is important that a
nucleus of professionally minded bureaucrats should succeeed in
separating itself from the network of patronage, but that is another
matter (Silcock, 1967: ch. 4 and App. B).

Thailand is fortunate also in its cultural capacity to assimilate its highly capable and industrious Chinese minority. The
Chinese business structure is a most effective instrument of development, providing—in highly competitive conditions—credit,
incentive goods, information, and market services to farmers
previously working on a subsistence basis (Skinner, 1957, 99-
109). This structure is, however, far less effective in carrying on
the business of the economy once an appreciable number of the
merchants acquire enough wealth and influence to affect local
political power. It is not inherently a competitive system, because
it lacks the West's cultural, social, and political barriers to the
invasion by wealth of the social and political process (Silcock,
1967: ch. 8).

Another special feature of Thai society is the expectation of
leadership from the government, especially from the king, in the
process of modernisation. This expectation was successfully built
up by the monarchy under the Chakkri dynasty, and it has made

the Thais more pragmatic and less millennial about change than the inhabitants of most development countries. There is no expectation that the expulsion of a few colonialists or neo-colonialists can usher in a golden age. This makes extension work relatively easier in Thailand, and lowers the obstacles to adaptation. It has, however, one disadvantage: the popular attitude of submission to the wishes of authority makes it more difficult for the bureaucracy to learn from the felt needs of the farmers, and from their local experience. The prestige of foreign degrees and training makes Thailand exceptionally subject to a Duesenberry effect of conspicuous consumption of capital-intensive gadgetry. It is in Thai industry that the cult of modernity in place of science does most harm (Silcock, 1967: ch. 11); but even in agriculture there seems to be a disproportionate promotion of tractors and mechanical irrigation pumps in comparison with new hand-tools, pest control techniques, and seed selection.

It has often been emphasised that the Thai government has concentrated a high proportion of its development funds on rural infrastructure investment, but it is not usually recognised that there are special circumstances which make the economy unusually responsive to such investment.

The Thai economy was traditionally one based on canal-fed irrigation for the cultivation of wet rice.[5] Modern canal locks were introduced by private enterprise and these led to the recognition by King Chulalongkorn, early in the twentieth century, that scientific irrigation could bring great advantages to Thailand. A Dutch engineer, I. H. Van der Heide, was invited to help, and as early as 1907 a scheme was recommended based on a high dam across the Chao Phaya River at Chai Nat (Ingram, 1955: 80-7). This scheme was delayed for over forty years and was even then cut down as too expensive, because of Thai fears that indebtedness to foreigners would threaten Thailand's sovereignty.

Similar considerations applied to the building of roads. Railways had been built for political purposes, and the royal government was determined that they should remain solvent. Hence long after

---

[5] It is not clear whether the Thais were already using canals for irrigation before they came from Central Asia to the northern part of modern Thailand. Canal irrigation was almost certainly a Thai practice in the Sukothai period, and when they were under Khmer rule they clearly absorbed many Khmer ideas about the central role of irrigation in the state.

an integrated system of government had been introduced throughout the country, the building of roads which might compete with
the railway was held up.

The railway network was completely focused on Bangkok. Road
links not related to Bangkok were almost non-existent, and trade
was almost wholly related either to export or to meeting the capital's needs.

A focus of this kind is relatively harmless in a subsistence
economy but, particularly after the forced efforts to industrialise
during World War II, the absence of road communications came
to be considered a serious handicap. In modern Thailand the
demand for transport of goods and passengers is acute; whenever
the season allows it, trucks and buses go far beyond the limits of
the existing road system, over any tracks that are available. Roads
are built in Thailand to meet an acute felt need.

While the recent period of rapidly developing transport has seen
increasing concentration of the main export crops, a different trend
is evident in the crops produced mainly for local consumption. In
many areas improved transport facilities have led almost immediately to experiments with new crops either for a market in a nearby
town or for national distribution. Instances already mentioned
include the spread of chillies and onions from the southwest to the
northern valleys; watermelons are spreading from the neighbourhood of Bangkok further out into the Central Plain and the northeast. Groundnuts are also being being planted in more and more
areas (*Crop Reports*, 1959-65).

This development may in part result from the increase of cash
income from exports as diversification has proceeded. Most rice
cultivators either grow kitchen garden crops for their own needs or
exchange rice for a few supplementary foods. Their rice surplus is
commonly sold in advance to settle debts incurred for emergencies
or household consumption, so that little is available to sell for
cash. The switch to export crops has probably meant that more
cash is available for buying supplementary foods.

The pattern of planting of these crops for local use changes
every year, but generally the proportion of the whole area planted
in the three leading provinces has declined over the last few years
for which figures are available (see ch. 5, t. 5.8). Clearly there is
a good deal of experimentation, but as yet the influence of specialisation is not sufficient to offset the two factors making for disper-

Table 8.1   Growth of principal types of crop by region compared with population, 1952-65

Crops	North	Northeast	Regions Central	South	Years
Area under maize, mung-	81	379	531	31	1952-4
beans, cassava, and	129	546	1,040	125	1956-8
sugar-cane in 000 *rai*	110	674	2,696	133	1960-2
	127	606	4,683	145	1963-5
Area under castor beans,	164	246	607	418	1952-4
groundnuts, sesame, soya-	143	370	851	478	1956-8
beans and coconuts in	205	447	1,056	560	1960-2
000 *rai*	270	455	1,204	678	1963-5
Area under cotton, kapok	21[a]	166[a]	94[a]	0[a]	1952-4
and bombax, jute, kenaf	41[b]	318[b]	230[b]	13[b]	1956-8
and ramie in 000 *rai*	59	1,359	370	8	1960-2
	97	1,861	470	13	1963-5
Area under garden crops,	122[c]	109[c]	78[c]	2,404[c]	1952-4
fruits, rubber, and tobacco	199[d]	250[d]	273[d]	2,840[d]	1956-8
in 000 *rai*	226[e]	436[e]	502[e]	3,244[e]	1960-2
	374	607	936	3,621	1963-5
Area under all non-rice	389[ac]	934[ac]	1,312[ac]	2,856[ac]	1952-4
crops in 000 *rai*	512[bd]	1,484[bd]	2,432[bd]	3,459[bd]	1956-8
	600[e]	2,932[e]	4,625[e]	3,944[e]	1960-2
	769	3,529	7,306	4,457	1963-5
Area under rice in 000	2,340	2,340	13,273	17,075	1952-4
rai	2,413	2,413	13,126	16,743	1956-8
	2,598	2,598	15,928	17,580	1960-2
	2,655	2,655	15,858	19,109	1963-5
Population estimates	2,381	7,280	8,125	2,534	1952-4
in 000[f]	2,728	8,350	9,335	2,834	1956-8
	3,024	9,275	10,278	3,332	1960-2
	3,238	9,848	10,986	3,512	1963-5
Non-rice area per head	0·16	0·13	0·16	1·13	1952-4
in *rai*	0·19	0·18	0·26	1·22	1956-8
	0·20	0·31	0·45	1·18	1960-2
	0·24	0·36	0·67	1·27	1963-5
Rice area per head	0·98	1·82	2·11	1·02	1952-4
in *rai*	0·88	1·57	1·79	1·00	1956-8
	0·86	1·72	1·71	0·90	1960-2
	0·82	1·61	1·74	0·93	1963-5

[a] Kapok and bombax not available.
[b] Kapok and bombax not available for 1956.
[c] Garden crops and fruits not available.
[d] Garden crops and fruits not available for 1956.

sion—increasing rural incomes and the increasing area which is accessible to the large Bangkok market.

In time, specialisation is likely to develop again, on a nation-wide basis, for these home-consumed crops. This can be expected to raise rural incomes further. At present a large number of new areas are being brought within reach of the national market, and this is the dominant influence.

(c) *Land resources and utilisation.* Of Thailand's total area of 514,000 square kilometres, or 320 million *rai*, some 60 million *rai* are watershed forest or otherwise unusable. Of the remaining 260 million *rai* of land area just under a third, or about 75 million *rai* are held in individual holdings (Krit, 1957: 3). The remainder is potentially available forest land. However, the area in individual holdings has nearly doubled since World War II. Though there is still land to spare, the government's policy at present is to limit the expansion of cultivation—for climatic and other reasons—to rather less than half the total area (N.E.D.B., 1964: 78).

The area of land occupied per head of population cannot be estimated year by year with any precision; in Table 3.8 the area under all crops, as given in the agricultural statistics, was compared with the total population. Coverage of the crops actually grown has improved during the period in view—e.g. cassava figures on a national basis are available only from 1956 and fruit and vege-tables from 1957. The true area per head in 1950 may have been 2·1 *rai* instead of 2·0. It appears, however, that over the post-war period the area per head has remained approximately constant, with a slight net fall to 1957, a rise during the period of Sarit's rule and a subsequent slight fall again. From 1947 to 1963 the population outside municipal areas rose from 15·76 million to 24·98 million, the municipal population having doubled (Silcock, 1967: 238-9). If we apply this growth rate to estimate for 1950 and 1965 the area in agricultural holdings per non-municipal inhabitant, this area has not changed, having been about 2¼ *rai* at the beginning and at the end.

---

e Garden crops and fruits not available for 1960.

f The regional population is not available for intercensal years. The *chang-wat* figures for 1947 and 1960 were used to derive regional figures and a straight-line trend fitted for each region.

Sources: Ministry of Agriculture, *Agricultural Statistics of Thailand, 1958, 1964* and *1965* and *Crop Reports* (Crop Series), 1961 and 1962.

In Table 8.1 we show the same material as in Table 3.8 but with more regional detail, for different points in time, so as to show how the different regions have responded and when. It is clear from this table both that the experience of the regions is different and that when area under the different types of crop is related to population the use of additional land is set in proper perspective. Only right at the end of the period has the area of non-rice crops increased markedly faster than population in every region. The rise in the Central Region has gone on fairly steadily, indicating a relative shift out of rice to almost every other variety of crop as a result of improved irrigation and transport and the low price of rice. In the North the increase in area of non-rice crops exceeds population growth only in the last period; but this is a slightly distorted picture. Better methods and better yields had come earlier, and the increase in area per head becomes possible with the opening up of Chiang Rai and the increasing settlement of upland areas (Chapman, 1967: 3; U.S.O.M., n.d.). The increase in the Northeast comes with the kenaf boom in 1961. In the South the main influence is the irregular increase in the planting of low-yielding smallholder rubber.

We know from the analysis by regions and crops that though similar and pervading pressures operated through the whole of this already loosely-structured economy—namely changes in infra-structure to facilitate development and high rice taxes to impel it—the immediate agents of change were different in different parts of the country.

In the Far North deliberate and skilled extension work, combined with irrigation, has been an important stimulus (see ch. 7). All over the country vegetable crops have been spread by small merchants following the new roads, and, by supplying fertiliser and pesticides, helping the farmers to expand the crops formerly grown in household gardens (see ch. 5). In the Northeast kenaf spread like a fire once the government factories had given the initial impulse; and some of its effects on the soil, and on quality levels, have been harmful, requiring government remedial action (see ch. 4). The main new export crops have been developed in a few limited areas, probably stimulated by the initiative of active entrepreneurs attracted to these areas by other profit opportunities (see chs. 5 and 6).

(d) *Land and irrigation ideologies.* In the management of both land and water resources Thai policy is strongly influenced by ideological considerations, which do not always coincide with the needs of economic development. Land policy is strongly committed to the idea of the independent, land-owning farmer. Irrigation policy is influenced by the idea that irrigation ought to be a free service. Both these policies can be presented in terms of a commitment to the welfare of the poorest citizens. Yet in fact Thai taxation is very regressive in its effects, and Thai overall planning policy gives little attention to the promotion of movement out of agriculture which is the chief way in which farmers benefit from economic progress.

We have seen that pledging of rice land sometimes led to ownership by middlemen usually interested in control of a source of supply, but sometimes merely in a traditional investment. The reaction of Thai specialists to this problem has been a political reaction, based on the need to guarantee the small Thai farmer the ownership of his land (Chaiyong, n.d.).

Highly elaborate schemes of registration, rent-control, pre-emption and the like have been suggested, designed to promote more land ownership by farmers in the Central Plain, and to allow only some very limited and controlled opening up of land on a plantation basis elsewhere. These schemes must be judged in the light of the inability of the existing Land Department to survey more than about half the land in the Central Plain over the past fifty years, and the fact that over the greater part of Thailand full legal titles to land are almost non-existent. Clearly any attempt to expand an underpaid civil service rapidly to undertake, in remote rural areas, tasks that run counter to strong economic pressures would merely lead to wholesale corruption and obstruction. A long step towards reality has been taken in the second development plan, which envisages a detailed land census over twelve years, with classification of land capability over twenty years (N.E.D.B., 1967: 131). Both of these were originally envisaged as short-term projects to be linked to a program of wholesale rent control, freezing of existing tenures, and land redistribution.

Moreover, in the south it has now been recognised that some method of grouping holdings together must be found. There has also been some shift of emphasis in the co-operative movement towards using co-operatives as instruments for development rather than as protection for the small farmer against indebtedness.

N

The basis of land policy in Thailand is further discussed in chapter 10.

The origins of the Thai attitude to irrigation have been discussed in chapter 1 and some of the problems, particularly in relation to rice, in chapter 4. Ever since the time of Van der Heide at the beginning of the century foreign advisers have suggested, from time to time, that irrigation could be more effective if farmers paid, in some measure, in relation to what they received. Yet the attitude that irrigation is a public service, to the maintenance of which farmers are expected to contribute labour in their own immediate neighbourhood, but for which they should not be charged, remains fundamental both in the Royal Irrigation Department itself and among farmers who benefit from its services.

The underlying concept is that the government should ultimately provide irrigation water to all those who need it, and the people should respond—and even be made to respond—by maintaining the channels to their villages and farms. In general, however, this system works well only in the Far North, where the irrigation systems are small, and have also mostly been in existence for many decades. In the Central Plain and in the Northeast far less than the engineering potential of the system is usually achieved because of unwillingness to maintain the channels beyond one's own farm. A good deal of effort is now being put into the improvement of ditches and dykes, but it is not unreasonable that the Royal Irrigation Department should regard the farmers themselves as responsible for the final stage of the distribution system.

Adaptation to this situation is in fact going on at the district and *tambon* level. Under the Ministry of the Interior local irrigation 'co-operatives' are being established by the administrative officers in the districts. These normally use mechanical pumps and are operated by paid labour financed by contributions from the beneficiaries. In the circumstances this is probably a satisfactory solution of the difficulty. One disadvantage is that the Ministry of the Interior is the great promoter of rice double-cropping, and as already indicated in chapter 4 it seems questionable whether the rice double-cropping program is usually a sound use of scarce resources.

(e) *Quantitative summary of rural development.* It has already been pointed out that the Ministry of Agriculture statistics, which are the only series available, cannot be regarded as wholly reliable.

However, an attempt is here made to use them to take an overall view of the components of Thai agricultural growth over the period from 1951-3 to 1962-4.

During this period the rural population increased by 31 per cent; the rural work force probably increased by 30 per cent for there was almost certainly a slight rise in the proportion of children. Rural trade, rural public works, transport, and government service in rural areas almost certainly expanded relative to total rural population, though the censuses do not show rural and urban figures separately. We can estimate that the farming population increased by 29 per cent.

During the same period the area under crops increased by 33 per cent as shown in Table 8.2. The 1951-3 figures are not all as given in the Ministry of Agriculture's *Agricultural Statistics of Thailand*. The adjustments are indicated in notes. The overall increase, however, differs little from the official figure.

It is interesting to compare the growth in real agricultural product (as estimated by weighting the proportional increase in output per *rai* by the average number of *rai* cultivated) for different parts of the rural sector, with the growth rate of the gross domestic product at constant prices for the economy as a whole. Columns (3) and (4) show the area and yield components respectively of an increase in output shown in (5) for rice, other export crops, rubber, semi-export crops, crops for local use, and tobacco. The growth in gross domestic product at constant prices for the same years was 90 per cent.

This table shows that all non-rice crops taken together increased three times as fast as the economy as a whole. The rural sector as a whole, however, increased only two-thirds as fast as the whole economy, because of the low rate of increase of rice. Indeed, if any earlier terminal three-year period had been chosen the effect would have been even more marked, for rice would then have shown no increase in yield per *rai*.

It is clear from the table that a small group of export crops has been responsible for a high proportion of the growth. These have not merely greatly increased their area under cultivation but also shown much the highest rate of increase in yield.

One feature of the table that needs explanation is the large increase in the area under crops for domestic use and the comparatively small improvement in yield per *rai*. In fact any increase

Table 8.2 Components of increase in output 1951-3 to 1962-4 by groups of crops

Groups of crops	(1) Area planted 1951-3	(2) (000 rai) 1962-4	(3) Increase in area %	(4) Average increase in yield per rai %	(5) Total increase % (100 + (3)) × (100 + (4)) − 100
Rice	36,457	41,262	13	15	30
Other export crops[a]	942	5,355	469	56	788
Rubber[b]	1,694	2,654	56	23	92
Semi-export crops[c]	1,164	1,714	50	40	110
Crops for local use[d]	564	2,785	392	26	520
Tobacco	292	277	−5	20	14
All non-rice crops[e]	4,656	12,785	175	40	284
All crops	41,113	54,047	31	21	59

	1951-3	1962-4			Increase %
Gross Domestic Product (constant prices)	33·3	64·0			90·2

[a] Maize, mung-beans, cassava, castor beans, kenaf, jute, ramie.
[b] Tappable area.
[c] Sugar-cane, groundnuts, soya beans, sesame.
[d] Cotton, chillies, onions, garlic, other vegetables, pineapples, watermelons, bananas.
[e] Excluding kapok and coconuts for which reasonable figures for 1951-3 cannot be estimated. In 1962-4 these occupied about ⅛ of the non-rice area.

Source: Ministry of Agriculture, Agricultural Statistics of Thailand, 1964. Chillies, onions, and garlic figures are available only from 1952, and the average of 1952/3 was substituted for the average of 1951/3. Cassava figures before 1956 are available for Chon Buri province only; an estimate for the whole kingdom was made on the basis of subsequent figures for Chon Buri and for the whole kingdom.

in yield of these crops represents a remarkable achievement. Highly capital-intensive methods have been developed for chillies and onions in the Ratchaburi area (see ch. 6), and the spread of these crops to the north and elsewhere could be expected to lower the yields per *rai*. The improved local market, generated partly by post-war industrialisation round Bangkok, partly by the development of new cash crops for export, has stimulated a great deal of development of vegetables in the regions, with both the government and private enterprise publishing handbooks on the cultivation of these crops, and with widespread adoption of pesticides, weed-killers, fertilisers, and seed selection.

The method of aggregating growth which is used here weights the different crops according to the area cultivated, not the value of the crop produced. This is unsatisfactory except as a rough measure, for the true significance of a crop's contribution depends on its value. However, it enables us to avoid the major difficulty which affects all Thai agricultural statistics—the depression of the value of rice within Thailand by the rice taxes to a little over half its international value. This means that in other methods of measuring changes in Thai national income the relatively slow rate of increase in rice is given a low weight and the relatively fast increase of other crops and of industry a high weight. This probably gives an unduly favourable picture of the growth of Thai national income in all official figures.

(f) *Role of agricultural exports.* The post-war period has seen the development of several 'miracle crops', which have greatly diversified Thailand's rural economy. The expansion of rubber may have come to an end. The long delay in introducing a replanting scheme, and the diversion of some of the replanting fund's resources to making good hurricane damage before the scheme was properly under way, prevented effective replanting during the period of relatively high prices for natural rubber, up to 1966. Maize, however, has continued to expand, and kenaf appears to have overcome the setbacks which followed the rapid expansion in 1960-1. Further expansion of maize into other parts of the north central plain can be expected, as Japan's demand for animal feed expands. Later Thailand may expand its own livestock industry, if the present political obstacles can be overcome. Kenaf takes more out of the soil, and there are dangers in planting it further and further afield, in search of new land, in the northeast. Though proper application of fertiliser can prevent exhaustion of the soil, this is a risky adventure for farmers near the margin of subsistence, in a region where rainfall is very uncertain. Kenaf is likely to expand further, but new crops will need to be sought in the long run, for kenaf can hardly be expected to compete indefinitely with synthetic packing materials. Sorghum is at present being tried in some northeastern areas.

Other probable growing points in the export trade are mung-beans, cassava, castor beans, and perhaps groundnuts. Thailand's exporters are keen to develop new markets, but for some products, such as kenaf and maize, quality control is likely to be a problem, while for others such as sugar and livestock free access to the international market may subject Thai producers and consumers to excessive fluctuations. Machinery for both quality control and export licensing exists, but it easily leads to monopoly when effectively enforced. The close relations existing between politicians and the leading exporters lead Thai economists generally to favour as little interference with the export trade as possible.

The chief purchasers of Thailand's export crops in recent years have been as follows: Indonesia is usually the chief buyer of rice, though Malaysia and Singapore together often buy more than Indonesia. The importance of Singapore and Hongkong in the rice market—together they take about a quarter of the total—makes the ultimate destination of much of Thailand's rice uncertain, since these are both primarily entrepôt ports. Japan usually buys 60 per cent or more of the maize, and the United States about the same proportion of the cassava, no one other country being of much comparative importance in these trades. Japan and the United States are also the chief buyers of Thai rubber, the relative share of Japan rising and that of the United States falling. Kenaf is sold chiefly to Japan but also to Germany and other European countries, with a rather rapidly falling share in its exports going to the United Kingdom for sack manufacture (N.S.O., 1965: 302-7).

9

Policy towards the Rural Sector

(a) *Strategy of rural development.* The basic strategy by which the Thai government attempts to promote rural economic development is to spend a fairly high proportion of its development funds on rural infrastructure projects, such as irrigation, roads, research and extension, and to promote competitive private enterprise to carry out the actual operations of production and marketing (N.E.D.B., 1964, 1967). The fact that the actual organisation of economic life sometimes differs from this pattern does not imply that the policy is purely a façade.

Policy in Thailand as elsewhere is made up partly of rational inferences from the values held by the ruling *élite* and the facts of their situation, partly by pressures of individual interests which derive special power from the structure of Thai politics. In democratic countries particular groups, perhaps of primary producers, are able to gain special influence because of the power of their organisations to win votes. Thailand is not in this sense a democracy; there is no distortion of policies by anything corresponding to—say—a maize farmers' lobby.

The corresponding situation in Thailand is the pressure exerted on Thai politicians to give patronage to certain business circles, the wealth of which enables the politicians to hold their power and contribute to the power of the ruling group.[1] Thai civil servants, and to some extent even the politicians themselves, recognise that this situation makes for weakness and inefficiency in the economy

[1] For more detailed discussion of this political structure see Wilson, 1962; Riggs, 1966; Evers and Silcock, 1967.

if the government is involved in a large part of the nation's economic activities. Hence in principle there is a good deal of support for a liberal policy and the encouragement of competition. This has in practice helped the maintenance of an expanding free market particularly in agricultural products. Yet it would be a mistake to regard this, without qualification, as the norm in Thai economic life.

This is not the place to discuss the Thai *élite* structure in any detail, but it is instructive to consider briefly the three main pre-war agricultural exports from the point of view of structure and policy. In rice and teak the Chinese had built up an intermediate position of oligopoly for their large rice-mills and sawmills, based on their relations with the European exporters and (for rice) on a network of supply reaching back to the farmers (Skinner, 1957: 104-5). In rubber a few large Chinese companies, mostly based in the Straits Settlements, had acquired a similar position of oligopoly, without any direct relation with Europeans, at least in Thailand.[2] Before the 1932 coup, Thai policy made no attempt either to take over these businesses or to ensure competitive conditions. After 1932 an attempt was made to set up a Thai Rice Company to break the Chinese hold over the rice trade, but the attempt to oust the Chinese was abandoned, as a result of Western diplomatic pressure in the post-war period (Silcock, 1967: 9).[3]

The present position is that for rice the former monopoly gains (and more) have been captured for public purposes after a struggle between the bureaucrats (led by the Bank of Thailand and assisted by international agencies) and the army politicians. For teak most of the profits have been captured for Thais, with the originally dominant Chinese families successfully working for them, but a much higher proportion of the profits goes to individuals in the form of inflated costs, with co-operative Chinese no doubt receiving a good share (Usher, 1967: 225-7). For rubber the oligopolistic position of Chinese merchants, mainly based in Malaysia, continues. This is partly because of the remoteness of the industry and the lack of understanding of it in Bangkok, partly because of

[2] Their position was, however, strengthened by ties with the European-run Singapore Rubber Market. For an account of this market see Wilson, 1958.

[3] Information on this was supplied to me in Bangkok by a number of business men and ex-officials, but I am not at liberty to cite sources.

intervention by these merchants, through the banking system, in the Thai political process.

It is noteworthy that these trades are not now the growing points of the Thai economy. The exploitation of the growing transport network, the expansion one after another of the new 'miracle crops', the building of new trading centres and the fostering of new seeds, pesticides, etc. for fruit and vegetable cultivation in their neighbourhood, have owed a good deal to the stimulus of independent Chinese entrepreneurs, not yet wealthy enough to build up a position of monopoly in collaboration with military-political leaders.

In some instances powerful leaders may press hard for a particular intervention in rural trade to further a particular business interest. However, it is clear that opposition to new monopolies is developing. The problems that pose special difficulties are those in which some case for intervention can be made on public grounds, but reasonably effective machinery for intervention is difficult because of Thai political structure. It is probably true, for example, that greater price instability would result from a completely free export of livestock than from the present monopoly, even though on the average both farmers and consumers might fare better (Muscat, 1966: 118 ff). Instability provokes a demand for intervention, and in Thai conditions this leads to monopolies from which many interests must draw their share. The sugar industry, having enjoyed a period of price support, will face the need for major readjustments if no scheme can be worked out for reducing costs and regulating the local market. Yet it is difficult to envisage any control system which will not in fact rapidly become a patronage network.

Close control over the cutting of teak is necessary if long-term supplies are not to be endangered (Puey and Suparb, 1955: ch. 5). This control could lead to substantial profits to the government, but the actual organisation of control leads to considerable leakages, and even worse to much waste of factors of production.

Maize exporters have from time to time suffered from the monopsonistic position achieved by Japanese buyers of Thai maize. Suggestions of cartel organisation among Thai exporters seem, on the whole, dangerous in Thai conditions, for they might well destroy the flexibility of the Thai market. More research directed to overcoming the moisture problem which prevents Thailand sending its maize to more distant markets would seem a more promising type of defence. Yet some defence may well be needed.

There is probably no fully satisfactory solution to these problems. In time the system of patronage may become more institutionalised, with better opportunities for limiting its effects. At present the attitude of the more professional of the civil servants, that Thailand should accept at least minor hazards of instability, deterioration of quality and the like, rather than introduce restrictive licensing or other controls, seems a sound one. It should, however, be encouraged, in some cases, as a lesser evil rather than as a solution to all Thailand's problems. There is a disposition in some foreign circles in Thailand to overpraise the *laissez-faire* attitude which the Thai government professes to adopt and to overemphasise the advantages of unrestricted competition in agriculture. There is—for fairly adequate reasons—remarkably little unrestricted competition in agriculture in the more developed countries. It may be wise, in Thai conditions, to limit interference with private business in agriculture, but it cannot be expected to be an easy or painless policy.

(b) *Agriculture in the national development plans.* There have been some fairly important changes in the position of agriculture in the Thai national development plans. Partly these are merely the result of a change in the character of national planning, but in part they represent a change in government attitudes.

It is worthy of note that the first national economic plan for the first three year period was simply a loose and rapidly put together co-ordination of different departmental plans, while the changes introduced in the second three year period—increased relative expenditure on communications, decreased relative expenditure on agricultural promotion—are not in accordance with the expressed aims of policy, which were, among other things, to give increasing emphasis to improving agricultural yields per *rai* and to discourage rapid opening up of new land (N.E.D.B., 1964, ch. 3, t. 1 and ch. 4, t. 1). Irrigation projects and roads were not assessed in terms of cost benefit ratios. These are now being applied, but are still rather crude and based on inadequate data.

The position may be summarised by saying that neither the decisions about the broad lines of policy nor the detailed choice of projects owed much to the formal techniques of planning. Yet this criticism, severe though it may seem, is really a comparatively trivial indictment of the effects of the first national plan on Thai rural development.

The influence of the plan depended not on its effect on the central process of decision-making, but on its impact on the conduct of government business and the redistribution of influence within ministries. The setting up of a Ministry of National Development, for example, was an extremely untidy piece of government re-arrangement, taking both Land Development and Irrigation away from the Ministry of Agriculture. It had a vivifying influence because it brought several well-trained Thais together, separating some of them from existing old-fashioned seniors, and giving them a substantial voice in the conduct of public affairs.

Similarly, within the existing ministries a demand was introduced for detailed schemes substantiated with statistical evidence, and containing targets that were both important and attainable. The officials who could prepare such schemes, and were interested in factual verification, gained in relative influence. This in turn increased the departments' capacity to obtain information. In the long run this is far more important than the formal efficiency of the means of co-ordinating information.

In relation to agriculture the second part of the first plan was still mainly based on proposals by ministries and departments, though there was some criticism from a national point of view, for example of the failure to follow up irrigation expenditure by distribution of the water to the farms. There was also some additional emphasis on regional work, especially the establishment of regional agricultural centres at Chai Nat and Khon Kaen (N.E.D.B., 1964: 67; 1967: 97).

Although targets were set and attempts made to anticipate demands for Thai exports, and the general growth rate was anticipated, there was little attempt to forecast in detail what would be needed apart from finance. Hence the overall strategy was not worked out after proper allowance for the shortages that it would generate. It was rather an agreed statement of objectives, while the actual provision of finance depended on *ad hoc* assessments of what could be done, for instance in expanding agricultural research or securing foreign aid for highway construction. The actual effect of responding to availabilities in this way was not to achieve the result of improving production by better yields and cutting down the expansion of acreage as laid down in the policy. Acreage panded rather more rapidly during the plan period, as shown in chapter 3, while the training of suitable research workers has taken longer than was anticipated, with adverse effects on the improvement of yields.

In the second plan there is evidence of some more technical appraisal of demands and resources, especially manpower (N.E.D.B., 1967: 80-8). It is not clear, however, that this has had much impact on the agricultural sector of the plan, except that a greatly increased local demand for fruit and vegetables is foreseen as a result of rising incomes, and the grouping of research centres is planned as a means of overcoming a shortage of agricultural specialists. There is not much consideration of the resource aspects, for example, of double-cropping of rice as against non-rice crops in the off-season, or broadcast sowing as against transplanting of rice in areas where mechanisation is changing the bottlenecks. Cost-benefit studies have now been undertaken in some of the highway and irrigation projects, yet planning is still undertaken in terms of completing the system and then settling down to a lower level of maintenance expenditure.

Even more important is the evidence that the realities of the rural situation have not been taken seriously into account in designing the overall policy. Formally there is a shift of emphasis in the second plan away from growth as such to the diffusion of the benefits of growth as widely as possible to the farmers. Yet the proportion of the population engaged in farming is planned to fall only from 80 per cent to 75 per cent while the proportion of the national income derived from farming is to fall from 31·6 per cent to 26 per cent over the same period. This has certain implications for what is meant by diffusion, which are neither spelt out in detail nor apparently acted on in the design of the detail of the policy. The main implication is that the average rate of growth of average individual incomes in the agricultural and non-agricultural sectors of the economy is to be approximately the same, roughly 3 per cent per year. Average incomes in the non-agricultural sector are to remain about eight and a half times as great as in the agricultural sector, but about one farmer in every hundred each year will transfer from agriculture to the non-agricultural sector, and the effect of this will be to raise average *per capita* incomes in the economy as a whole from 3 per cent (which it would be without the transfer) to 5 per cent.

This is, in a sense, a diffusion of the benefits of growth, but it is not raising the relative position of the farmer, except in the sense that some of the farmers each year are transferring into the much better paid non-farm sector. Without the transfer of farmers out of agriculture about half of the gain actually envisaged would be swallowed up by population growth; yet the Second Plan certainly does not give the impression that much attention was paid to the importance of this transfer. The government report on migration even suggests that there is some preoccupation with keeping farmers on their farms. The report itself is factual, but indicates a good deal of anxiety about these movements (Dept of Labour, 1965).

This is not the place to discuss Thai industrialisation policy; but the foregoing comment suggests that relatively labour-intensive industries, absorbing more rural labour per unit of available capital, would be more in line with expressed policy.

In some of its details, however, the agricultural section of the Second Development Plan shows improvements on the first. The projects for both research and infrastructure development appear to be more detailed and realistic than in the first plan, as well as being expanded in scope. The 800 million *baht* allocation for Aid to Farmers, though it will probably be directed to politically sensitive areas, does give more scope for focusing resources on sites with good prospects for development.

The plan also shows rather more localised interest in regional problems. Instead of drawing up regional plans by the main administrative regions the government has appointed regional committees for the Northeast, North, and South, but in the Central area has established East and West Region committees, roughly covering the East and West Sub-regions considered in chapter 6. In addition special foreign aid is being given to three areas all adjacent to the growing points already described in the North Central Region, the East, and the West. The United States is giving special assistance in the Saraburi-Phetchabun area and in Rayong *changwat*, while Israel is assisting a project in Phetchaburi and Prachuap Khiri Khan near the Ratchaburi growing point.

(c) *Position in public finance.* A measure of the importance given in official policy to the rural sector is its role in the public finance of Thailand. Table 9.1 gives an indication of the importance of different parts of the rural sector both in the revenue of Thailand

Table 9.1 Estimates of direct revenue from, and expenditure on, the rural sector in the Thai government budget, 1965 (million *baht*)

Revenue Actual			Expenditure Estimates	
Total taxes		10,283	General administration	934
Sale of goods and services		313	Defence, internal and external	2,850
Revenue from government enterprises		224	Debt service	688
Other revenue		377	Education primary	1,211
Total revenue		11,197	Education other	917
of which			Public health and welfare	1,865
Rice premium	1,257		Economic expenditure	3,370
export duty	197		Other	584
milling duty[a]	about 80		Total expenditure	12,419
Total rice		1,534	of which	
Rubber export duty	164		Roads	1,028
licences	19		Railways	99
Total rubber		183	Other rural transport[c]	335
Tobacco: total revenue from local tobacco[a]		about 700	Irrigation	696
			Other agriculture	264
Livestock: export duty on hides	5		Forestry	87
epizootic control levy	6·5		Fisheries	37
Total livestock		11·5	Total economic expenditure, rural sector	2,546

Forestry: teak export duty	10·5
teak royalty	7
other export duty	4
other royalty	50
forest duties	53
sale of forest produce	14
profits of Forest Industry Organisation	14
sawmill duty[b]	about 40
Total forestry	192·5
Fisheries: licences	5·5
Total direct revenue, rural sector	2,626·5

[a] Total revenue from government tobacco monopoly and private producers, reduced by 10% to allow for use of some imported leaf (approx. 10% by weight).

[b] Total business tax on milling divided 2 : 1 between rice milling and sawmilling.

[c] All air transport excluded, but all other transport expenditure included.

Sources: Budget Documents 1967 (Thai language), Bangkok, Budget Bureau, Vols. 1 and 2 for 1965 actual revenue. Budget in Brief 1965, Bangkok, Budget Bureau, supplemented by Budget Documents 1965 for Expenditure Estimates. (Actual expenditures are not broken down appropriately in the Budget Documents, and in 1965 actual expenditure appears to have differed relatively slightly from the original estimate.)

its public expenditure. Generally speaking Thai financial , though quite detailed, are insufficiently annotated to enable ᴜ.. .. reconcile figures from different sources, but the figures as given suffice to show a number of important facts about the economy.

The first of these is the great importance of rice as a source of revenue. The rice premium, yielding 1¼ billion *baht*, yields more than the whole income tax, and more than twice as much as the income tax on individuals. Tobacco is in most countries a source of revenue; in Thailand most of the raw tobacco is locally grown. This revenue—about seven hundred million *baht*—is collected through a government monopoly, though a few private individuals are allowed to prepare tobacco for sale on payment of duty, and probably many more prepare it for sale or use without permission or payment.

The forests are also an important source of revenue. As we have shown in chapter 5 by no means all the revenue accrues to official government funds. However, we can see from the table that the official revenue from the forests exceeded 190 million *baht*.

In comparison with rice, tobacco, and forest products, rubber— the untaxed export value of which was in 1965 about two-thirds of that of rice—is relatively lightly taxed. It contributed to the government official budget less than 10 per cent of the export value. Like forestry products, however, rubber pays a number of unofficial levies.[4] Chinese committees levy one *baht* for every five sheets for the support of Chinese schools—the rubber merchants are all Chinese. A further 300 *baht* is paid to customs officers for every ship carrying rubber cargo. Further unofficial payments, in addition to the official ones, are paid in respect of the many licences required in the rubber business.[5]

It could be argued that the unofficial levies on teak and rubber, though they lower the real incomes of producers, are not part of the taxation system. Such an argument completely misrepresents the structure and motivation of Thai politics (Evers and Silcock, 1967). It is, however, true that the only influence of these payments on the expenditure pattern is that they collectively help to reduce

[4] Information on these was given to me when I visited south Thailand in December 1964.

[5] Moreover, in the remote southern areas most rubber producers and traders pay taxes to the communist armies there.

the general level of salaries paid to Thai civil servants. It is impossible to estimate the total of unofficial levies in all sectors. The available evidence suggests that there are considerable opportunities for irregular income in communications and in the industrial sector (I.B.R.D., 1959: 198-200) and these probably have an influence on development policy.

The derivation of some 25 per cent of the official revenue more or less directly from the rural sector represents a fairly heavy burden when the sector earns rather less than a third of the income and employs three-quarters of the population, especially as some of the large items which cannot be clearly allocated—e.g. the 900 million *baht* from petroleum products, the 400 million from imports of rough cotton cloth and perhaps the 150 million from the state lottery—can be expected to fall predominantly on the rural sector.

How far is the expenditure in fact directed to rural development? Not enough explanation of the budget figures is published to enable one to go much beyond the breakdown given in the Budget in Brief (published annually in English) (Office of the Prime Minister, 1962: 18-19). The expenditure section of Table 9.1 does not attempt to show all the government funds spent in the countryside, any more than the revenue section can show all the funds derived from it. Of the three thousand million *baht* spent on primary education and on public health and welfare, almost certainly more than half would be spent for the benefit of farming communities, even though the standard of service in the country is lower than in the towns. Within the economic sector an approximate allocation is easier.

The approximate equality between the amount taken directly from the rural sector and the amount spent on it is coincidental and of no real significance. It is more important that about three-quarters of the economic expenditure is devoted to the rural sector, and that the economic sector as a whole is more than a quarter of all the revenue.

Perhaps the most striking feature of the expenditure figures is that over half of the economic expenditure is devoted to the two headings of roads and irrigation. This has already been explained in terms of the past history of Thai economic development (see ch. 1).

(d) *Foreign aid in agricultural development.* Foreign aid has influ-

Q

enced the development of Thai agriculture in four ways. First it has contributed to total funds available and so given the Thai government more freedom of action and enabled it to help agriculture more. Next it has introduced certain biases into Thai policy —mainly favourable to rural development—as a result of the greater willingness of foreign governments and international agencies to aid certain types of development rather than others. Thirdly the stricter supervision and sometimes greater technical efficiency of foreign aid projects has strengthened the impact on the rural economy of such intention as exists in the Thai bureaucracy to improve rural conditions. Finally the indirect effects of military aid in certain rural areas have probably been substantial.

It could be argued that the effect on total funds available is the least significant part of foreign aid. Thailand is in the peculiar position of having received very considerable gifts and loans from international agencies and from the United States, Japan, Australia, and European countries, yet having gold and foreign exchange reserves of its own greater than the total of all such gifts and loans. About a third of Thai development expenditure during the decade to 1965 has come from foreign grants and loans; but the addition to Thai reserves during the same period has been almost equal to the aid and loans received. Its total reserves at the end of 1965 were worth 15,380 million *baht* while the total grants it had received from foreign governments were about 8·5 thousand million *baht*, together with fourteen loans from the International Bank with a total principal of 4·5 thousand million *baht* (of which under two thousand million was actually outstanding in 1965) and under three thousand million *baht* of other government borrowing (Corden and Richter, 1967: 128-50).

However, given the strong belief of the Thai bureaucracy and the Bank of Thailand in international reserves, it is probable that these would have been built up—though perhaps not quite so far —if there had been no foreign aid. Moreover the increased reserves have removed anxieties about foreign exchange and so strengthened the liberal element in Thai policy making. They have probably also helped to bring in foreign capital, some of which may have helped rural development indirectly.[6]

In estimating the total effects of aid we must also add the indirect

[6] The strength of the currency is mentioned in Bangkok Bank, 1966: 33-4.

effects of military aid. Figures are not available, but it is unlikely that these are small. In terms of foreign exchange, Thailand gains by being able to sell farm produce, some manufactures, services, and the use of accommodation, for foreign currency. The gains in terms of real income will be considered later.

It is difficult to determine in what ways, and to what extent, foreign aid has influenced the overall direction of Thai policy. It has certainly introduced a bias towards private enterprise and against state enterprises, as shown in more detail in Appendix I. This has probably not been very important in the rural sector, though it may have weakened the tendency to form cartels in the export market. Probably a more important effect has been a shift in emphasis away from certain nationalistic aims—reducing indebtedness to middlemen, building up Thai competitors to the Chinese trade network—towards other aims in which more capital and technique were needed. The Thai civil service was certainly aware, without foreign aid, of the importance of agricultural research, transport, and irrigation; but the availability of foreign aid has steadily increased the attention it has given to them.

Foreign aid has strengthened Thai agricultural technique in a number of respects, probably the most important being the great expansion of research into more suitable rice seeds, the introduction of the Guatemala type of maize, improvement of the breeds of livestock, and the strengthening of agricultural economics research at Kasetsart University and in the government's own ministries.

Transport has been given increasing attention from the time of the first International Bank loans in 1950 for railway improvement and port development. In addition a large proportion of the aid of foreign governments has gone into road construction. The strategic implications of this aid have probably been overemphasised though they have some importance. It is more important that internal expenditure on road construction and maintenance is one of the most difficult types of expenditure to control. This leads not merely to leakages but to the kind of conflict between the Ministry of Finance and the operating agencies that causes roads to be left unfinished or unmaintained (Corden, 1967). Foreign aid has reduced these difficulties; though there have been serious delays in negotiation, particularly with West German aid (N.E.D.B., 1966: 40-5).

This draws attention to perhaps the most important features of foreign aid in Thailand, the introduction of technical expertise and the control of expenditure. To a very limited extent this represents intervention by foreign governments in the general interest of economic development against the financial interests of prominent individuals. For the most part it represents a deliberate use by Thai bureaucrats themselves of the disciplines of the international money market and the treasury control techniques of foreign governments for the benefit of the Thai economy. This represents a strengthening of the internal structure of the Thai government. Probably the most important example of technical expertise is in the research programs where, in addition to improved varieties of rice and maize already mentioned, the breeds of livestock have been improved and considerable new work initiated on marketing. The most important examples of expenditure control—apart from the road programs already mentioned—have been in railway and port equipment.

Finally we must refer to the important indirect effect of the local expenditure of army units and individuals. These expenditures, particularly those outside Bangkok, are beneficial in two ways. In so far as the earnings of the factors producing goods and services are higher than these factors could earn elsewhere there is a net gain to the Thai national income equal to these differences in earnings. There may well be, however, an additional effect. In so far as shortage of local capital or enterprise is a bottleneck in development, the expenditure of considerable sums in country areas on rentals, personal services, and local produce is likely both to create capitalists and entrepreneurs locally and to attract them out from the metropolis. This is not to say that such expenditures in rural areas are always beneficial. In Thailand, however, with its large income differential between town and country and its availability of mobile Chinese enterprise wherever prospects are sufficiently attractive, it is unlikely that serious local inflationary effects will develop, while the favourable effects in country areas are more likely than in other less developed countries.

(e) *Rice premium policy.* The statistical aspects of the Thai policy of taxing rice exports have been fairly fully discussed, and some of its adverse effects on rice production have been considered (see chs. 2 and 4). From the point of view of other agricultural products, however, this is a cost reducing policy, with effects rather similar to those of a devaluation of the currency. These aspects need some further consideration.

Is the policy a deliberate one aimed at diversification of the economy and a move away from subsistence agriculture? It is impossible to give a clear-cut affirmative or negative answer to this question. Certainly the policy was not originally adopted with this end in view. The rice premium came into being as a result of the compulsory post-war deliveries of rice and its aim was revenue. When the premium was first raised after 1955 to prevent a shortage of rice in Thailand the objective was rather stabilisation of the cost of living than a deliberate forcing of it down for the sake of achieving either industrialisation or agricultural diversification. It was the junior civil servants in Bangkok rather than the incipient industries—let alone rubber or maize growers—whose voice was heard by the politicians (Mousny, 1964: 35-44).

This is not, however, a completely negative answer. The government is well aware of the connection between rice prices and wages, and no doubt realises that the low price maintained by the premium is helpful to Thai industry against import competition. There is also general awareness that Thailand's main exports are agricultural, and that there is a symmetry between export promotion and import substitution. All that can be clearly denied is that this policy is explicitly used as a policy to promote agricultural diversification. It is never mentioned as such in the Thai economic literature.

The main point of this argument is that, although an important cause of agricultural diversification in Thailand is the rice taxation policy, it does not appear to be a consciously planned policy with any deliberate substitution of other crops for rice. The notion of substitution is unacceptable, and the stereotype of the rice-growing farmer as the backbone of the country remains in spite of the very considerable importance of the shift to other crops in the pattern of change of the economy. A more deliberate policy would be likely to achieve more success.

It is, of course, difficult to discourage subsistence farming without discouraging rice growing altogether. Indeed, it could be argued that what the rice premium discourages is precisely production of rice for sale, and that the true subsistence farmer is unaffected (Corden, 1967). What is actually happening is that development is not reducing the consumption of the farmer's own rice as much as might be expected, but farmers are not putting maximum effort into growing a rice surplus but are growing auxiliary crops for cash where they can. A still small, but probably increasing number are being encouraged by cash yields to move out of rice altogether, in marginal areas.

The policy of exaggerating the inducements to move out of subsistence agriculture, so as to accelerate the change to a more rational and specialised form of farming, would be a commendable policy if it were deliberately adopted for the purpose. In so far as the policy is accidental it is likely to have some deficiencies in achieving a more efficient market structure. Insufficient attention may be given to the need to treat partial cash-cropping as an intermediate stage, and to adapt extension services accordingly. Moreover sufficient attention may not be given to the need, in planning, to correct for the undervaluation of rice. This is not a matter which can be adequately dealt with by a shadow price for rice, however necessary this may be conceptually. The right kind of specialised farming of rice for cash needs to be encouraged in appropriate areas, by subsidising irrigation and transport and modifying land tenure. Recent policy of deliberately returning an increased proportion of the rice premium to rice growers is on the right lines; but to accord with the general trend away from subsistence to market agriculture it will need to be more precisely directed.

It is important to appreciate that the rice taxes are beneficial— in so far as they are beneficial at all—for dynamic, not static reasons. They act in much the same way as an infant industries tariff. In general terms the cheapness of rice encourages the production and discourages the consumption of vegetables and other components of the Thai cost of living (Silcock, 1967: ch. 10; Usher, 1967). On the supply side labour is pushed out of rice growing to seek other sources of income, including cultivation of fruits, vegetables, etc.; on the demand side both reduced income and substitution of rice for other items in the diet tend to reduce the consumption of these other items and make them available for the towns. This keeps down the wage level and stimulates both manufactures and other export crops.

In terms of comparative static analysis, of course, since trade must balance, this distortion would produce a situation in which Thailand was deprived of some of the advantage of the division of labour, the income of the producers of rice (in which it enjoys the greatest comparative advantages) being reduced in terms of international trade goods. Thailand would produce instead, by relatively labour intensive methods, other crops and also industrial products which it could have obtained more cheaply in exchange for rice. Comparative statics is not, however, the relevant analysis for Thailand's current situation. In dynamic terms, the encouragement of new exports and the discouragement of imports provides a favourable balance for the import of capital goods and the stimulus to change—towards new crops and new industrial products—gives the inducement to import this equipment. Much of the advantage generated, directly and indirectly, by keeping down the price of rice and of labour in terms of imported goods, has undoubtedy been wasted in consumption of luxury goods for a small and politically powerful middle class. More is probably wasted on imports of relatively inappropriate capital goods (Silcock, 1967: ch. 11). Yet the taxes create a pressure for change in the right direction, provided a deliberate policy of development is based on them.

10

Conclusions

(a) *Rice price policy*. We have seen that the rice premium policy was not adopted as a deliberate device to diversify agriculture and promote industrialisation, but rather came about as a result of a series of adaptations in this general direction. Such merits as the policy has are analogous to those of an infant industry tariff, diverting resources away from an allocation which in terms of static equilibrium analysis would be superior, to one with a greater potential for growth. Commercial farming for export or industrialisation may be statically inferior to the cultivation of rice for subsistence plus an export surplus; but commercial farming carries stronger and more apparent inducements to change old techniques, while industrialisation trains technicians and creates capital, with high external economies. On the whole it is more likely that the policy of taxing the export of rice will promote development if its dynamic merits are exploited and if some of its static harmful effects are corrected.

Perhaps the basic techniques of cost-benefit analysis could be applied, for example in irrigation plans, to the effects of the rice taxes. One way of allowing for harmful static side effects is to adopt a uniform shadow price of rice based on (though not necessarily identical with) the international price, which could be used in all policy calculations related to output, subsidies, taxation, etc. Differences between the actual price and this notional price could be allowed for in all policies affecting the cost of production of rice or rice substitutes. This would enable a number of schemes to be assessed not in terms of the gains to the participants but in terms of the gain to Thailand from the rice produced. Certainly such a price should be taken into account.

However, it is not clear that an adjusted price could simply be fed into a mathematical model to assess policy, unless the model is made exceptionally sophisticated. The aim must be to try to secure the dynamic effect of the rice taxes in promoting diversification, but to eliminate erroneous comparisons of benefits to be achieved —as between rice and other crops—where these dynamic effects can be neglected. If we are assessing the relative benefits of the Klawng River scheme and a scheme on the Chao Phaya, should we value the fruit and vegetables produced in the Ratchaburi area under the former and the rice produced under the latter at prices that would prevail if there were no rice taxes? If we are interested only in the immediate yields of vegetables and rice such a valuation would be appropriate; but if we judge that Chao Phaya irrigation would help to keep a number of subsistence farmers in existence, who would respond relatively slowly to new opportunities, there would be a case for incorporating this as a negative factor into the model.

We may apply this line of thought to the problem of the relation of rice prices to fertiliser use, already considered in chapter 4. It is desirable to offset the effect of the rice premium on the inducement to use fertiliser which would double the yield of rice. Applying a notional price of rice approximately equal to the international price we infer that if the risk and extra labour of applying fertiliser would be worth incurring at that price it would be worth while, from the point of view of Thailand, for the fertiliser to be applied. We should therefore seek for a policy which will achieve this result without destroying the pressure to substitute more commercial crops for rice on the farms where this is possible. This can be done by subsidising fertiliser, provided not too large a proportion of the fertiliser is wasted.

Clearly, in the example given in chapter 4, if no fertiliser were wasted the subsidy would cost the government nothing; for the gain in rice premium would be more than enough to pay for the subsidy: rice production would increase by an amount worth six times the cost of the fertiliser subsidy and even if consumption increased it would be extremely unlikely that less than half the additional production would be added to Thailand's exports (see p. 63 n. 4). Since about a third of the proceeds would be premium the subsidy would cost nothing. In fact considerable leakage would be likely, but most of this would add something to productivity elsewhere and not be a total loss.

(b) *Population and land policy.* Like many of the less developed countries, Thailand's population is growing relatively rapidly; but unlike most of them it is not experiencing very rapid urbanisation (Caldwell, 1967). A transfer of population on a larger scale out of agriculture into industry would be, in Thai conditions, one of the most effective sources of income growth, but policy is certainly not designed to accelerate this.

The relative concentration of Thai development effort on the agricultural sector is partly a cause and partly a consequence of the relatively slow urbanisation of the Thai population. On the whole, however, the explanation of the tendency of Thais to remain in the rural areas is probably social rather than economic: the barrier of the Chinese lower middle class, the centralisation of the Thai economy on Bangkok under the absolute monarchy, and the fact that education was indigenous not colonial in character. These factors create population pressure in rural areas themselves, and the result is large-scale migration to new land.

Moreover, though good land is still available it is not unlimited; and the decline of the teak industry due to overcutting in the post-war period, combined with fears about the effects of deforestation on Thailand's climate and water table, led the government, in 1956, to begin extensive forest reservation and to lay down a policy of limiting agriculture to half the land area. This has focused increasing attention on raising the yield per *rai*.

It has been shown that the area cultivated per head has remained fairly constant (see t. 3.8 and 8.1). If the rate of expansion of the total area cultivated is to fall, the area per head in the rural areas will depend on what happens to urbanisation. This in turn partly depends on industrialisation policy. At present Thai industrialisation—at least in the sectors promoted by the government—is very capital intensive. Saving in the Thai middle class is now fairly satisfactory, but the government has set limits on the proportion of foreign borrowing and it may be difficult, even in the future, to provide employment for more than a small influx from the country to the towns. If existing methods of industrialisation are used, the capital will just not be available to absorb many into industry.

Thailand is thus faced with the prospect of a rapid growth of the rural population at the same time as it is directing attention to restricting the opening up of new land. It may be expected that in time this will lead to a population policy of encouraging the growth of family planning (Caldwell, 1967). However, this is not the basis of present policy as the army group which controls the government is (for mistaken military reasons) lukewarm about family planning. Moreover, even a rapid change of population policy would not affect the immediate pressures.

This suggests that the Thai bureaucracy's concern about the level of rural rents, particularly in the Central Plain, is mainly concern about a symptom. The cause of the symptom is the rapid growth of population. This is not at present running up against any actual shortage of land. The main barrier at present is probably not yet government policy limiting the future alienation of land, but simply inertia combined with very rapid population growth. Accelerating movement out of relatively congested areas would be the most effective way of dealing with the problem.

This is perhaps the main reason why the strong hostility of the Thai bureaucracy to tenancy seems something of a barrier to economic growth. It prevents active concern with the conditions that would assist mobility, fair sale prices for land, and development-minded landlords. Clearly one of the main reasons for delay in proper registration of land titles and an efficient system of valuing and transfer of land is the secretiveness of landlords, who feel that the government is hostile to them and are often in a position to bribe officials to leave them undisturbed.

With Thailand's very flexible social system a satisfactory register of land transactions, and steps to ensure that a farmer wishing to sell his land will have a good market for it, should be high priorities. Moreover the fact should be faced that for some time to come there will in fact be a good deal of tenancy. More could then be done about promoting an economically efficient division of responsibilities between landlord and tenant, and conducting extension work among landlords to promote a more developmental attitude to land as an investment.

In both the Central Plain and the South there are indications that relatively large-scale landholdings may be beneficial—in the Central Plain allowing the successful rice farmer, growing a large surplus, to expand his operations quickly to the optimum size he can work by renting land and using his capital for equipment (see ch. 6); in the South allowing replanting to be done by capitalists who can afford to wait (see ch. 7).

The economic case for small-scale ownership rests mainly on conservation arguments which are weak in the Central Plain and irrelevant in the South. Separation of ownership from farming may be useful when large areas need to be planned together. Moreover, as land becomes scarcer and the economy more complex, allocation of land between alternative uses may become relatively more important, in comparison with optimum conservation. Landowning becomes a separate function, and ways must be found to make landlords themselves more interested in development. Perhaps the most effective way of doing this is by improving registration and the market for real estate, and showing that encouragement of landlords or opposition to them depends on their active interest in developing their land and finding productive tenants. Resistance to landlords on principle makes it more difficult to devise suitable institutions for a real estate market which could ensure that farmers obtained a reasonable price for their land. Such institutions could, in addition, open up the possibility of large-scale land development, perhaps by subsidiaries of banks.

(c) *Growth centres and regionalism.* Previous chapters have suggested that transport has been an important factor in growth in Thailand. It also seems probable that growth is exceptionally likely to occur if, in addition to favourable transport facilities, there are also local expenditures to attract entrepreneurs from elsewhere. It may be impossible to generate further considerable centres of foreign expenditure, but some of those planned in the immediate future seem specially likely to attract new growth. The Phetchaburi-Prachuap Khiri Khan scheme, with Israeli help, the American schemes in the Sattahip and Lomsak-Saraburi areas, all seem likely positions for growth to emerge.

If this analysis is sound, it may well be good strategy to give special attention to research into the problems of growth of their special products, and to see that their extension services are, for the time being, staffed to a standard considerably higher than the average for the kingdom. This was, indeed, a point to which Field Marshal Sarit as Prime Minister devoted a good deal of attention, with his regional centre at Khon Kaen.

For this purpose the two new regional centres, at Tak for the North and at Pattani for the South, seem rather less likely to be centres of vigorous growth. It seems unlikely that establishment of a regional centre as such would be sufficient to give the stimulus, and neither of these appears to have enough growth potential apart from that contributed by the government.[1]

(d) *Cost-benefit analyses.* For two reasons it is now becoming more important to scrutinise carefully the machinery for assessing the effects of government investments (Silcock, 1967: ch. 10). One reason is that the relatively obvious preliminary works have been undertaken. There is no lack of possible schemes to achieve further improvement, but it is becoming much more difficult to arrange them in order of priorities. The second reason is that the rice taxes make it unwise to rely either on the working of the price system or on highly sophisticated planning techniques, without a good deal of prior analysis.

The Chai Nat and Phumiphon dams have been built, and once the ditches and dykes scheme is completed choices must be made among a number of other projects none of which is clearly essential to the others. The main road system will soon be completed, making a unified network covering the whole kingdom. Even this may involve sacrifices in feeder roads or in maintenance expenditures that should have been given priority.

The basic techniques of cost-benefit analysis have been applied, both to roads and to irrigation, but so far without much success. It seems important that in any future schemes close attention should be given to allowing for the effects of the rice taxes as already indicated.

(e) *Techniques with little capital.* A final point that can hardly escape the attention of anyone who has travelled in rural Thailand is the comparative lack of interest in techniques which improve the productivity of rural labour by scientific methods using relatively little capital. Thai senior civil servants are increasingly going for study to the United States, a country which is certainly far

[1] Tak is, in this respect, probably better than Pattani, though at first sight the choice looks less promising. Tak is an area with new land and irrigation potential, not far from an existing growth centre, and though as yet there is little commercial activity there, it is possible that a government centre here could be a catalyst releasing new commercial activity and rural development. Pattani is a long established town with a port that needs constant dredging and with a few factories. There appear to be limited prospects for mining, but it is hardly a potential centre of independent growth.

ahead of the other developed countries in capital equipment per head, but the claim of which to leadership in applied science is much more questionable and in pure science still more so. Naturally abundant capital equipment per head becomes identified with modernity, in the minds of the Thai *élite*.

The Thai farmer's impression of the modern world is derived from junior civil servants who naturally model themselves on seniors who have studied abroad. They are the ones in immediate contact with the farmers, but they are apt to lack even the familiarity with scientific principles that a second-rate degree in an average or below-average American university gives to many of their seniors in the *changwat* capitals. Naturally they pass on to the farmers the values that they have acquired. It is not only professional motives that prompt them to foster expensive equipment; unfortunately, because of grossly inadequate salaries, they often have personal motives also.

Hence a farmer who can afford to invest only little is apt to think the world of science is not for him but for the more fortunate farmers with good and abundant land and hence high incomes.[2] The poorer farmer has been effectively convinced that there is nothing between two buckets slung on a pole and a diesel-operated irrigation pump, nothing between a buffalo pulling a wooden plough and a twenty-five horse-power tractor, nothing between a traditional all-purpose hoe and a motorised garden tractor. Millions of man-hours a day are wasted by Thai women which could be saved by simple hand pumps and plastic tubing; and it is hard to believe that either new policy or new equipment could not be devised to eliminate many of the arduous bodily movements of transplanting rice in Thai conditions.

[2] The evidence for this was the replies to the questionnaire on economic opportunity (see Appendix II).

Appendix I

ECONOMIC EFFECTS OF THAI POLICY AT THE END OF WORLD WAR II*

Among those who enjoy setting up object lessons for the leaders of the less developed countries, Thailand is coming to be cited as the virtuous example who wins all the prizes.[1] She has a growth-rate of national income of about eight per cent, her currency is strong, she is attracting foreign investors, new crops come forward, one after another, every few years to help her diversify her agriculture. These happy consequences are alleged to follow from Thailand's observance of certain simple received rules. She has a liberal trade policy, she controls credit strictly and balances her budget, she does not nationalise industries, and she fosters agriculture by roads and irrigation instead of building up elaborate heavy industry. Clearly therefore her success is the simple reward for virtue.

It is not the purpose of my paper to depreciate this ridiculous caricature. In fact Thailand has a relatively flexible internal market economy which she protects by a tax that forces down the price of

* A paper presented at the Fortieth Annual Congress of the Australian and New Zealand Association for the Advancement of Science, January 1968, and subsequently published in *Australian Outlook*, April 1968. Permission to reproduce it as an appendix to this book is acknowledged with thanks.

[1] This refers mainly to popular articles in magazines and newspapers; A. Mousny, *The Economy of Thailand*, Bangkok, Social Science Association Press, 1964, strikes a similar note, and also R. J. Muscat in 'Growth and the Free Market: a Case Study in Thailand', *Malayan Economic Review*, XI, 1, April 1966, though his *Development Strategy in Thailand*, New York, Praeger, 1966 gives a much more reasoned account.

rice and the cost of living;[2] her credit system is the result of the interplay of a highly professional central bank (enjoying much international support), with local bankers who can be partly controlled by it because they need foreign aid;[3] Thailand's attitude to nationalisation is not a result of any strong regard for private enterprise; rather it springs from unfortunate experiences with a particularly pervasive form of government affiliated businesses.[4] The purpose of this paper is to present some material recently produced in Thai by the Bank of Thailand,[5] the Thai war-time ambassador to Japan[6] and the remarkable ex-civil-servant Thawi who was caretaker-prime-minister of Thailand during a critical fortnight[7] and to show that many features of the present Thai economy arise from the peculiar circumstances of Thailand at the end of World War II. I have discussed elsewhere what I believe to be the reasons for the relative success of the Thai economy.[8] Here I want to show that the structure of this economy emerged not because of any particular virtue in terms of Western values, but because of certain constraints imposed by Thailand's special situation of being a liberated country to the Americans and a defeated enemy to the British.

During the War, Thailand had first rather half-heartedly resisted a Japanese invasion, and then even more half-heartedly fought on the Japanese side, with an underground movement (led by Pridi the Regent himself) passively resisting the Japanese,[9] and the Bank of Thailand thwarting, as best it could, Japanese attempts to milk the Thai economy.[10] The Japanese gave back to Thailand

[2] T. H. Silcock, *Thailand: Social and Economic Studies in Development*, Canberra, A.N.U. Press, 1967, ch. 10.

[3] Ibid. ch. 8.   [4] Ibid. ch. 11.

[5] Bank of Thailand *Wiwatanachai Anusorn* (A Memoir on Prince Viwat) Bangkok, private issue, 1961.

[6] Direk Jayanama *Thai kab songkhram lok khrang thi sawng*. (*Thailand in World War II*) Bangkok, Phrae Pittaya 1967. This work includes, in Part II, sections by Thawi Banyaket, Puey Ungphakorn and Phra Phisan Sukhumvit.

[7] Thawi Bunyaket in Direk, op. cit.

[8] T. H. Silcock, op. cit., ch. 12.

[9] I have seen no adequate account in English of the Free Thai Movement. See Direk, op. cit., especially sections by Puey Ungphakorn and Thawi Bunyaket; also Chantana *XO Group* Bangkok, Prayun Phisnakha, 1964 (in spite of the English title this book is wholly in Thai).

[10] Viwat Memoir, op. cit., Pt. I, pp. 76-82, 89-104, Pt. II passim.

British and French territory in Malaya and Indo-China that Thailand had given up during the period of colonial expansion. This was one factor making Britain more hostile than America to Thailand in the post-war period; but other factors were also important. First, the British had a better understanding of the detailed structure of Thai society than the Americans. British Advisers had been working in Thailand for many years, and it was fully appreciated in Britain that the army group around Field Marshal Phibun had considerable sympathy with nationalist dictatorship of the Japanese type, and moreover had not been thrown out by a revulsion of popular feeling. Pridi had first outwitted Phibun in the Parliament and installed a more neutral figure to patch up the feud between them. Phibun had retained control of the army and kept it poised in Lop Buri ready to bring him back to power. As the war turned against Japan, however, he accepted the appointment of Thawi, a prime minister more likely to be acceptable to the United Nations.[11] The Americans had accepted the point of view of Seni, the democratic Thai Ambassador to the United States, that Thailand's declaration of war on the United States was made under pressure, and was invalid and against the wishes of the Thai people.[12] Had they foreseen in September 1945 that the wartime leader Phibun, then heading the list of Thai war criminals, would be back as Prime Minister, with very little public opposition, within three years, their attitude would almost certainly have been different. Both Britain and America were, in 1945, trying to settle the future in terms of the war they had just fought, the Americans generously and with faith in democracy, the British more guardedly

[11] This comes out clearly in the account of political parties in Thailand published by Pla Thawng under the title of 'Sarakhadi' in the Thai newspaper Siam Rath: see the issue of 10 Aug. 1964. The series has since been published as a book on Thai political parties.

[12] Pridi Phanomyong, the leader of the Free Thai movement, had, as one of the members of the Council of Regency, contrived to avoid signing the declaration of war to render it invalid. This point was later brought out by the Government of Khuang Aphaiwong. The Thai Ambassador in the U.S.A., Momrachawong Seni Pramoj, however, based his repudiation of the declaration of war on the ground that it was made under duress. In actual fact, as Thawi makes clear, there was no duress. Phibun entered the war voluntarily, with the consent of most of the powerful Thais (though not Pridi) and no expressed popular opposition, because Japan was victorious everywhere at the time, and Thailand hoped for advantages from joining the attack, see Direk, op. cit., pp. 360-1.

P

and with better information. American generosity to Thailand has paid good dividends, but not in terms of democracy; probably neither America nor Britain now attaches as much importance to democracy abroad as they did in 1945.

The main aim of Thai policy at this time was to avoid being treated as an enemy country by the British.[13] Thailand was within the British, not the American, zone of operations; and the British were plainly much less willing than the Americans to accept the Free Thais as genuinely in control of Thailand. They wanted British troops in Thailand, not only to disarm the Japanese forces, but also to disarm, or at least reorganise and retrain, the Thai armed forces.[14] Moreover they wished to impose stiff economic demands; Thailand's productive capacity was relatively undamaged in comparison with Malaya's and Burma's. Thailand's rice surplus and productive capacity in tin, teak and rubber could help the hard-pressed British Imperial economy, once Lend-Lease Aid from America came to an end.[15] Britain had the means to enforce these demands, not only because Thailand was within the British zone of operations but because Britain held most of Thailand's reserves frozen in London.

Pridi, the Regent, missed his opportunity to form a government-in-exile overseas in June 1943 when his supporter Thawi was elected President of the Parliament; a clean break at this time would almost certainly have forced British recognition, but Thawi and Pridi missed the opportunity by attempting too much.[16] The

---

[13] Puey, in Direk, op. cit., p. 431.

[14] Direk, op. cit., p. 492.

[15] Tin and rubber had been among the most important sources of dollars before America entered the war (Malaya was known locally as a 'dollar arsenal') and one of the reasons for a lack of consultation between Britain and America over Thailand may well have been pressure from the British Treasury to ensure that the dollars earned by Thai rubber and tin should accrue to the reserves in London.

[16] Thawi, in Direk, op. cit., pp. 363-5. Pridi and Thawi planned to set up a government-in-exile, which would consist of Pridi as Regent, Thawi as President of the Parliament, and Kri Dechatiwong, a Minister in the Phibun Government, all of whom were willing to escape from Thailand and go abroad. Thawi actually secured election, but Pridi wanted Phibun to ratify the election; Phibun was able to browbeat the Members of Parliament into another election, and the chance of some show of legality was lost. It is strange that Phibun's consent should have been considered important in the conditions of the time.

Free Thai leaders remained within Thailand, in close contact with Free Thais overseas; their relations with the Thai Government gradually shifted, and, because of the surrender of the Japanese, were never marked by any sharp break. The first step in trying to secure neutral or allied status was to send Major Puey, now Dr Puey Ungphakorn, Governor of the Bank of Thailand, but then a Thai officer in the British Force 136, back to London in June 1945.[17] The Phibun Government had fallen, and the new Prime Minister was taking a much more neutral stance in the War.[18] Major Puey was asked to contact Anthony Eden, the Foreign Secretary, but had neither the time nor the diplomatic standing to gain access to him; he did however see Professor Laski, the Chairman of the British Labour Party which Puey confidently expected to win the forthcoming election. Laski unfortunately failed to pass Puey on to anyone with more influence, but himself later bombarded Ernest Bevin with ineffectual letters on behalf of the Free Thais. Thailand paid heavily for Laski's delusions of grandeur, for Puey certainly had the personality to impress Attlee or Bevin directly had he had the chance, while Laski of course was just Laski with one of his crazes.

After the surrender of Japan an openly Free Thai Government, under Thawi as caretaker Prime Minister, was appointed to administer the government until Ambassador Seni, the leader of the American Free Thais, could come and take over.[19] Thawi tried to negotiate with the British in Kandy, but they would accept only a military mission.[20] Indeed they stated that it was only out of respect for the honour of the Thai government that they allowed it to send a mission voluntarily instead of demanding that one come to receive the terms on which the state of war could be ended.[21] The Thais, however, handled the negotiations with great skill. The leader of their mission was General Senanarong, the most successful of the leaders of the short-lived original opposition to the Japanese invasion; the secretary was Major Puey, in the uniform of a British Major of Force 136.[22] The mission was briefed as a good-

[17] Puey, in Direk, op. cit.

[18] Pla Thawng, op. cit.

[19] Pla Thawng, op. cit., issue of 11 Aug. 1964.

[20] Personal interview (1967) with Dr Puey Ungphakorn, secretary of the mission at the time.

[21] Direk, op. cit., pp. 488-9.

[22] Puey, in Direk, op. cit., p. 433.

will mission with no political negotiating powers;[23] and it gave great publicity to the hospitable treatment it was receiving.[24] The British commanders presented twenty-one demands, which would have given Britain complete control of the military, political and economic life of Thailand, and demanded that the Thais immediately accept them.[25] Probably these demands had been drawn up for presentation to a Thai government and army that would have been actively fighting, on the side of the Japanese, against British and Free Thai armed forces. In such conditions the demands would have made sense. There is a good deal of evidence that the secrecy surrounding the atomic bomb kept at least the political planners of British post-war policy in South-East Asia ignorant of the likelihood of a sudden and (locally) non-violent end of the war.[26] Both in Malaya and in Thailand there was insufficient time to re-think the policy, and previously planned policies were implemented with no essential change.

The Thai delegation reacted first by claiming that they had no authority to discuss political matters; next they contacted local American representatives and convinced them that previous Thai contacts with the American Office of Strategic Services had led the mission to think it had come over merely to make joint arrangements for receiving the Japanese surrender.[27] In this context the

[23] Interview with Dr Puey.

[24] Press interview by negotiating team reported in Thai newspapers, 5 Sept. 1945.

[25] Direk, op. cit., pp. 489-94.

[26] No doubt it was known that the Americans hoped to develop new weapons that could end the war quickly; but both in Thailand and in Malaya the policy actually attempted seems to have been worked out on the basis of terms of capitulation after the local liberation of the countries, with Chinese guerrilla aid in Malaya and Free Thai aid against Phibun and the Japanese in Thailand. In fairness to the British it must be emphasised: (a) that strict secrecy in America was essential; (b) the British, not the Americans, were actually responsible for the detailed plans for South-East Asia, which was in their zone; (c) there had been a change of government in the U.K.; (d) a delay of even one month in the readiness of the atomic bombs would have meant that the British plans were appropriate. The British actually landed in Malaya on the very day they had expected to do so. Because Japan had surrendered there was no resistance. The failure to adjust within a few days is intelligible, but nevertheless caused great harm. Cf. W. L. Holland, *Asian Nationalism and the West* pp. 298-300, where I discuss the effects in Malaya.

[27] A careful reading of Direk, op. cit., shows that the Thais knew the aims of the British in sending for this mission, and deliberately briefed it,

British demands were made to appear quite outrageous. Cables hurriedly flew round the world and pressure via Washington and London compelled the British delegation to allow the Thais to accede merely to the strictly military demands, and negotiate over the rest.[28]

These subsequent negotiations lasted from September 1945 to 1st January 1946 when the Formal Agreement was signed. They were conducted by an exceptionally able Thai, Prince Viwat, who had built up the Bank of Thailand and carried on a skilful defence of the Thai economy against Japanese pressures. Prince Viwat, a tough and courageous negotiator[29] was strongly supported by Seni the new Prime Minister in Bangkok, a shrewd analyst of American policy with an understanding of the possibilities of judicious leakage of information to the American press.[30] Between them they succeeded in evading most of the political demands. The Americans were to be associated in the bodies that controlled exports and collected the rice,[31] and this meant that even the economic demands —on which they had to give way—could be renegotiated later.[32] In order to secure these concessions they had to agree to deliver, free of charge, the full 1½ million tons of rice that the British demanded.[33]

---

nevertheless, as a goodwill military mission. The Thai Government could hardly have known in advance how little the Americans had been consulted; but it was a piece of brilliant strategy in an uncertain situation, and achieved excellent results.

[28] Compare Puey, in Direk, op. cit., p. 433, Phra Phisal in Direk, op. cit., p. 458 and Direk, 497-8. This confirms information given me by a reliable American source (whose name I may not quote) and by Dr Puey and M. R. Seni in interviews, that American pressure was exercised at this time.

[29] Viwat Memoir Part I pp. 34-5 gives a vivid account of the stand he took in the negotiations over the 'Emerald Buddha'.

[30] M. R. Seni himself told me in an interview (1967) that he had given information to American journalists to influence the later stages of the negotiations; cf. E. Snow, 'Secrets from Siam', *Saturday Evening Post*, Jan. 1946.

[31] Direk, op. cit., p. 508.

[32] There is a hint of this in the interview with the American ambassador —see Direk, loc. cit.—and M. R. Seni and Dr Puey both confirmed that Pridi wanted to settle Thailand's status and renegotiate the economic terms with American help later.

[33] This amount included the amount already freely offered by Seni, and was formally not an indemnity but an earnest of willingness to co-operate with the United Nations.

It must be emphasised that the Thai government was forced to resist even temporary political control because of the severity of the economic demands, and the danger that such control would give a dominating position in Thai economic life to the British trading firms. The Thais feared (not unreasonably) that they would be reduced to a virtually colonial status. The great strength of Thailand in maintaining its independence has been its understanding of the colonisation process. Just as King Chulalongkorn clearly understood the different significance of a British adviser recruited from England and one appointed from Singapore,[34] so Seni understood the difference between an obligation to deliver rice as an agreed contribution by a Thai government to the United Nations and an obligation direct to a British-controlled Agency enforced by political controls through the British Embassy. The latter would in fact have generated (whether London intended it or not) strong local interests with the power to dominate Thai economic and political life.

Yet there is some evidence that if the economic demands had not been so stiff, Pridi at least might have found it acceptable to yield to some interference with the armed forces, which were his chief opposition.[35] Seni, however, who had never accepted the declaration of war and knew little of the internal forces in Thai politics, was quite unwilling to submit to such pressure, and would have been a much more serious obstacle.

The reserves backing the Thai currency at this time were held in London, New York and Tokyo.[36] Neither Major Puey nor Prince Viwat succeeded in securing the release of any of the funds blocked in London; even the envoy who had been flown out to America in 1945, failed to get the reserves in America released before early 1946, and also failed to get Thailand included among the countries which were to obtain help from U.N.R.R.A.[37] Thus the Thais at

[34] Negotiations on this question between King Chulalongkorn and the British Foreign Office are mentioned by Dr E. Thio in an unpublished Ph.D. thesis 'British Policy in the Malay Peninsula 1880-1909', London University, 1956.

[35] Pridi could not, of course, have been expected to agree without some show of pressure. However (a) he did not mention the status of the army when briefing Major Puey; (b) he was quite prepared to go into a government in exile and take up arms against Phibun.

[36] Bank of Thailand *Thi-ralük wan-khrob-rawb pi thi-yi-sib* (*20-year Memorial*) Bangkok, Bank of Thailand, 1962, p. 11.

[37] Phra Phisan in Direk, op. cit., pp. 366-71.

first had great difficulty in re-equipping their transport system and obtaining essential imports such as medical supplies.[38]

I must now proceed to show how the special characteristics of the present Thai economy arose directly from the experiences of Thailand in this immediate post-war period. I shall divide the argument into three parts. First I shall show how the obligation to deliver rice, combined with the political structure which the negotiations produced, led to the system of developing the economy by heavy taxation of rice. Next I shall show how the structure of Thai banking was dominated by the experience of these negotiations. Finally I shall show how these negotiations produced the present peculiar situation in which a large part of the Thai economy is controlled (indirectly through the Departments) by the Thai political leaders, and yet the policy is a liberal one of opposing nationalisation.

First, however, I must emphasise that such democratic elements as there were in the Free Thai movement had a very short-lived influence. There had been no radical change in Thai social structure, and Field Marshal Phibun was able very soon after being acquitted as a war-criminal, to use armed force once again to become dictator of Thailand. His ideas of government had changed little. Like almost every Thai he put the independence and sovereignty of Thailand first, and was both supple and resolute in maintaining it;[39] like the Chakkri kings, whom he had helped to overthrow, he had a strong modernising impulse;[40] and like most of the 1932 revolutionaries he believed that the fruits of power should go to those who were trained to use the apparatus of power, and not to a hereditary monarchy.[41] This was approximately the limit of his democratic sentiment.

The free delivery of one and a half million tons of rice proved unworkable, as Pridi had foreseen. Within five months a new agreement was negotiated offering a price of £12.14.0 per ton for

[38] Phra Phisan, loc. cit., Bank of Thailand, op. cit., pp. 29-30.

[39] Though more sympathetic to Japanese ideas than many Thais, Phibun was no puppet. For example he supported Prince Viwat's efforts to restrict Japanese economic demands, kept the Thai army intact, and would not allow the Japanese access to prisoners taken by Thais.

[40] Sometimes this took rather ridiculous forms, e.g. compelling Thai ladies to wear hats; Thawi in Direk, op. cit., p. 363; Rayne Kruger, *The Devil's Discus*, London, Cassell, 1964.

[41] Pla Thawng, op. cit., 1 and 3 Aug.

the rice,[42] though this was still far below the free market price. Smuggling, which had been carried on for survival during the Japanese Occupation, was now big business in which several United Nations soldiers and civil servants took a hand.[43] Before the 1932 revolution only the King had large sums of money in Thailand. Now really wealthy Chinese and Thais began to emerge, depositing their money in the new banks and investing in new undertakings. The Thai Rice Bureau, to which all export rice legally had to be sold, was at this time an honest institution, but its powers were inadequate to obtain much rice until a further agreement almost doubled the price to £20 a ton.[44] This was still well below the free market price, but at this price rice began to be exported in fairly large quantities through official channels.

An attempt was made by the Thai government to monopolise the milling of rice in 1949, but this was successfully resisted by the Chinese millers and European exporters, who mobilised diplomatic pressure against such a reversion to national socialist tactics.[45] Phibun learnt his lesson. The Rice Bureau was an accepted instrument in Government-to-Government transactions. If he wanted to derive a profit from rice for the ruling army group, he had to gain control of the Rice Bureau. International allocation of rice ended at the end of 1949, but most governments still wanted to control the buying of rice. The Rice Bureau was taken over by the politicians, and throughout the sellers' market of the Korean War its accounts were never published.[46] It was an open secret that the profits from rice were one of the main sources of the dictator's power to buy support.

The Thai politicians thus had both a personal and a political interest in keeping the internal price of rice low during the whole period of the Korean War, when the international price of rice was high. This is the main reason for the present pattern of the Thai economy, with low internal prices of rice keeping the cost of living low. Once the internal price of rice had been kept low through all

[42] Bank of Thailand, op. cit., p. 29.

[43] Stories of this smuggling—some of them circumstantial—were common currency in Singapore in 1946, but difficult to substantiate. The statement in the text represents the minimum that can hardly be doubted.

[44] As from 1 January 1947. See Bank of Thailand, *Annual Report, 1947.*

[45] Information based on interviews with businessmen (whose names cannot be published) during 1965 and 1967.

[46] J. C. Ingram *Economic Change in Thailand since 1850*, Stanford U.P. 1955, p. 186.

the post-war turmoil, a rise would have introduced new disturbances in the real earnings of junior civil servants—an important class in maintaining the government's power. The machinery for maintaining the disparity had originally been imposed on Thailand; later it became a source of wealth and power for the government; now it has become an important instrument in Thai economic development.[47]

There have subsequently been substantial changes in the way in which the margin between the external and internal price is used; and since these have a bearing on development we may consider them briefly here. From 1954 onward the Rice Bureau was faced by a buyers' market for rice.[48] Increasingly private traders were allowed to seek markets, paying a premium for their breach of the Bureau's monopoly. At the beginning of 1955 the whole rice trade was returned to private hands and the premium became the normal form of the margin between internal and external prices.[49] Largely under pressure from the Bank of Thailand, this premium nearly all found its way into official government funds, not private pockets. However a rise in the external price of rice began to lead to internal shortages. Quotas were imposed on exporters, and the allocation of these was a new source of wealth to the politicians, helping them to tide over until new sources of political income became available, such as the National Economic Development Corporation and the expanding government enterprises.[50] Ultimately discontent with the quotas led to their abolition, and the premium was deliberately adjusted from time to time in response to changes in the internal cost of living.[51]

The proceeds of the rice premium are now wholly (or at least mainly) collected for public purposes. It is official policy to return an increasing proportion of this revenue indirectly to the farmers in the form of irrigation, extension services etc.[52]

[47] The rice premium's effects on diversification and other matters are discussed more fully in T. H. Silcock, *Thailand*, chapters 9 and 10.

[48] A. Mousny, op. cit., pp. 35-45.

[49] W. M. Corden, in T. H. Silcock, *Thailand*, chapter 7.

[50] International Bank for Reconstruction and Development, *A Public Development Programme for Thailand*, Baltimore, Johns Hopkins Press, 1959, pp. 93-4.

[51] A. Mousny, loc. cit., W. M. Corden, loc. cit.

[52] National Economic Development Board 'Report of the Thai Delegation to the Consultative Committee on Thailand, October 4th, 1965, Washington D.C. Sponsored by the I.B.R.D.', Bangkok, mimeo, p. 8.

The effects of the premium are by no means all favourable to development. Probably it discourages the application of fertiliser in rice cultivation. It may lead to some misallocation of land and some miscalculation of irrigation benefits. Yet for good or ill it has become a critical element in the development of the modern Thai economy.

If we ask how the Bank of Thailand came to have both the will and the power to interfere with the politicians' use of rice profits we are led back again to the post-war negotiations, to Prince Viwat and Major Puey, and the effect of the post-war situation on the influence of the Bank in modern Thailand. Thailand probably owes her development at least as much to the constructive efforts of the Bank as to the rice premium; but the role of the Bank might well have been very different if it had not been for the experience of these negotiations.

Prince Viwat was Cambridge-educated, and when he built up the Bank of Thailand he modelled it on the Bank of England, complete with separate Issue and Banking Departments.[53] War-time experience, however, had convinced him that anything like sound money and balanced budgets would be achieved in Thailand only if the Bank had some additional strength within the political structure. He was probably worried by Pridi's disposition to use commercial Banks as a source of political power and influence.[54] Banks were easy to establish in the inflationary conditions of war-time Thailand. Just as Phibun had brought the army into Thai politics, Pridi, who established both the Bank of Asia and the Bank of Ayuthaya as sources of political influence, brought banking into Thai politics. Prince Viwat's training might well have led him to seek a sterling link to reinforce his influence, provided the Bank of England and the British Government had been willing to give him some moral support in relation to internal credit, combined with respect for Thai sovereignty. He had moved some Thai reserves out of sterling into dollars in the early years of the war,[55] and would probably have been a fairly independent member of the

---

[53] The Viwat Memoir, op. cit., includes (Pt II, pp. 53-71) the first two chapters, in English, of a book drafted by the Prince, but left unfinished, on the origins of the Bank of Thailand, as well as much material in Thai setting out his thoughts on the establishment of this Bank.

[54] This is not explicit in the Viwat Memoir, and of course Pridi's name is not mentioned in the contemporary documents cited there; but see pp. 53-4, 97-114, 135-74.

[55] Viwat Memoir, op. cit., pp. 28, 66-7.

sterling area system. However, Major Puey brought a copy of the Bretton Woods White Paper back from London with him before the end of the War,[56] and this appears to have convinced Prince Viwat that membership of the International Bank and Fund was important as a support to Thailand's internal financial soundness. The tough attitude of the British towards Thailand's sterling reserves must have added a powerful external reason. An international authority would threaten Thailand's sovereignty less.

Thailand was admitted to the International Bank and Fund in May 1949.[57] From then on the Bank of Thailand was able to use Thailand's international standing as a powerful weapon in internal politics, particularly after the politicians saw the improvement in negotiating power that resulted from the transfer of the U.N. Economic Commission for Asia and the Far East from Shanghai to Bangkok in the same year. At the same time the urgent need to rebuild the reserves forced the Bank to take a strong deflationary position in internal finance. The method adopted was a multiple exchange rate system, under which exporters of rice surrendered the whole, and exporters of rubber and tin a part, of their foreign exchange proceeds at a low official rate, while the Bank sold foreign exchange at a little below the higher free rate to the commercial banks for general imports.[58] The Bank's exchange profits were usually higher than the Government's deficits. In addition that part of the profit of the Rice Bureau which went into private hands was mainly hidden away, with only a part spent on current consumption. These deflationary influences helped to prevent inflation from resulting from the build up of the currency reserves in a time of heavy Government spending. Later, when rice was returned to the private trade the Bank simultaneously abolished the obligation to deliver rice at a low exchange rate. This gave the Bank some power to take a hand in the establishment of the fund which was to replace both the Rice Bureau and the Bank's exchange profit, and to see that it all went into public, not private, hands.[59]

[56] Interview with Dr Puey, 1967.

[57] Viwat Memoir, op. cit., Pt I, p. 116.

[58] The multiple exchange rate is described in detail in S. C. Yang, *A Multiple Exchange Rate System*, Madison, Wisconsin U.P., 1957; cf. also W. M. Corden in T. H. Silcock, op. cit., ch. 7, and A. Mousny, op. cit.

[59] The strategy adopted was, on the one hand to set up an account in the Ministry of Economic Affairs, and on the other to bring pressure to bear via the International Monetary Fund to reform the Budgetary System in 1956.

If we turn to ask why the Bank should set itself up to be an upholder of Thailand's financial virtue, using international influences to help it in its task, the reason was probably, in the first instance, the great expansion in Thai commercial banking during the War, the involvement of these banks in Thai politics, and the consequent recognition by Prince Viwat that some help would be needed if the Bank was to exercise its basic function of controlling the credit system. The resulting structure of private banks, headed by aggressive entrepreneurs and supported by politicians who derive revenue from them, kept partly in check by a professional central bank with some international support, has probably provided constructive tension for Thailand's development.[60] It was largely the result of the Anglo-American differences, carefully fanned by the Thais, concerning what was to be done about the national-socialist influences within the Thai social structure.

We have already seen that the Americans hoped for democratic pressures from the Free Thai Movement, and that these hopes came to nothing. (The British did rather more for Pridi, in helping his escape from Phibun than the Americans did;[61] but the Free Thais could have been supported only by considerable outside intervention which would have greatly lessened their appeal to the Thais.) The British plan to reorganise both the army and the economy carried (as has been explained) grave dangers of creating a colonial group of merchants and administrators in control of the political and economic life of the country. This danger—in the post-war world and with a Labour Government in London—might have been less than the Thais feared, though with their history they could hardly be expected not to fear it. In any event, the severity of the initial economic demands and the American complete acceptance of the invalidity of the Thai declaration of war made the success of such a plan impossible.

The negotiations ensured that the Americans should oppose almost every British effort to modify Thai political or economic life, while they lacked the knowledge themselves to help reform and strengthen Thai democratic forces. Nothing remained to prevent the dictator taking over. The structure of Thai politics con-

[60] There are however drawbacks in the system; see T. H. Silcock, *Thailand*, chap. 8 for fuller discussion.

[61] For a dramatic account of the incident see Rayne Kruger, op. cit., pp. 117-21.

tinued to depend on leaders who could control the army;[62] but Pridi's introduction of the commercial banks into Thai politics helped to ensure that banks, managed mainly by energetic Chinese, should become one of the important instruments in controlling the army and the civil service.[63]

Another important instrument, that had been growing in the years immediately before the war, was a group of government owned enterprises, notably the state railways, the Thai Rice Company and provincial trading companies.[64] When Phibun Songkhram returned he realised, as a result of the post-war negotiations and his own experiences as a person barely acquitted of war crimes, that at all costs he must avoid antagonising the Americans. Successful British opposition to the monopolising of rice may have contributed to his fear of any direct Government ownership of industry; for the Americans, on this occasion, did not support Thailand.

At this time, however, mere hand-outs from the profits of the Rice Bureau were not enough to hold the loyalty of his supporters. Jobs in government industries were necessary, and he could not afford to abolish the supposedly strategic industries controlled by the Army, the remaining provincial trading companies, and other features of a war economy that had survived the post-war purge. Indeed the War Veterans' Organisation was creating new positions.[65] In the early fifties Phibun split off many of these industries into semi-independent corporations, with ministers and senior civil servants occupying ex-officio positions on their boards and drawing profits from them; the state budget supplied much of the capital.[66] As long as Phibun actively opposed communism and all state planning, these public corporations aroused only mild disapproval.

In recent times the leading politicians have found participation

[62] D. A. Wilson, *Politics in Thailand*, New York, Cornell U.P., 1962, esp. chapters 4 and 6.

[63] F. W. Riggs, *Thailand: the Modernization of a Bureaucratic Polity*, Honolulu, East-West Centre Press, 1966, chapter 9; T. H. Silcock, op. cit., chapters 4 and 8.

[64] The Thai Budget Documents 1967 give, in Volume 4, brief accounts of the origin of the different public enterprises, from which some of the earliest ones still surviving can be identified. Other information is based on Annual Reports of the Ministry of Industry and on interviews with business men.

[65] T. H. Silcock, op. cit., Appendix A, Chart III.

[66] Ibid., text and Table A.I.

in the private sector of the economy more rewarding than control of the government enterprises. They play a protective role on the boards of industries and banks and have often developed private businesses, usually in the names of close relatives.[67] They have come to realise how wasteful many of the Government-affiliated industries are, and are now prepared to support in principle the Bank of Thailand's long campaign against them.[68] Nearly all the politicians, however, have loyal supporters in their Departments who are involved in these industries, and the more liberal policy is still far from effective.[69]

The present structure of the Thai economy seems to be relatively stable, and to have achieved an enviable rate of growth, from which most members of the population are benefiting, though by no means equally. It is hardly, from an American point of view, an ideal regime. Nevertheless the increasing power of an honest King, the great increase in the number and the influence of professionally trained Thais, and the great expansion in basic education since World War II, will probably ensure that the abuses of Government diminish.

Any Thai would probably draw from this story the moral that Thailand's tutelary deity still watches over the nation's welfare. A British economist may be permitted to observe that generosity without intelligence sometimes—in this necessarily uncertain world —pays better dividends than intelligence without generosity.

[67] There is virtually no restriction on the business activities of political public servants; bureaucrats can hold positions openly on public industries, where they commonly serve *ex officio* and nevertheless draw revenue from them. Private interests of bureaucrats sometimes need to be covered by the name of a close relative to avoid prosecution.

[68] Government industries have been the subject of adverse comment by the Bank of Thailand since 1954; see Bank of Thailand *Annual Reports*, 1954, 1958; Puey Ungphakorn *Speeches*, Bangkok, Bank of Thailand, 1964.

[69] The difficulty of eliminating abuses, because of personal interests of those concerned, is summarised in the Thai proverb 'Pass your hand over your face, you encounter your nose'.

Appendix II

QUESTIONNAIRES USED IN VILLAGES

Notes on Use of Questionnaires

1. There were eight separate questionnaires[1]
   - (a) General background information on the village
   - (b) Education
   - (c) Village Trading
   - (d) Irrigation[2]
   - (e) Sequence of Change
   - (f) Economic Opportunity

2. The first 5 (a to e) were filled in for 'the village', i.e., the village was the sample unit. In three cases, however, (e, g, and h) approximately ten farmers per village were *also* interviewed. For questionnaire f *only* individual farmers were interviewed. (In practice it was usually possible only to ask g *or* h—in addition to e and f—of any one farmer.)

3. Notes on use of Village Trading questionnaires
   - a. Question 8 was asked of (the required number of) merchants.
   - b. Question 9 was asked of the manager of the village co-operative (marketing) society, if any.
   - c. Question 10 was asked of merchants.

[1] Questionnaires d-f were prepared by Dr D. H. Penny and are being used in international comparisons. All the questionnaires were translated into Thai by Mr. Chumnian Boonma of Kasetsart University.

[2] This questionnaire was abandoned as it proved inapplicable in most villages and difficulties arose over the translation.

4. Notes on use of Economic Opportunity questionnaire

    a. The quantities of rice mentioned in questions were translated into local value (money) terms.

    b. Question 4 was not asked if *all* answers to question 3 showed that the money would be used solely for productive purposes in agriculture.

a. GENERAL VILLAGE QUESTIONNAIRE (Complete one only for each village studied. Interview village head or other reliable village informant.)

1. Name of village
   Sub-district

   District
   Province

2. Population of village
   < 15 years > 15 years
   Total
   Men
   Women
   Total

3. Total village agricultural land
   Wet rice fields (irrigated fields) Ha
   Unirrigated arable land
   House gardens/land in perennials
   Total

4. Average farm size (by land types)
   Irrigated fields

   Unirrigated arable land
   House gardens, etc.

   (Total) average

5. Soil type(s)

6. Average annual rainfall mm

7. Height above sea-level metre

8. Distance from
   Regional market   km
   'Major' local market   km
   Nearest local market   km

9. a. Distance of village centre from
     Main road   km
     Railway station   km
   b. i Specify if trucks can come to village centres:
     Yes/No

10. Number and type of vehicles owned in the village
    Truck
    Automobile

    Pickup

ii All year round?
                Yes/No   Buses
iii If not, how far to   Tractors (large $>$ 25 Hp)
     nearest road?   km   (small $<$ 25 Hp)

11. Number and type of
information sources
available in village:
Radio   Extension agencies:
  Note % owned by   resident agent Yes/No
  farmer %   agent visits
Newspapers (number   times per year
  bought/delivered daily)   village co-op. Yes/No
Coffee shops/restaurants   Other (specify)

b. EDUCATION (Complete *one* per village. Interview village head, village schoolteacher or other reliable informant.)

1. a. Number of primary
schools in the village
b. Total number of pupils
2. a. Distance of village
from nearest junior
high school (or
equivalent) km
b. Distance of village
from nearest senior
high school (or
equivalent) km
c. Distance of village
from nearest university
(or equivalent) km
3. Number of village children
currently attending:
a. junior high (or
equivalent)
b. senior high (or
equivalent)
c. university (or
equivalent)
4. In what year did a child
from this village begin to

7. In what year did the *child
of a farmer* from this
village first graduate from
a. junior high (or
equivalent)
b. senior high (or
equivalent)
c. university (or
equivalent)
8. How many children from
this village have ever
graduated from
a. junior high (or
equivalent)
b. senior high (or
equivalent)
c. university (or
equivalent)
9. How many of those
enumerated under 8 live
in the village?
a. Those graduated from
university (or
equivalent)

attend, for the first time,
a. junior high (or equivalent)
b. senior high (or equivalent)
c. university (or equivalent)

5. In what year did a *farmer's* child from the village begin to attend, for the first time,
    a. junior high (or equivalent)
    b. senior high (or equivalent)
    c. university (or equivalent)

6. In what year did a child from this village first graduate from
    a. junior high (or equivalent)
    b. senior high (or equivalent)
    c. university (or equivalent)

b. Those graduated from senior high (or equivalent)
c. Those graduated from junior high (or equivalent)

10. What do the people enumerated under 9 do for a living? Give details

11. Estimate, and rank in appropriate order of importance (1, 2, 3, etc) the sources of money used to finance the schooling of *farmers'* children outside the village:
Source of funds
    Trading
    Farming
    Borrowing
    Assistance from family
    Assistance from neighbours
    Other (specify)

12. What do farmers of this village in general think about the usefulness of higher education (i.e. schooling above primary level) for their children?

13. a. Name and position of person(s) interviewed
    b. Name of interviewer
    c. Date of interview

c. VILLAGE TRADING (Interview village leaders, traders and managers of co-operatives, and farmers (where necessary)).

1. How many shops or stores are there in the village?

2. Who owns/runs these stores?
    a. People born in the village   %
    b. People from outside the village   %

3. Is there a co-operative in this village that sells agricultural requisites (fertiliser, insecticides, agricultural implements, etc).

4. Which type of store (private or co-operative) was the first to supply and sell the following to farmers in this village?

	Private Store	Co-operative
a. Artificial fertiliser		
b. Insecticide (or other chemicals)		
c. Knapsack sprayer		
d. Agricultural implements (specify)		
e. Improved seeds		

5. Do co-ops or private stores have in stock *at the present time* any of the following?
   a. Fertiliser
   b. Insecticides
   c. Knapsack sprayers
   d. Agricultural implements (specify)
   e. Improved seeds

6. If the agricultural requisites specified in 4 above, are *not currently available*, find out when each was last available for sale in the village.

	Month	Year
a. Fertiliser		
b. Insecticides		
c. Knapsack sprayers		
d. Agricultural implements (specify)		
e. Improved seeds		

7. In what year(s), were the following first stocked/made available by private stores or the co-op?

	Year
a. Fertiliser	
b. Insecticides	
c. Knapsack sprayers	
d. Agricultural implements (specify)	
e. Improved seeds	

8. If it was a private store (or stores) that first supplied/sold

modern agricultural requisites, find out from the store keep-er(s) involved

   a. The source of information regarding the profitability
       of selling

                                   Source of information
       i Fertiliser
       ii Insecticides
       iii Other (specify)

   b. Where did you (he) get the funds to finance the pur-
       chase, storage and sale of your (his) first supplies of:

                                   Source of finance
       i Fertiliser
       ii Insecticides
       iii Other (specify)

9. If it was the co-op that first supplied/sold modern agricultural
    requisites, find out from the manager

   a. The source of information regarding the profitability
       of selling:

                                   Source of information
       i   Fertiliser
       ii Insecticides
       iii Other (specify)

   b. Where did you get the funds to finance the purchase,
       storage and sale of your first supplies of

                                   Source of finance
       i Fertiliser
       ii Insecticides
       iii Other (specify)

10. (Ask the following questions of (some) private merchants
    and the manager of the co-operative)

   a. Are farmers willing or reluctant to buy these modern
       inputs?
       Why are they willing/reluctant?
       Informant A   Informant B   Informant C
       Informant D

   b. Which farmers in your view are most willing to buy
       modern inputs? (list 3 in order of importance)

                                   Informants: A B C D

    i   Old farmers
    ii Large farmers
   iii Educated farmers
   iv Rich farmers
    v Medium farmers
   vi Poor farmers
  vii Tenant farmers
 viii Sharecroppers
   ix Other (specify)

Note: please indicate the meaning each respondent gives to the terms 'old', 'large', 'poor', etc. Informants A B C D

c. Do most farmers usually buy for cash or on credit? Informants A B C D

d. Has a farmer ever come and placed a firm order for a modern input that you (ask the leading storekeeper—A—and the Co-operative manager—B) did not have in stock at that moment?

      Type of input (specify)   Ever ordered A B

e. Have there ever been cases where farmers have *not* ordered such production requisites from a store, or the co-operative, even though it is clear that they intend to buy such goods? Why did they not place orders with you? (Ask the respective managers and also a few farmers.)

11.   a. Names of persons interviewed   Name   Occupation
       b. Name of interviewer
       c. Date of interview

d. IRRIGATION (not listed here, see p. 223 n. 2).

e. SEQUENCE OF CHANGE (To be used for the 'village as a whole', and also for ten farmers)

Innovation/ New technology	Year first used[3]	Type of crop or livestock

[3] 'Year first used' is the year in which any farmer (or the individual farmer being interviewed) first started using the innovation on a continuous basis.

1. Artificial fertiliser (specify)
   a.
   b.

2. Bought livestock feed (specify)
   a.
   b.

3. New and important cash crops[4]

   (specify)
   a.
   b.
   c.

4. Chemical pesticides (specify)
   a.
   b.

5. Animal medicines/vaccines
   a.
   b.

6. New methods for old crops (e.g. formerly broadcast, now transplanted; weed more intensively; use compost, etc.) (specify)
   a.
   b.
   c.
   d.
   e.

7. Use new agricultural implements[5]

   (specify)
   a.
   b.
   c.
   d.

[4] Cash (or commercial) crops, are usually industrial raw materials, but they may also be food crops, for example maize in Thailand which was introduced with the *primary* aim of selling the output on the market.

[5] New tools and equipment: for example, the sickle for the cutting knife, steel for wooden plough, tractors, etc.

8. Buy improved seeds or other planting materials[6]
    a.
    b.
    c.

9. a. Name and position of person interviewed
    b. Basic data on the farm (for individual farmer inter-
       viewed); Size of farm, soil type, main crops grown,
       number of dependants, land tenure (land rented, etc),
       total production last year, age of farmer.
    c. Name of interviewer
    d. Date of interview.

f. ECONOMIC OPPORTUNITY

1. Have you ever borrowed—money, rice, etc.—to meet an economic need?

2. a. Are you in debt at the present time?
   b. (If 2a yes), for what did you borrow the money, rice, etc.,
      the last time you borrowed?
   c. (if 2a yes): suppose you were given *as a gift* a sum of
      money exactly equal to your present total debt (including
      accrued interest), how would you use the gift money?

3. a. Suppose you were given a *gift* of money to the value of 60
      kilogram of paddy, how (or for what) would you use the
      money?
   b. (Same: but gift to the value of 600 kg paddy)
   c. (Same: but gift to the value of 3,000 kg paddy)

4. a. If such gifts could only be used to finance productive ex-
      penditure (i.e. could be only used for agricultural pur-
      poses), how (or for what) would you use gift money to the
      value of 60 kg of paddy?
   b. (Same as 4a: but gift to the value of 600 kg paddy)
   c. (Same as 4a: but gift to the value of 3,000 kg paddy)

5. Have you *bought* any of the following agricultural requisites:

Type	This year	Last year	2 years ago
Fertiliser			
Pesticides			

[6] For all crops. Improved seeds, etc., should be of guaranteed quality for,
in some cases, e.g., rubber, planting materials brought in to the village from
outside are of low/unknown quality.

Pure seed
Modern agricultural
implements (specify)

6. a. (Ask *only* to farmers who have ever bought and used artificial fertilisers).
What is your per hectare (or other unit area) yield of

	If fertilised	Not fertilised
Paddy		
Maize		
Other (specify)		

Note amounts and types of fertiliser used

b. (Ask *only* to farmers who have *never* used fertilisers). In
your estimation, how much output (calculation on a per
hectare, or other unit area basis) would you get if you used
artificial fertiliser?

If used on	If fertilised	If not fertilised
Paddy		
Maize		
Other (specify)		

7. a. Which in your view is the best (most profitable) way or
ways of using your own spare money capital in agriculture?[7]
(to buy fertiliser? to repair the irrigation system? to buy
pure seed? etc.)

b. Would it be more profitable to use any spare money capital
you had directly in agriculture (see 7a.) or to lend it to a
farmer or other person?

8. a. Name of person interviewed, and some basic data on his
farm (see questionnaire on 'sequence of change')

b. Name of interviewer

c. Date

g. TRANSPORT AND PRICE CHANGES

1. In the past ten years has there been any important change in
transport conditions in this village?

a. Any new road built, or road improved, to the village?

b. Any new road built, or road improved, to your local
village local market centre?

---

[7] His 'spare capital' may be a lot or a little.

    c. Any new water transport channel, or any improvement in water transport?

    d. Any new development or improvement in goods transport services?

    e. Any new development or improvement in passenger transport?

    f. Any other transport improvement? Specify.

2. How are the main products of the village shipped out to consumers? (What transport route, what vehicles?)

    a. Is the service convenient whenever it is required?

    b. Has there been any change in this respect in the past ten years?

    c. During the past ten years have merchants or their agents come more than before to buy produce in the village?

    d. Do farmers or other villagers go to the local market more than before or not?

    e. Please state the difference in 1957 between the price villagers received here for their main product and the Bangkok price.

    f. Please state the corresponding difference in 1967.

3. How do branded goods (e.g. cigarettes, Coca Cola) reach this village (what transport route, what vehicles?)

    a. Is the service convenient whenever it is required?

    b. Has there been any change in this respect in the past ten years?

    c. During the past ten years have travelling salesmen visited this village more than before?

    d. Please say what proportion of the villagers go to buy goods more than 10 kilometres away at least once a year.

    e. Please state the purchase price in this village of (a) a litre of petrol, (b) a chopper, (c) a toothbrush.

    f. If you went to buy a, b, and c above at a major market, more than 10 kilometres away, how much would you save?

    g. What difference would there have been in the savings mentioned in f. if you had bought in the market ten years ago?

4. What price changes have been most discussed in this village in the past three years?

    a. How many farmers change the crops they plant because of price changes?

    b. Which types of farmers respond most to price changes? (see Question 10b on Village Trading) (This was mistranslated as 'How do farmers respond . . . (see 9, 10b on Village Trading)' and I usually failed to make contact!)

5. In the past ten years what change has there been in the number of villagers who have *never*

                                    Now   Ten years ago

    a. Been to Bangkok

    b. Been outside this Region

    c. Been outside this Province

Please describe any recent changes and specify the types of travel.

6. Please state the number of families who

    a. Have moved in to live in this village in the past three years?

    b. What was the occupation of these families?

    c. Have moved out of the village in the past three years?

    d. Please state the reasons why these families moved.

    e. How many of the families in c went to stay with relatives in Bangkok?

    f. How many of the families in c went to stay with relatives in a town in another province?

7. How many villagers in this village

    a. Have been to work for short periods in Bangkok?

    b. Go almost every year to work for short periods in Bangkok?

    c. Have been to work for short periods in a town in another province?

    d. Go almost every year to work for short periods in a town in another province?

    e. Have been to work in the country around here, more than 20 km away?

h. OPERATIONS OF GOVERNMENT

1. Have attempts been made in the past three years to set up any of the following in your village:
    a. Co-operatives?
    b. Young Farmers' Clubs?
    c. Other Associations to help farmers?
    d. Have any of these been established successfully?
    e. Do these help the farmers?
    f. Please mention any failings of these institutions in your village.

2.   a. Please give the name of the Economic Officer of your Province
    b. Has he visited your village for any purpose during the past two years? (Specify)
    c. Has he taken any action during the past two years to increase your income? (Specify)
    d. Has he taken any action during the past two years to reduce your income? (Specify)

3.   a. Please give the name of the Agricultural Officer of your Province
    b. Has he visited your village for any purpose during the past two years? (Specify)
    c. Has he taken any action during the past two years to increase your income? (Specify)
    d. Has he taken any action during the past two years to reduce your income? (Specify)

4.   a. Please give the name of the Rice Officer of your Province
    b. Has he visited your village for any purpose during the past two years? (Specify)
    c. Has he taken any action during the past two years to increase your income? (Specify)
    d. Has he taken any action during the past two years to reduce your income? (Specify)

5. Has any District Official given you personal assistance in your work in the past two years?
    a. Assisted you without charge at your own request
    b. Assisted you without charge on his own initiative

    c. Given you any assistance in return for payment of expenses of any kind. Please specify.

6. What expenditure by the government do you think helps most to raise your income?

7. What government tax do you consider the heaviest?

8. Please suggest any way in which the government should help you more than at present to earn more income.

References

Allen, G. C. and Donnithorne, A., 1959. *Western Enterprise in Indonesia and Malaya*, London.

Bacon, G. H., 1964. 'Report on the Rice Department's Statement on Double Cropping of Rice', Ministry of Agriculture mimeo., Bangkok.

Bangkok Bank, 1966. *Facts and Figures: An Investor's Guide to Thailand*, Bangkok.

Bank of Thailand, 1949-55. *Annual Reports*, Bangkok.

——, 1961. *Wiwatanachai Anusorn* (Viwat Memorial), Bangkok.

——, 1962. *Thiralük wan-khrob-rawb pi thi-yi-sib* (20-year Memorial), Bangkok.

Bauer, P. T., 1948. *The Rubber Industry*, London.

Boeke, J. H., 1953. *Economies and Economic Policy of Dual Societies as Exemplified by Indonesia*, New York.

Brown, L. R., 1963. *Agricultural Diversification and Economic Development in Thailand*, United States Department of Agriculture, Foreign Agricultural Report, Washington.

Bureau of General Statistics Annual (before World War II). *Statistical Year Book of the Kingdom of Siam*, Bangkok.

Caldwell, J. C., 1967. 'The Demographic Structure', ch. 2 in T. H. Silcock (ed.), *Thailand: Social and Economic Studies in Development*, Canberra.

Chaiyong Chuchart, n.d. *Land Reform Evaluation for Thailand*, Bangkok.

—— and Suphan Toosoonthorn, 1957. *Costs and Returns in Korat Farm Enterprises*, Bangkok.

R

—— *et al.*, 1959. *Economic Survey of Land Cooperatives in the Northeast, 1959*, Kasetsart University, Bangkok.

—— *et al.*, 1961. *Production and Marketing Problems Affecting the Expansion of Kenaf and Jute in Thailand*, Kasetsart University, Bangkok.

—— *et al.*, 1962. *Production and Marketing Problems Affecting the Expansion of Corn Growing in Thailand: A Preliminary Report*, Kasetsart University, Bangkok.

Chamberlin, E. H., 1950. *The Theory of Monopolistic Competition*, 6th ed., Cambridge, Mass.

Chantana, 1964. *XO Group*, Bangkok.

Chapman, E. C., 1967. 'An Appraisal of Recent Agricultural Changes in the Northern Valleys of Thailand', mimeo., a paper delivered to the Sixth Academic Conference of the Agricultural Economics Society of Thailand, Kasetsart University, Bangkok, 30 January.

—— and Allen, A. C. B., 1965. 'Internal Migration in Thailand', a paper presented to the ANZAAS Conference in Hobart.

Chira Phanupongse, 1964. 'Report of the Study of Conditions in the Irrigation Tanks in the Northeast', Ministry of National Development, mimeo., Bangkok (in Thai).

Corden, W. M., 1967. 'The Exchange Rate System and Taxation of Trade', ch. 7 in T. H. Silcock (ed.), *Thailand: Social and Economic Studies in Development*, Canberra.

—— and Richter, H. V., 1967. 'Trade and the Balance of Payments', ch. 6 in T. H. Silcock (ed.), *Thailand: Social and Economic Studies in Development*, Canberra.

Cornell Research Centre, 1956. *The Social Sciences and Thailand: A Compilation of Articles on Various Social-Science Fields and their Application to Thailand*, Bangkok.

Department of Customs, 1966, 1967. *Annual Statements of Foreign Trade of Thailand*, Bangkok.

Department of Industrial Promotion, 1959. *Annual Report for 1959* (in Thai), Bangkok.

Department of Labour, Ministry of the Interior, 1965. *Study of the Facts Concerning the Migration of the Population in Thailand* (in Thai), Bangkok.

Department of Rice, Ministry of Agriculture, *Annual Report on 1961 Rice Production in Thailand* (in Thai, tables in Thai and English), Bangkok.

————. *Annual Report on 1962 Rice Production in Thailand* (in Thai, tables in Thai and English), Bangkok.

Direk Jayanama, 1967. *Thai kab songkhram lok Khrang thi sawng* (Thailand in World War II), Bangkok.

Evers, H. D. and Silcock, T. H., 1967. 'Elites' and Selection', ch. 4 in T. H. Silcock (ed.), *Thailand: Social and Economic Studies in Development*, Canberra.

Figart, D. M., 1925. *The Plantation Rubber Industry in the Middle East*, Washington.

Firth, R. W., 1966. *Malay Fishermen: Their Peasant Economy*, 2nd ed., London.

Fisk, E. K., 1967. 'Rural Development Policy', ch. 8 in T. H. Silcock and E. K. Fisk (eds.), *The Political Economy of Independent Malaya*, Canberra.

Freedman, M., 1961. 'The Handling of Money: A Note on the Background of the Economic Sophistication of Overseas Chinese', ch. iv of pt 1 in T. H. Silcock (ed.), *Readings in Malayan Economics*, Singapore.

Gajewski, P., 1965. 'The 1963 Census of Agriculture and the National Income Accounts', mimeo., Bangkok.

Gamba, C., 1956. *Synthetic Rubber and Malaya*, Singapore.

Graham, W. A., 1924. *Siam: A Handbook of Practical Commercial and Political Information*, London.

Hancock, W. K., 1942. *Survey of British Commonwealth Affairs*, vol. ii, pts 1 and 2, London.

Hanks, L. M., 1962. 'Merit and Power in the Thai Social Order', *American Anthropologist*, vol. 64, pp. 1247-61.

Holland, W. L., 1953. *Asian Nationalism and the West*, New York.

Hsieh, S. C. and Ruttan, V. W., 1967. 'Environmental, Technological and Institutional Factors in the Growth of Rice Production: Philippines, Thailand and Taiwan', Stanford, Food Research Institute Studies, vol. VII, no. 3.

Ingram, J. C., 1955. *Economic Change in Thailand Since 1850*, Stanford.

I.B.R.D., 1959. *A Public Development Program for Thailand*, Baltimore.

I.L.O., 1965. Regular Programme of Technical Assistance, *Report to the Government of Thailand on Internal Migration*, ILO/OTA/Thailand/R26, Geneva.

Joint Thai-United States Operations Mission Study, 1963. *Prelimi-*

nary Assessment of Education and Human Resources in Thailand, Bangkok.

Judd, L., 1964. *Dry Rice Agriculture in Northern Thailand*, Cornell Data Paper 52, South East Asia Program.

Keyes, C. F., 1967. *Isan: Regionalism in Northeast Thailand*, Cornell Data Paper 65, South East Asia Program.

Krit Samapuddhi, 1957. *The Forests of Thailand and Forestry Programs*, Bangkok.

Kruger, Rayne, 1964. *The Devil's Discus*, London.

Lee, S. Y., 1963. 'Recent Developments in Thailand's Maize Trade', *Bangkok Bank Monthly Review*, October, pp. 120-33.

Long, J. F. *et al.*, 1963. *Economic and Social Conditions among Farmers in Changwat Khon Kaen*, Bangkok.

McFadyean, A. (ed.), 1944. *The History of Rubber Regulation 1934-43*, London.

McFarland, G. B., 1954. *Thai-English Dictionary*, San Francisco.

McHale, T. R., 1961. 'The Competition between Synthetic and Natural Rubber', *Malayan Economic Review*, vol. vi, 1, pp. 23-31.

Meth Ratanaprasidhi, 1963. *Forest Industries and Forestry of Thailand*, Bangkok.

Ministry of Agriculture, 1953-65. *Agricultural Statistics of Thailand*, Bangkok, annual.

———, 1964. *Rai-ngan kan-süksa rüang phawa Talad lae rakha phlid-phon kasetkam lae pasusat nai phak tawan awk chiang nüa khawng prathet Thai* (Market Survey Report on Agriculture and Livestock in Northeast Thailand), Bangkok.

———, *Sa-thi-ti kan-pluk phüt-rai lae phüt-phak* (Statistics of the Planting of Upland Crops and Vegetables), usually referred to as *Crop Reports*, Bangkok, annual, 1961-5 (figures for 1959 supplied in mimeo.).

Ministry of Industry, 1959. *Annual Report, 1959*, Bangkok.

Mousny, A., 1964. *The Economy of Thailand*, Bangkok.

Muscat, R. J., 1966a. *Development Strategy in Thailand*, New York.

———, 1966b. 'Growth and the Free Market; a Case Study in Thailand', *Malayan Economic Review*, vol. xi, 1.

Myint, H., 1967. 'The Inward and Outward Looking Countries of Southeast Asia', *Malayan Economic Review*, vol. xii, 1, pp. 1-13.

Nakhon Sawan Provincial Government, 1964. *Annual Report* (in Thai).

N.E.D.B., n.d. Committee on the Development of the Northeast, *The Northeast Development Plan, 1962-66,* Bangkok.

———, n.d. Committee for the Development of the South, *Phaenphatana phak tai 2507-2509* (Southern Region Development Plan 1964-66), Bangkok (in Thai).

———, Office of the Prime Minister, 1964. *National Economic Development Plan, 1961-1966. Second Phase, 1964-66,* Bangkok.

———, *Review of Progress During the Fiscal Year 1964* (Evaluation Report of the First Economic Development Plan), mimeo., Bangkok.

———, 1965. 'Report of the Thai Delegation to the Consultative Committee on Thailand', mimeo., Bangkok.

———, 1966. *Performance Evaluation of Development in Thailand for 1965 under the National Economic Development Plan, 1961-66,* Bangkok.

———, 1967. Office of the Prime Minister, *Provisional Second National Economic and Social Development Plan, 1967-1971,* Bangkok.

———, National Income Division, n.d. *Regional Gross Domestic Product,* Bangkok.

N.S.O., 1963a. *Census of Agriculture, 1963,* Bangkok (76 vols.).

———, 1963b. *Advance Report, Household Expenditure Survey, B.E. 2506,* Bangkok.

———, 1963c. *Household Expenditure Survey, B.E. 2505-6 (1962-3).* Vols. for Whole Kingdom, Bangkok-Thon Buri, and North, Northeast, East, Central, and South Regions, Bangkok.

———, 1963d. *Report of the Labour Force Survey (Round 1),* Bangkok.

———, 1963e. *Report of the Labour Force Survey (Round 4),* Bangkok.

———, 1964. *National Income Statistics, 1964,* Bangkok.

———, 1946-64. *Statistical Year Book of Thailand,* Bangkok, annual.

Office of the Prime Minister, 1962-5. *Budget Documents,* Bangkok, annual.

———, 1962. *Budget in Brief,* Budget Bureau, Bangkok.

Platenius, H., 1963. *The Northeast of Thailand: Its Problems and Potentialities*, N.E.D.B., Bangkok.

Pridi Phanomyong, 1947. *Khao Khrawng Sethakid* (The Economic Plan), Bangkok.

Prot Panitpakdi, 1967. 'National Accounts Estimates of Thailand', ch. 5 in T. H. Silcock (ed.), *Thailand: Social and Economic Studies in Development*, Canberra.

Puey Ungphakorn, 1956. 'The Application and Potential Value of Economics to Thailand', a paper in the Cornell Research Centre's *The Social Sciences and Thailand: A Compilation of Articles on Various Social-Science Fields and their Application to Thailand*, Bangkok.

——, 1964. *Speeches*, Bangkok.

—— and Suparb Yossundara, 1955. *Sethakid Haeng Prathet Thai* (The Economy of Thailand), Bangkok.

Ratchaburi Provincial Government, 1962. *Annual Report* (in Thai).

Riggs, F. W., 1966. *Thailand: The Modernization of a Bureaucratic Polity*, Honolulu.

Robinson, Joan, 1956. *The Accumulation of Capital*, London.

Royal Irrigation Department, 1964. *Annual Report*, Bangkok.

Rowe, J. W. F., 1936. *Markets and Men*, Cambridge.

Rubber Division, Ministry of Agriculture, 1966. 'Sathana khawng yang thamachat nai anakhot kab kan-phatana suan yang' (The Natural-Rubber Situation in Future, and the Development of Rubber Holdings), mimeo. in Thai, Bangkok.

Schumpeter, J. A., 1949. *The Theory of Economic Development*, Cambridge, Mass.

Sharp, L. *et al.*, 1953. *Siamese Rice Village: A Preliminary Study of Bang Chan, 1948-1949*, Bangkok.

Sherwood, P. W., 1956. 'Export Duties and the National Income Accounts', *Economic Journal*, vol. lxvi, 26 March, pp. 73-83.

Silcock, T. H., 1949. *Economy of Malaya*, Singapore.

—— (ed.), 1964. *Readings in Malayan Economics*, Singapore.

—— (ed.), 1967. *Thailand: Social and Economic Studies in Development*, Canberra.

—— and Fisk, E. K. (eds.), 1963. *The Political Economy of Independent Malaya: A Case-study in Development*, Canberra.

Skinner, G. W., 1951. *Chinese Society in Thailand: An Analytical History*, Ithaca, N.Y.

Somsri Lelanuja, 1961. *Economic Survey of Business Firms that Exported Corn from Thailand in 1959*, Kasetsart University, Bangkok.

Sundrum, R. M. and Daroesman, Ruth, 1960. *Education and Employment in Thailand*, Kuala Lumpur.

Thio, E., 1956. 'British Policy in the Malay Peninsula, 1880-1909', Ph.D. thesis, University of London.

Trescott, P. B., 1968. 'Some Observations on Rice Production in Thailand', *World Crops*, vol. 20, Sept., pp. 49-56.

U.S.O.M., Private Enterprise Division, 1966. *A Report on the Thailand Fertilizer Situation and Potential*, prepared for the Royal Thai Government Board of Investment, 10 May.

U.S.O.M., Research Division, 1960a. *Economic Survey of the Korat Nongkhai Highway Area*, Bangkok.

——, 1960b. 'A Cost-Benefit Study of Roads in North and Northeast Thailand', mimeo., Bangkok.

——/N.S.O., 1965. *Changwat-Amphur Statistical Directory*, Bangkok.

Udhis Narkswasdi, 1963. *Agricultural Credit Systems in Certain Countries*, Bangkhaen.

United Kingdom Commissioner-General's Office, 1946-9. *Bulletins*, Singapore.

Usher, D., 1963. 'The Transport Bias in Comparisons of National Income', *Economica* (New Series), vol. xxx, no. 118, pp. 140-58.

——, 1965. ' "Equalising Differences" in Income and the Interpretation of National Income Statistics', *Economica* (New Series), vol. xxxii, no. 127, pp. 253-68.

——, 1966. 'Income as a Measure of Productivity: Alternative Comparisons of Agricultural and Non-Agricultural Productivity in Thailand', *Economica* (New Series), vol. xxxiii, no. 132, pp. 430-41.

——, 1967. 'The Thai Rice Trade', ch. 9 in T. H. Silcock (ed.), *Thailand: Social and Economic Studies in Development*, Canberra.

Van Roy, E., 1967. 'An Interpretation of Northern Thai Peasant Economy', *Journal of Asian Studies*, vol. xxvi, no. 3, pp. 421-32.

Vella, W. F., 1955. *The Impact of the West on Government in Thailand*, Los Angeles.

Wales, H. G. Q., 1931. *Siamese State Ceremonies: Their History and Function*, London.

———, 1965. *Ancient Siamese Government and Administration*, New York.

Wharton, C. R., 1967. 'Rubber Supply Conditions: Some Policy Implications', ch. 6 in T. H. Silcock and E. K. Fisk (eds.), *The Political Economy of Independent Malaya*, Canberra.

White, G. F. *et al.*, 1962. *Economic and Social Aspects of Lower Mekong Development*, a Report to the Committee for Co-ordination of Investigations of the Lower Mekong Basin, Bangkok.

Wijeyewardene, G., 1965. 'A Note on Irrigation and Agriculture in a North Thai Village', *Felicitation Volumes of Southeast Asian Studies*, vol. ii, Bangkok.

———, 1967. 'Some Aspects of Rural Life in Thailand', ch. 3 in T. H. Silcock (ed.), *Thailand: Social and Economic Studies in Development*, Canberra.

Wilson, D. A., 1962. *Politics in Thailand*, Ithaca, N.Y.

Wilson, Joan, 1958. *The Singapore Rubber Market*, Singapore.

Wittfogel, K. A., 1957. *Oriental Despotism: a Comparative Study of Total Power*, New Haven.

Wu, H. S., 1967. *Report and Project for Rationalisation and Modernisation of Thailand Sugar Industry*, Bangkok.

Yang, S. C., 1957. *A Multiple Exchange Rate System*, Madison.

Zimmerman, C. C., 1931. *Siam Rural Economic Survey, 1930-31*, Bangkok.

Index

245

T. H. Silcock, Emeritus Professor of the University of Malaya, is the author of ten previous books on Southeast Asia. In recent years he has concentrated most of his attention on Thailand, having edited *Thailand: Social and Economic Studies in Development* in 1967 and written (in lighter vein) *Proud and Serene: Sketches from Thailand* in 1968.

This book is based mainly on a study of material in the Thai language and on a series of visits to interview farmers and other country people in most parts of Thailand. On these visits Professor Silcock, who speaks Thai, travelled alone, and divided his time between formal interviews and informal conversation.

Since leaving Malaya in 1960 Professor Silcock has been mainly associated, in various capacities, with the Australian National University.

Set in 10 pt Linotype Times Roman, 2 pt leaded and printed on 85 gsm Burnie English Finish by Brown Prior Anderson Pty Ltd.
Designed by the A.N.U. Design Section.

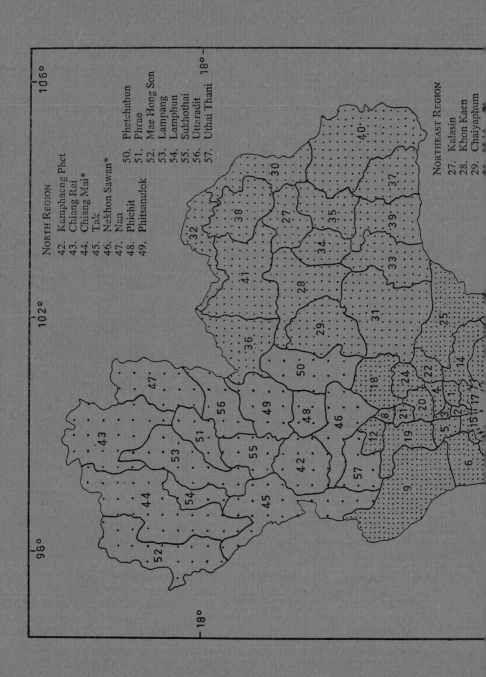

NORTH REGION

42. Kamphaeng Phet
43. Chiang Rai
44. Chiang Mai*
45. Tak
46. Nakhon Sawan*
47. Nan
48. Phichit
49. Phitsanulok
50. Phetchabun
51. Phrae
52. Mae Hong Son
53. Lampang
54. Lamphun
55. Sukhothai
56. Uttaradit
57. Uthai Thani

NORTHEAST REGION

27. Kalasin
28. Khon Kaen
29. Chaiyaphum